P9-DCI-746

2/18

DATE DUE

WITHDRAWN

BRODART, CO.   Cat. No. 23-221

THE BEST OF

Knitter's

MAGAZINE

edited by Nancy J. Thomas

shawls
and scarves

photography by Alexis Xenakis

AN XRX BOOK

PUBLISHER
Alexis Yiorgos Xenakis

CHIEF EXECUTIVE OFFICER
Benjamin Levisay

EDITOR
Nancy J. Thomas

INSTRUCTION EDITING
Traci Bunkers

PHOTOGRAPHER
Alexis Yiorgos Xenakis

PUBLISHING DIRECTOR
David Xenakis

GRAPHIC DESIGNER
Bob Natz

BOOK PRODUCTION MANAGER
Debbie Gage

DIGITAL COLOR SPECIALIST
Daren Morgan

PRODUCTION ARTISTS
Jay Reeve
Lynda Selle
Carol Skallerud

MARKETING DIRECTOR
Tad Anderson

FIFTH PRINTING, 2007; FIRST PUBLISHED IN USA IN 1999 BY XRX,
INC.
PO BOX 1525, SIOUX FALLS, SD 57101-1525

ISBN 10: 096463916-5
ISBN 13: 978-096463916-4

Produced in Sioux Falls, South Dakota, by XRX, Inc., 605.338.2450

Printed in China

shawls
and scarves

In the beginning

After almost 15 years and a lot of great issues, we stepped back to look at our magazine. We discovered an enormous amount of material that many readers may have never seen. Some issues are now out-of-print, but certainly not forgotten. We also discovered two types of readers: those with complete sets of magazines and those searching for the often-unobtainable issues.

The challenge was clear. How can we best resurrect these sought-after designs, stories, and projects? In the publishing world, reprinting an entire issue of the magazine is almost unheard of. So we turned to books.

We believe our *Best of Knitter's* series, culled from our greatest hits, is an ideal forum. *Knitter's Magazine* has established a reputation for presenting thematic issues in a cohesive manner. The *Best of Knitter's* provides us with a venue to offer this timeless material in a logical format.

New and improved

Knitter's Magazine has evolved over the years. At each step along the way, we've worked to improve and simplify our presentation. For the *Best of Knitter's*, we've endeavored to combine new and old material in a consistent manner. We've included charts and written words for most patterns; clarified and simplified instructions, and incorporated errata. The *Best of Knitter's* truly offers you the best of both worlds—old and new.

What's Inside

Shawls and Scarves is a timeless journey that spans issue #2 through issue #50. The voices we've included come from every vantage point. You'll find the guru of all knitter's, Elizabeth Zimmermann, talking about ageless techniques. On an untraditional avenue, you'll find Lily Chin. The list of featured designers reads like a "Who's Who" in the knitting world. So you know you're in good hands with names like Meg Swansen, Joan Schrouder, Priscilla Gibson-Roberts, and Deborah Newton. You'll note that lacemaster, Eugen Beugler has more entries than any other designer. He's a pro when it comes to shawl and scarf making!

Shawls and Scarves follows a logical progression, beginning with some history, where we delve into traditional Shetland and Faroese shawls. From there we've organized chapters according to shape. Our final chapter, "*Taking it One Step Beyond*" brings you to a nice conclusion with an array of lively, untraditional projects which incorporate principles you've learned along the way.

Similar to the magazine

In many ways, *Shawls and Scarves*, follows the example of *Knitter's Magazine*. Throughout the book, you'll find references to *The Knitter's School* on page 100, which features abbreviations and illustrated techniques. We've also included helpful information specific to shawl and scarf making. Even though we've given generic yarn material quantities by yardage and meters, there's a list of material suppliers on page 103. Along with the yarn companies, you'll find a list of publishers for books mentioned in articles and projects. Keep in mind that we've updated the listing and that they are current as of the publishing date.

Ready, get set— knit!

This is an unforgettable journey! Enjoy your shawl and scarf making.

Nancy J. Thomas
Editor, Knitter's Magazine

Issue 2 • Spring/Summer 1985
Features Elizabeth Zimmermann's Shetland shawls: *In the English Tradition* and *Stonington Shawl* shown on pg. 16.

Issue 9 • Winter 1987
The famed Shawl and other casual covers issue. Most projects are featured on these pages.

Issue 23 • Summer 1991
From this issue, an elaborate christening shawl from Priscilla Gibson-Roberts, *Christening Chrysalis* is shown on pg. 22.

Issue 42 • Spring 1996
Lace knitting resurfaces in this issue with five splendid shawls. The cover wrap, *Featherweight Fantasy* appears on pg. 84.

Issue 50 • Spring 1998
Amazing lace was the theme. Both *Dayflower Daydream* (pg. 54) and *Faroese-Style Lace* (pg. 34) come from this issue.

foreword

contents

For as long as there have been shoulders, there have been shawls.

Lizbeth Upitis

ah, shawls

First came the shape. Before knitting, sewing, or the loom, man used an animal skin as a flat garment to be draped about the body: a shawl. Still before knitting, man used the loom to produce cloth for protection and ornamentation. Looms easily produce squares and rectangles, but all other shapes are difficult: most require cutting and sewing and waste valuable fabric.

Every culture has some form of fabric draped as covering. Neolithic cave paintings (c. 4000-1500 B.C.) elegantly depict women wearing shawls while riding cattle. *Himation, toga, palla, tablion, serape, rebozo, manta, mantilla, cape, cloak, and mantle* are but a few of the names given to this ubiquitous garment.

Our name for it comes from the Persian *shal.* In Kashmir, a shawl was a gift of princes and the word means gift. These Kashmir shawls were made from the finest, softest wool from the belly of the Tibetan goat or 'shawl goat.' The country gave its name to the goat, cloth, and garment: cashmere.

Beginning in 1798, many exquisite cashmere shawls were sent home by officers during Napoleon's Egyptian campaign. Josephine is credited with owning three to four hundred! Delicate neo-Grecian gowns of the Directoire period had short sleeves

But for vanity, surely the shawl would be wrapped snugly around the shoulders of this Directoire beauty—detail of a painting by Francois Gérard.

A Scots lady of the Victorian age, complete in black lace shawl and poke bonnet—Lady Mary Ruthven

and low necks making the soft cashmere shawls not only an accessory but nearly a necessity.

Businessmen of the British East India Company gained control over much of India by 1757, and Kashmir shawls were available to most of Europe. Wellington gave Napoleon his Waterloo in 1815, and power shifted from France to England: from Emperor Napoleon's armies to Queen Victoria's industrialists. As new textile industries blossomed, some began to copy the Persian masterpieces. Queen Victoria loaned several of her Indian shawls to the mill in Paisley, Scotland, which became the finest and most famous of the shawl producers. Because many fine replicas of Indian textiles with the pomegranate motif were woven at the Scottish mill, the design became known as 'paisley.'

The shawl had become a European fashion. It was a necessary part of a woman's wardrobe for more than 100 years—needed to complement skimpy Directoire styles or to give balance to the huge hoops or crinolines of later years. Victorian ladies took classes from Spanish instructors in graceful and enticing ways to wear shawls.

When hands had other tasks, shawls could be fastened and forgotten—Sleeping Spinner, a painting by Gustave Courbet.

Elaine Rowley

beginnings both sides of a stitch

Small beginnings

Most shawls start small. Casting on a large number of stitches at uniformly relaxed tension and keeping track of their number (do you make yourself arrive at the correct number two times out of three before proceeding?) is always an irritation when what you really want is to get on with the knitting.

But there's an even better reason to avoid a long cast on when knitting a shawl. Shawls need to stretch all over, not just in their middles, so the cast-on and bound-off edges need to have as much give as the body of the shawl. This is not easy to accomplish, but a good method is to make the difficult edges short, involving as few stitches as possible. When that is not done, take extra care to make the cast-on stitches loose. Invisible cast on (see School, pg. 100) is the best choice if the stitches are to be picked up later.

Circular shawls knit from the center out are lots of fun except at the very beginning. With almost as many needles as stitches, the first few rounds test patience and dexterity. And often it shows. For a tidy center, try Emily's circular beginning (pg. 100).

Borders

On shawls, borders serve most of their usual functions; they enhance the design and prevent rolling, but they are not used to firm the edges. Instead, a wide edging adds the bit of weight to the shawl's border that makes it drape better when worn. A border can form the beginning of a shawl whose stitches are picked up along it rather than being cast on (see Deborah Newton's shawl, pg. 10). This is a common method for Shetland shawls. Very frequently a border is worked sideways to the outside edge of the shawl, and knitted onto its un-cast-off stitches, avoiding the final firm edge. Borders are an valuable weapon in this fight against rigidity.

But, as you might expect, there is one little problem with the borders, and, although we discussed it with many knitters, we found no answer. The problem is how to deal with the beginning and end of the border itself. The border stitches must be cast on and the end joined to the beginning. Most often, an invisible cast on is used, the stitches are not bound off, and the beginning and end are grafted together. The difficulty is that often this does not happen on stockinette or garter stitch, but right in the middle of lace. And, while we may understand the lace well enough to knit it, even to correct errors in it, the chances that we can hold three rows of it in our heads at once (the two on the needles and the one being grafted) are slight.

Everyone we discussed this problem with tries to graft on a plain row and then just does their unscientific, but practical best to make it look correct. The tension on the grafting row can be adjusted, and a bit of extra attention given this spot in the blocking will pay off. As a result, if you look for the graft, it can be found, but it is usually less obtrusive than a seam. The only reference I've found dealing with this problem is in *Knitted Lace Doilies* by Tessa Lorant.

Blocking

Not all shawls are lace; not all shawls require blocking. (Yes, there is a connection.) For some a simple steaming, or less, will do. But for most, a proper blocking is required for the best appearance. All that is required is a damp shawl; rust-proof T-pins or wig pins (more than you have); a place (Emily Ocker says this can be no more than a bread board covered with soft fabric if the 'shawl' is really a small doily, or a bed, or flat carpet covered with plastic sheeting and a sheet, if larger); the dimensions (frequent blockers may want waterproof concentric circles, squares, or whatevers marked on their blocking surface); time (the object needs to dry completely before unpinning); and courage (stretch further than you think).

Between times

Like kimonos, shawls are too pretty to fold away between wearings. They are flat shapes that look as good off the body as on it. Shawls can double as table, couch, and bed wear. Make yours serve double-duty.

Deborah Newton

on designing:
shawls and scarves
in two dimensions

Shawls and scarves can be extremely easy to make, or challenging in terms of shaping and patterns. They can offer a rare chance to experiment spontaneously, to ignore gauge and swatching considerations, simply because they don't have to fit the body like a sweater. Anything that can be done to create an interesting shawl can be applied to scarf design, just on a smaller scale.

Shawls and scarves are perhaps the most common of flat knitting project, but need attention to detail to make them special. Shawls must overcome a sterotypical old age/knitting image. And scarves often suffer from dullness, in shape and fabric. But these accessories can offer rewards not always found in three-dimensional garments.

There are no standard measurements for shawls and scarves—all decisions are left up to your personal choice. A scarf can be as small as a cuff that circles the neck, or as long as *Dr. Who's* stripey wrap. And very often you don't have to decide the length of a shawl or scarf ahead of time, unless you have a pattern repetition that must end in a certain place, or have a limited amount of yarn available. An educated guess predicts the number of stitches to cast on with a familiar yarn. More complex projects demand a small swatch at least, and a large shawl that requires blocking benefits from working a swatch and blocking it, too. But if your gauge changes and the piece measures a little more or less—for once, who cares? Relax and enjoy this freedom.

I'd like to introduce you to design approaches that will help you to revitalize your notions of shawls and scarves.

Yarns
All yarns have possibilities for scarf- and shawl-making, as long as they are not too heavy. As a beginning knitter, I once went too far by creating a warm scarf from a heavy yarn; the fabric was so thick that it defied wrapping around the neck. If you want a blanket-like 'stadium shawl,' use a heavy yarn, but in most cases remember that the pull of gravity will cause unsightly stretch in a large piece. Lovely, light-weight mohair and springy lightweight wools are always dependable for shawls, especially when knit on a larger needle size.

Size
Measurements may not be crucial in most of these projects, but it's a good idea to aim for an approximate size. In planning shawls, I find it helpful to play with a length of fabric to find an appropriate size; obviously, this can work for scarves too. After you start knitting, you can stop wherever you want, or your pattern repeat or sequence may dictate the length. For lace shawls, blocking is essential to open up the patterns. Expect your shawl to stretch farther than you would imagine, even a bit more than a swatch might indicate.

Shape
You can really have fun with the shape of flat projects making the shawl or scarf transcend any mundane stereotypes. The most obvious—and easiest—is the rectangular shape, formed by casting on, then working to desired length before binding off. For a variation, rectangles can also be sewn together in strips to form larger pieces, and blocks can be connected patchwork-style. Be aware that your sewing or joining technique can be an important design feature: will it be unobtrusive, or become a decorative part of the design?

Shapes can be further explored by using increases and decreases in unique ways. Triangular shawls can start with one stitch or more, increasing regularly at each edge (does it always have to be the edge?) until a desired width is reached at the top. I recently created an interesting shawl by casting on enough stitches for a lace panel (about 5-6" worth) then working increases to either side as the panel continued. The width of the panel formed a flat edge rather than a point on the triangle-type shawl. The triangular shawl can be further shaped after reaching its widest point, to add decorative bands or ties.

Square and circular shawls can be begun in the middle and worked out to their perimeters (see Elizabeth Zimmermann's wonderfully easy pi shawl pg. 50). Any of the books that describe how to work doilies or berets from the center lend ideas that can be applied to small scarves and large shawls. Often these shawls are folded in half to drape across the shoulders. Think about ways you might approach creating a half-circle shawl to omit the extra layer.

Fabric
Shawls and scarves often look best when both sides are attractive, so choose stitch patterns that you think makes a good visual impression from both right and wrong sides. If stranded Fair Isle colorwork doesn't fit the bill, think about working the scarf in a circular tube to be flattened. Or consider slip-stitch color patterns that look good, often different, on both sides. Double knitting makes great flat reversible projects, with colors switching positions on either side. Lace usually looks interesting from both sides, but garter stitch lace patterns tend to be more reversible than those that are worked with a stockinette stitch foundation. And don't eliminate cabled knitting because it has a right and wrong side. Recently I stood behind a man wearing the most intriguing Aran-style sweater: I puzzled over the wonderful patterns until I realized he had it on inside out!

Pattern combinations and edges
Flat projects have a large surface area that you can work in an allover pattern or divide into areas of pattern. Common stripes come to mind when thinking of scarves, but they need not always be in color. Make your piece serve double duty as a sampler of patterns you haven't tried before. If you plan to alternate patterns which require different stitch counts, this could affect the shape of your piece. Blocking will even out pattern irregularities in some cases, but if this isn't possible, the wavy edge could be considered as a design feature.

Borders can be worked at the same time or added after completion. You may omit an added border entirely if your fabric is suitably flat. The traditional Shetland shawl is divided into two parts: a square central section, which is often surrounded by a border more significant in terms of design. We often consider edging functional and discrete, but switching traditional proportions to emphasize border is an interesting notion.

And there is always the fringed edge, borrowed from weaving, that commonly borders shawls and scarves. Instead of hooking on cut yarn strands, try a more knitterly approach, using a loop-type stitch at the beginning and end of your piece.

Making a Shetland-patterned shawl

My shawl was developed from a number of ideas that eventually merged. I wanted a shawl large enough to be used over a coat as a giant scarf, and light enough to be a summer wrap. I also wanted to use Shetland patterns in an un-Shetland way. Editor, Elaine Rowley helped me choose a fine 100% wool. The finished shawl was composed of as much air as wool when worked in very open Shetland patterns on a size 6 (4mm) needle.

For once, I swatched to become familiar with pattern and fabric 'drape,' not primarily to obtain a gauge. I had already used the wonderful Old Shale pattern and its relatives often (very reversible!). And I was familiar with the stockinette-based, Shetland lace patterns. But I had little experience with the garter-stitch, Shetland lace patterns that I felt would be more reversible. I also wanted an edging pattern that was garter-stitch-based too, to balance the central portion. I turned to Sarah Don's *The Art of Shetland Lace* (Unicorn), one of my favorite knitting books (the 1980 edition of this book, you may be sorry to learn, is riddled with pattern errors that have been corrected in the later editions).

I found that some of the beautiful, more complicated patterns required incredible concentration: I wanted this project to be more accessible and less time-consuming. I tried combining some of the smaller patterns in sequence. This yielded a field of motifs resembling an allover pattern, but still allowed for a natural break in the knitting after each pattern was complete.

I noticed that many of these Shetland patterns were panels of 15 stitches, or multiples of 14 plus 1 (which could easily be adapted to panels of 15 stitches). By combining them I could use 90 stitches throughout the main section without having to increase or decrease when changing patterns. I began to see how these compatible patterns had been combined over the years by the creative Shetland knitters to form some of the more complex patterns I had been trying to avoid!

Then, fearing that the surface would become boring because of the regularity of these patterns (which might appear to form columns), I planned to insert another pattern occasionally, worked over fewer stitches, to provide a visual break. I'd been hoping for years to use the 'Eyelid' pattern, simply because I think it has the most curious name of all knitting patterns. Here it would serve a purpose suited to its name: to 'blink' across the surface of the shawl.

What about the shape? I planned two sections for the shawl: the center (which was to be the field of motifs) and the border (also a garter stitch lace pattern from the Don book). I hoped to work the border at the same time, although it could have been added later. I wanted a rectangular feel, but didn't want to deal with the border going around truly square corners.

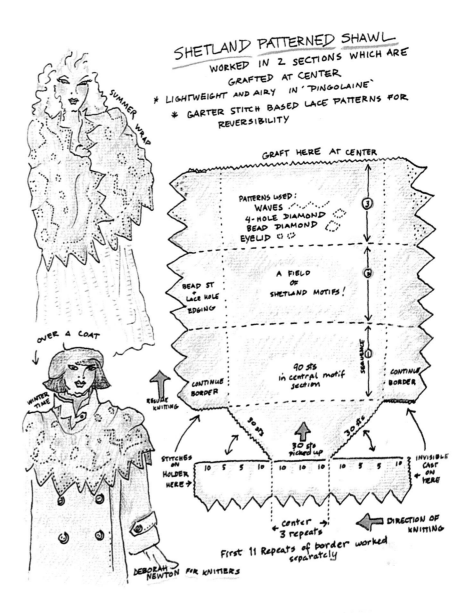

So, with all of these concerns in mind, I worked a detailed plan out on paper first, then passed it on to an expert knitter, Pat Yankee from Seekonk, MA, to see if it would work. And it did! Pat also enjoyed adapting the seemingly long patterns to short graph form, which we think makes them much easier read. Above is a much simplified 'cartoon' of the process for this shawl—see if you can figure out the concept! (The complete instructions begin on pg. 10.)

Note

For those interested in how others reduce actions to words and symbols without charting, take a look at Don's book. After I converted her lace instructions to more commonly used terminology, I was surprised at how long they became: for example, her simple T becomes k2tog. Barbara Abbey's *Knitting Lace* [Schoolhouse Press] also has a curious set of symbols that I like for reducing row by row instructions.

Deborah Newton

Using Shetland patterns in an "un-Shetland" way was the premise that inspired Deborah's shawl. She uses patterns that make this project not too boring or too complicated—the result is a beautiful piece that was worthy of the cover of the famous *Knitter's,* Issue 9 (Winter '87).

lace shawl

Notes

1 See *School*, pg. 100 for SK2P, invisible cast-on, and garter stitch grafting. **2** When picking up sts from edging, 1 'bump' or edge st equals 2 rows of edging. **3** Shawl is worked in 2 sections, then grafted tog at center.

Shawl

First Section

Cast on 18 sts using invisible cast-on, k 1 row. *Beg Bead Stitch and Lace Hole Edging Chart* Work Bead Stitch and Lace Hole Edging Chart for 4 reps (80 rows), end with a WS row. Mark beg of next row and work 3 more reps (60 rows). Mark beg of next row and work 4 more reps. Place sts on holder; break yarn.

Pick up sts from edging

With RS facing, slide a very fine needle through each bump or edge st along each garter st ridge between markers—30 edge stitches on fine needle. Do not turn. *Beg Bead and Diamond Chart* Work rows 1 and 2 of Bead Diamond Chart over 30 sts (2 pat reps). *Next row* (RS) Insert tip of RH needle into 2 bumps in edging and knit them tog, place marker (pm), work Chart row 3 over 30 sts to end, pm, then before turning, insert tip of RH needle into 2 bumps and k2tog—32 sts. *Next row* (WS) K1, sl marker, work in pat to marker, sl marker, k1. Keeping center sts in pat as established and working new sts in garter st, k 2 bumps tog at each end of every RS row 4 times more—40 sts; knit up 1 st in 1 bump at each end of every RS row 20 times—80 sts; then k 2 bumps tog at each end of every RS row 5 times—90 sts; At same time, when 18 rows of Bead Diamond Chart are complete, end with a WS row, beg new pat as foll: *Beg Eyelid Chart* (RS) Mark center 36 sts. Work as established to marker, work Eyelid Chart over center 36 sts (4 pat reps), work to end. When 2 chart reps (16 rows) of Eyelid Chart are complete, end with a WS row, beg new pat as foll: *Beg Waves Chart* (RS) Mark center 60 sts. Work as established to marker, work Waves Chart over center 60 sts (4 pat reps), work to end. When 3 chart reps (18 rows) of Waves Chart are complete, end with a WS row, knit 2 rows. *Beg Eyelid Chart* (RS) Mark center 72 sts, work as established to marker, work Eyelid Chart over center 72 sts (8 pat reps), work to end. When Row 7 of Eyelid Chart is complete, all edge sts of edging should have sts knit up into them, end with a RS row—90 sts. *Beg Bead Stitch and Lace Hole Edging Chart* (WS) K to end, pm, then slip cast-on sts from edging to a needle, and work Row 1 of Bead Stitch and Lace Hole Edging Chart across these 18 sts. *Beg 4-Hole Diamond Chart* (RS) Work Bead Stitch and Lace Hole Edging Chart row 2 to marker, sl marker, work row 1 of 4-Hole Diamond across next 90 sts (6 pat reps), pm, then work row 1 of Bead Stitch and Lace Hole Edging Chart from holder sts. *Next row* (WS) Work row 2 of edging to marker, sl marker, work row 2 of 4-Hole Diamond Chart to marker, sl marker, then work row 3 of edg-

ing to end. Cont to work in pats until 14 rows of 4-Hole Diamond are complete, end with a WS row. Cont working sts outside of markers in Bead and Lace Hole Edging Chart and sts inside markers in foll pat sequence: 2 reps of Wave Chart (12 rows); 1 rep of Bead Diamond Chart (18 rows); 1 rep of Eyelid Chart (8 rows); 1 rep Waves Chart (6 rows); k2 rows. Cont in edging pats on each end, rep entire sequence twice more beg with 4-Hole Diamond Chart. Sl rem sts to holder—one section of shawl complete.

Second Section

Work as for first.

Finishing

With RS facing up, and center of 2 sections tog, garter stitch graft sts from holders loosely to match tension in garter stitch. Block shawl.

Skill level Advanced
Finished Measurements 80" x 40" (blocked)
Yarn 1,540 yds (1,386m) of fingering-weight yarn.
Original Yarn: (No longer available)
Pingouin • Pingolaine
100% wool
1¾ oz (50g) 220yds(198m)
7 balls in #66 Tropique
Needles Size 6 (4mm) needles, *or size to obtain gauge*
Extras One very fine knitting needle for picking up edge stitches—approx size 1 (2¼mm) • T pins for blocking • stitch markers and holders
Gauge 25 sts and 50 rows to 8" (20cm) over Bead Diamond pat (based on final shawl size: swatching yielded a slightly tighter gauge than was obtained in full size shawl)
Original swatch yielded 30 sts and 60 rows to 8" (20cm)

Bead Stitch and Lace Hole Edging Chart *Beg on 18 sts*

Row 1 K3, yo, k2tog, yo, k1, k2tog, yo twice, k2tog twice, yo, k1, k2tog, yo, k2tog, k1. *2* K2, yo, k1, k2tog, yo, k4, p1, k2tog, yo, k3, yo, k2tog, k1. *3* K3, yo, k2tog, k2, yo, k2tog twice, yo twice, k2tog, k1, yo, k2tog, k1, yo, k2. *4* K2, yo, k1, k2tog, yo, k4, p1, k2tog, yo, k1, k2tog, k2, yo, k2tog, k1. *5* K3, yo, k2tog, k3, yo, k2tog twice, yo twice, k2tog, k1, yo, k2tog, k1, yo, k2. *6* K2, yo, k1, k2tog, yo k4, p1, k2tog, yo, k1, yo, k2tog, k3, yo, k2tog, k1. *7* K3, yo, k2tog twice, yo, k3, yo, k2tog twice, yo twice, k2tog, k1, yo, k2tog, k1, yo, k2. *8* K2, yo, k1, k2tog, yo, k4, p1, k2tog, yo, k5, [yo, k2tog, k1] twice. *9* K3, yo, k2tog, k1, yo, k2tog, k1, k2tog, yo, k1, yo, k2tog twice, yo twice, k2tog, k1, yo, k2tog, k1, yo, k2. *10* K2, yo, k1, k2tog, yo, k4, p1, k2tog, yo, k3, yo, SK2P, yo, k4, yo, k2tog, k1. *11* K3, yo, k2tog, k2, k2tog, yo, k5, yo, k2tog twice, yo twice, k2tog, k1, yo, k2tog, k1, yo, k2. *12* K1, k2tog, yo, k2tog, k1, yo, k2tog, k1, p1, k3, yo, k2tog, k1, k2tog, yo, k1, yo, k2tog, k3, yo, k2tog, k1. *13* K3, yo, k2tog twice, yo, k3, yo; SK2P, yo, k1, k2tog, yo twice, k2tog twice, yo, k1, k2tog, yo, k2tog, k1. *14* K1, k2tog, yo, k2tog, k1, yo, k2tog, k1, p1, k3, yo, k2tog, k4, [yo, k2tog, k1] twice. *15* K3, yo, k2tog, k1, yo, k2tog, k1, k2tog, yo, k1, k2tog, yo twice, k2tog twice, yo, k1, k2tog, yo, k2tog, k1. *16* K1, k2tog, yo, k2tog, k1, yo, k2tog, k1, p1, k3, yo, SK2P, yo, k4, yo, k2tog, k1. *17* K3, yo, k2tog, k2, k2tog, yo, k1, k2tog, yo twice, k2tog twice, yo, k1, k2tog, yo, k2tog, k1. *18* K1, k2tog, yo, k2tog, k1, yo, k2tog, k1, p1, k3, yo, k2tog, k3, yo, k2tog, k1. *19* K3, yo, k2tog twice, yo, k1, k2tog, yo twice, k2tog twice, yo, k1, k2tog, yo, k2tog, k1. *20* K1, k2tog, yo, k2tog, k1, yo, k2tog, k1, p1, k3, [yo, k2tog, k1] twice. Rep rows 1-20 for Bead Stitch and Lace Hole Edging Chart.

Bead Stitch and Lace Hole Edging

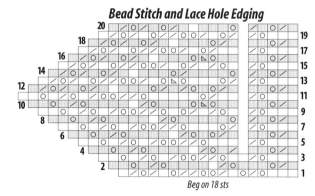

Beg on 18 sts

Bead Diamond Chart *15-st rep*

Rows 1-4 Knit. *5* K5, k2tog, yo, k1, yo, k2tog, k5. *6* K4, k2tog, yo, k3 yo, k2tog, k4. *7* K2, k2tog, yo, k1, yo, k2tog, k1, k2tog, yo, k1, yo, k2tog, k2. *8* K1, k2tog, yo, k3, yo, k3tog, yo, k3, yo, k2tog, k1. *9* K2, yo, k2tog, k1, k2tog, yo, k1, yo, k2tog, k1, k2tog, yo, k2. *10* K3, yo, k3tog, yo, k3, yo, k3tog, yo, k3. *11* K5, yo, k2tog, k1, k2tog, yo, k5. *12* K6, yo, k3tog, yo, k6. *13-18* Knit. Rep rows 1-18 for Bead Diamond Chart.

Bead Diamond

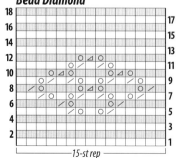

15-st rep

Eyelid Chart *9-st Rep*

Row 1 K2, k2tog, yo, k1, yo, k2tog, k2. *2* K1, k2tog, yo, k3, yo, k2tog, k1. *3* Knit. *4* K2, yo, k2tog, yo, k3tog, yo, k2. *5* Knit. *6* K3, yo, k3tog, yo, k3. *7-8* Knit. Rep rows 1-8 for Eyelid Chart.

Eyelid

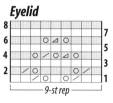

9-st rep

Waves *15-st Rep*

Row 1 K5, k2tog, yo, k1, yo, k2tog, k5. *2* K4, k2tog, yo, k3, yo, k2tog, k4. *3* K3, k2tog, yo, k5, yo, k2tog, k3. *4* K2, k2tog, yo, k7, yo, k2tog, k2. *5* K1, k2tog, yo, k9, yo, k2tog, k1. *6* K2tog, yo, k11, yo, k2tog. Rep rows 1-6 for Waves Chart.

Waves

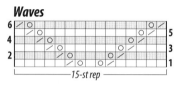

15-st rep

4-Hole Diamond *15-st Rep*

Row 1 K5, k2tog, yo, k1, yo, k2tog, k5. *2* K4, k2tog, yo, k3, yo, k2tog, k4. *3* K3, k2tog, yo, k5, yo, k2tog, k3. *4* K2, k2tog, yo, k1, k2tog, yo twice, k2tog, k2, yo, k2tog, k2. *5* K1, k2tog, yo, k5, p1, k3, yo, k2tog, k1. *6* K2tog, yo, k1, k2tog, yo twice, k2tog twice, yo twice, k2tog, k2, yo, k2tog. *7* K2, yo, k2tog, k2, p1, k3, p1, k2tog, yo, k2. *8* K3, yo, k2tog twice, yo twice, k2tog, k1, k2tog, yo, k3. *9* K4, yo, k2tog, k2, p1, k2tog, yo, k4. *10* K5, yo, k2tog, k1, k2tog, yo, k5. *11* K6, yo, k3tog, yo, k6. *12, 13, 14* Knit. Rep rows 1-14 for 4-Hole Diamond Chart.

4-Hole Diamond

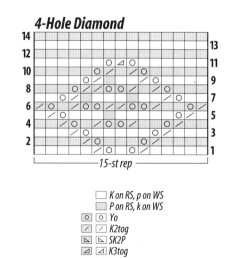

15-st rep

| | K on RS, p on WS |
| | P on RS, k on WS |
| Yo |
| K2tog |
| SK2P |
| K3tog |

Of Shetland shawls, Elizabeth Zimmermann says: "Make way for the Shetland Shawl! This most knitterly creation represents the quintessence of lace to a knitter." Without cast-on or bound-off edges, these shawls from the faraway Shetland Islands begin in the center with a square block surrounded by a border and then are completed with a narrow edging. This chapter includes Shetland versions and variations from a host of notable designers including Elizabeth Zimmermann. The Shetland shawl technique is diagramed on page 16.

shetland shawls

"You have heard of the legendary Shetland shawl. Light as a feather, elegant, and warm. Anybody worth his salt insists on one from the beginning, and people of all ages find them indispensable, comforting, and beautiful. Mary Thomas gives full traditional directions on pgs. 187-196 of her excellent *Knitting Book* (Dover). I have had the temerity to make a few changes—to call them improvements would be conceited indeed."

Elizabeth Zimmermann

in the english tradition

The relationship of the Shetland shawl to its individual elements—fabric, stitch, and construction methods—has the inevitability and coherence of a true classic. So it will come as no surprise that its traditional method of construction has been preserved. As described by Mary Thomas, "A Shetland shawl has neither cast-on nor cast-off edges but is built up from one corner of the lace border. The method is ingenious and accounts for the remarkable elasticity of all the edges, and the soft, caressing feel of the shawl as it enfolds the shoulders."*

*Mary Thomas's Knitting Book, (Dover) 1972. pg. 192

A Traditional Shetland Shawl

Cast on at A; work lace border to B; pick up stitches along inside edge of AB. Knit C, decreasing at corners; make row of holes and knit garter square, D. Do not bind off. Work lace border/side sections E, F, and G in the same manner. Graft the pieces together.

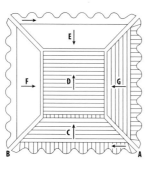

Note See *School*, pg. 100 for invisible cast-on and garter stitch grafting.

Shetland shawl

A true Shetland shawl has three essentials: it is made of fine wool from the Shetland Isles; it is knitted at a loose, relaxed gauge; and it is totally elastic—no casting-on or binding off.

Overview

Step 1: Center Square Start at corner A of the center square by (whisper) casting on 2 sts. Work in garter stitch, increasing 1 stitch at the beginning of each row until you have the diagonal width (distance from C-B) you want, then decrease down to 1 stitch again, by knitting 2 together at the beginning of every row, until you are at D with 1 stitch left. Pick-up and knit along DC, 3 stitches for every 2 garter stitch ridges (1 stitch in first ridge, 2 stitches in second).

Step 2: First border Work first trapezoidal side, increasing 1 stitch at beginning of every row. When side is as deep as you want, put all stitches on hold on a piece of wool (E-F). Pick up and knit 1 stitch in each ridge from F-C.

Step 3: Second border Now pick up and work second side as first, but increase only on side A-G; on side F-C work 1 more of the picked up stitches every other row.

Step 4: Third border Work third side as second.

Step 5: Forth border On fourth side, pick up a stitch or bump from E-D or H-B at end of every row.

Step 6: Edgings completed Now don't break the wool; the lace border is made with the same continuous thread.

Lay out the shawl and consider how wide the edging should be (Raphael's is 5" wide). Take stitches E-F from wool holder and put on a needle, at E cast on the necessary stitches for edging, preferably by the invisible method. If you have cast on invisibly, then end may be woven to the beginning, and you will have achieved an un-bound-off, un-cast-on shawl (if we agree to ignore those 2 whispered stitches at the beginning) with one continuous thread. Knit one preparatory row, knitting the last stitch together with its neighbor, an un-bound-off stitch. When edging is complete, dampen, and block severely, pinning out each point.

Before you begin

Try a shawl swatch. The knitting of this shawl is so simple to understand and comfortable to do that if you've the least confusion or hesitation, let me recommend that your initial swatch be in the form of a tiny shawl. A dress rehearsal. Follow Step-by-step directions (pg. 18). Increase until there are 24 stitches. For first side knit up 18 stitches. Increase to 25 stitches.

Complete all four sides. You may want to add a border, in this case the Double Circle Edging is a better choice since it has a rep of 12 rows. Practice washing and blocking this little square too.

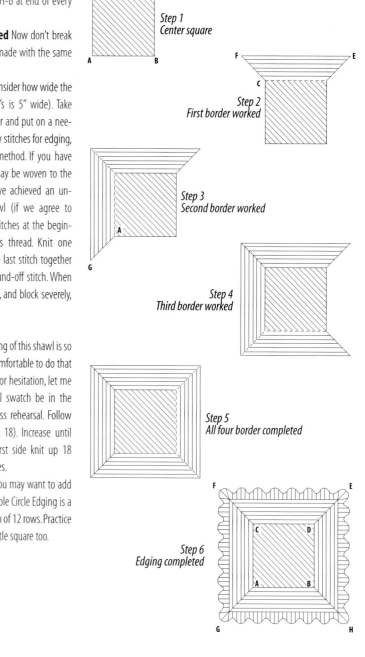

Step 1
Center square

Step 2
First border worked

Step 3
Second border worked

Step 4
Third border worked

Step 5
All four border completed

Step 6
Edging completed

Make way for the Shetland Shawl! This most knitterly creation represents the quintessence of lace to a knitter. Elizabeth Zimmermann's Stonington Shawl, shown here, made in two weights of wool.

"Courage, blind followers; here are step-by-step directions for the shawl."

Elizabeth Zimmermann

This wonderful piece can be made in two weights of wool that results in two different-sized shawls. Read Elizabeth's "In the English Tradition" to learn about the art of making traditional Shetland shawls and variations à la Zimmermann.

stonington shawl

Notes

1 See *School*, pg. 100 for M1, ssk, SK2P, invisible cast-on, and garter stitch grafting. **2** Shawl is worked in garter st throughout (k every row) with garter st lace edging. **3** Do not break wool throughout. **4** The center of the shawl is patterned with concentric squares of eyelet. **5** After shawl is made, edging is attached as it is worked.

Shawl

The center square can be worked as follows, but in plain garter st. But, for those of you who dread knitting a piece of plain garter st, work a bit of eyelet to hold your interest—concentric squares will do nicely. As for the edging, I used Raphael Stinson's Lace Border. The Double Circle Edging from *Knitting Lace* by Barbara Abbey, is also a fine alternative edging for Shetland and other shawls.

Step-by-step
Center Square

Start at corner A of center square. Cast on 2 sts. *Beg Concentric Squares Chart A* Follow chart, inc 1 st every row and sl last st with yarn in front (wyif) as if to p, until 145 sts rem. *Beg Concentric Squares Chart B* Follow chart, dec 1 st every row and sl last st wyif as if to p, until 1 st rem—center square complete.

First border

Pick up and knit along edge D-C at the rate of 3 sts for every 2 bumps (*pick up and k1 st in first bump; k1, M1, in 2nd bump; rep from*)—105 sts. Work back-and-forth in garter st on these sts, inc 1 st at beg of each row as foll: *Row 1* K2, yo, k to last st, wyif, sl last st as if to p. Rep until 145 sts; end at F; place all stitches on hold on a piece of wool (E-F).

Second side

Continuing with same strand of wool, pick up and k1 st in each bump down edge F-C. Pick up sts as for D-C along C-A. Work same as first side, except that instead of sl last st at F-C, you will work last st tog with next picked-up st from F-C each time you come to them: *Row 1* Working from A to C, k2, yo, k to last A-C st, wyif, sl next F-C st; turn, leaving rem sts unworked. *2* K2, yo, k to last st, wyif, sl last st. *3* K2, yo, k to last worked st, k last worked st tog with next F-C st, turn. Rep rows 2 and 3, working last worked st tog with next unworked F-C st each time, until 145 sts are on needle; this maneuver joins the two sides to at F-C as you go. End at G; place all stitches on hold on a piece of wool (F-G).

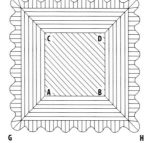

Third side

Work in same manner as second side. Pick up and k 1 st in each bump from G-A; 3 sts for every two bumps from A-B. When you have 145 sts on needle, end at H; place G-H sts on hold.

Fourth side

Work same as second and third side, except join to both first side at D-E and to third side at B-H: With same side of shawl facing, beg at E, and using a spare needle, pick up E-D bumps. Continuing with same strand of wool as third side, pick up and k sts along H-B, then B-D as for other sides, working last B-D st tog with next picked-up st from E-D; turn, leaving rem sts unworked. *Row* 1 Working from D to B, k2, yo, k to last D-B st, k last st tog with next H-B st; turn, leaving rem sts unworked. *2* K2, yo, k to last worked st, k last worked st tog with next E-D st, turn. Rep rows 1 and 2 until all picked-up sts and bumps are worked, end at E—145 sts. Place E-H sts on hold.

Sideways lace edging

Starting at E, cast on (preferably with invisible cast on) 18 sts. K17, k2tog (2nd st being first un-bound-off st from side E-F). Turn. *Beg Raphael Stinson's Lace Border Chart* Work Raphael Stinson's Border, working last st of all even-numbered rows tog with 1 un-bound-off st of sides. Toward the end, at row 18, count rem shawl sts. If they are not a multiple of 9, cheat a bit so that they are and the pattern will come out even. Garter st graft end to beginning. Break wool for first, last and only time.

knitter's pattern
• in other words •

Concentric Squares Charts A and B *Beg on 2 sts*

Notes This isn't as complicated as it looks. Basically increase 1 st every row to 14 sts, then eyelets beg (row 13). A new eyelet square begins every 14th row after that. Work in this manner until there are 145 sts, then beg dec every row and closing squares up until 1 st rem.

Chart A: Row 1 K1, M1, wyif, sl 1 as if to p. *2-11, 14 and all even rows through 142* K1, M1, k to last st, wyif, sl 1 as if to p. *13* K1, M1, k5, yo, ssk, k5, wyif, sl 1 as if to p. *15* K1, M1, k4, k2tog, yo, k1, yo, ssk, k5, wyif, sl 1 as if to p. *17* K1, M1, k4, k2tog, yo, k3, yo, ssk, k5, wyif, sl 1 as if to p. *19* K1, M1, k4, k2tog, yo, k5, yo, ssk, k5, wyif, sl 1 as if to p. *21* K1, M1, k4, k2tog, yo, k7, yo, ssk, k5, wyif, sl 1 as if to p. *23* K1, M1, k4, k2tog, yo, k9, yo, ssk, k5, wyif, sl 1 as if to p. *25* K1, M1, k4, k2tog, yo, k5, place marker, k6, yo, ssk, k5, wyif, sl 1 as if to p. *27* K1, M1, k4, *k2tog, yo, k5; rep from* to 1 st before marker, k1, yo, ssk, **k5, yo, ssk; rep from** to last 6 sts, k5, wyif, sl 1 as if to p. *29* K1,

Skill Level Intermediate
Finished Measurements 54" x 54" in Shetland wool • 44" x 44" in lace-weight Shetland wool
Yarn 2,240 yds (2,016) of Shetland wool • 1,800 yds (1, 620) laceweight Shetland wool
Original Yarn: Schoolhouse Press • Shetland
100% wool 16 oz (448g)
Schoolhouse Press • Laceweight
100% wool 8 oz (224g)
Needles Size 9 (5½mm) circular needle for Shetland, *or size to obtain gauge*
Size 7 (4½mm) circular needle for laceweight, *or size to obtain gauge*
Extras One spare needle • stitch marker • lengths of wool for stitch holders
Gauge 16 sts to 4" (10cm) over garter st in Shetland
20 sts to 4" (10cm) in laceweight

Concentric Squares Chart B

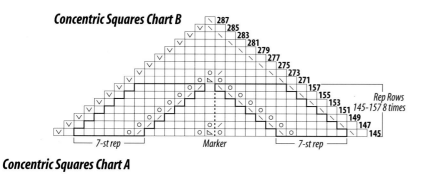

287
285
283
281
279
277
275
273
271
157
155
153
151
149
147
145

Rep Rows
145-157 8 times

7-st rep   Marker   7-st rep

Concentric Squares Chart A

7-st rep   Marker   7-st rep

39
37
35
33
31
29
27
25
23
21
19
17
15
13
11
9
7
5
3
1

Rep Rows
27-39 8 times,
then rep Rows
27-31 once

Cast on 2 sts

Key:
- ☐ K on RS
- ▨ K on WS
- ⊙ Yo
- ⁄ K2tog
- ◺ Ssk
- ◹ SK2P
- ◿ K3tog
- Ⓜ M1
- ☑ Sl1 purlwise wyif
- ⌒ K last st from chart tog with 1 st from shawl

Chart Note
Concentric Squares Chart and Double Circle Edging Chart show odd numbered rows only. K even numbered rows.

M1, k4, *k2tog, yo, k5; rep from* to 2 sts before marker, k2tog, yo k1, yo, ssk, **k5, yo, ssk; rep from** to last 6 sts, k5, wyif, sl 1 as if to p. **31** K1, M1, k4, *k2tog, yo, k5; rep from* to 3 sts before marker, k2tog, yo, k3, yo, ssk, **k5, yo, ssk; rep from** to last 6 sts, k5, wyif, sl 1 as if to p. **33** K1, M1, k4, *k2tog, yo, k5; rep from* to 4 sts before marker, k2tog, yo, k5, yo, ssk, **k5, yo, ssk; rep from** to last 6 sts, k5, wyif, sl 1 as if to p. **35** K1, M1, k4, *k2tog, yo, k5; rep from* to 5 sts before marker, k2tog, yo, k7, yo, ssk, **k5, yo, ssk; rep from** to last 6 sts, k5, wyif, sl 1 as if to p. **37** K1, M1, k4, *k2tog, yo, k5; rep from* to 6 sts before marker, k2tog, yo, k9, yo, ssk, **k5, yo, ssk; rep from** to last 6 sts, k5, wyif, sl 1 as if to p. **39** K1, M1, k4, *k2tog, yo, k5; rep from* to 7 sts before marker, k2tog, yo, k11, yo, ssk, **k5, yo, ssk; rep from** to last 6 sts, k5, wyif, sl 1 as if to p. **41-143** Rep rows 27-39 7 times more, then rep rows 27-31 once— 145sts .

Beg dec

Chart B: Rows 144 and all even rows K1, ssk, k to last st, wyif, sl 1 as if to p. **145** K1, ssk, *k5, yo, ssk; rep from* to 6 sts before marker, k5, yo, SK2P, yo, k5, **k2tog, yo, k5; rep from ** to last 2 sts, k1, wyif, sl 1 as if to p. **147** K1, ssk, *k5, yo, ssk; rep from* to 6 sts before marker, k4, ssk, yo, k5, **k2tog, yo, k5; rep from ** to last 2 sts, k1, wyif, sl 1 as if to p. **149** K1, ssk, *k5, yo, ssk; rep from* to 4 sts before marker, k9, **k2tog, yo, k5; rep from ** to last 2 sts, k1, wyif, sl 1 as if to p. **151** K1, ssk, *k5, yo, ssk; rep from* to 3 sts before marker, k7, **k2tog, yo, k5; rep from ** to last 2 sts, k1, wyif, sl 1 as if to p. **153** K1, ssk, *k5, yo, ssk; rep from* to 2 sts before marker, k5, **k2tog, yo, k5; rep from ** to last 2 sts, k1, wyif, sl 1 as if to p. **155** K1, ssk, *k5, yo, ssk; rep from* to 1 st before marker, k3, **k2tog, yo, k5; rep from ** to last 2 sts, k1, wyif, sl 1 as if to p. **157** K1, ssk, *k5, yo, ssk; rep from* to marker, k1, **k2tog, yo, k5; rep from

** to last 2 sts, k1, wyif, sl 1 as if to p. **159-269** Rep rows 145-157 7 times more— 19 sts. **271** K1, ssk, k5, yo, SK2P, yo, k6, wyif, sl 1 as if to p. **273** K1, ssk, k4, k2tog, yo, k6, wyif, sl 1 as if to p. **275-283** K1, ssk, k to last st, wyif, sl 1 as if to p. **285** K1, ssk, wyif, sl 1 as if to p. **287** Ssk.

Raphael Stinson's Lace Border Chart *Beg on 18 sts*

Row 1 K3, yo, k2tog, k9, yo k2tog, yo k2. **2** Yo, k2tog, k6, [yo, k2tog] twice, k6, k next st tog with 1 st from shawl. **3** K3, yo k2tog, k10, yo, k2tog, yo, k2. **4** Yo, k2tog, k8, [yo, k2tog] twice, k5, k next st tog with 1 st from shawl. **5** K3, yo, k2tog, k11, yo, k2tog, yo, k2. **6** Yo, k2tog, k10, [yo, k2tog] twice, k4, k next st tog with 1 st from shawl. **7** K3, yo, k2tog, k12, yo, k2tog, yo, k2. **8** Yo, k2tog, k12, [yo, k2tog] twice, k3, k next st tog with 1 st from shawl. **9** K3, yo, k2tog, k17. **10** Yo, k3tog, [yo, k2tog] twice, k14, k next st tog with 1 st from shawl. **11** K3, yo, k2tog, k1, [yo, k2tog] twice, k11. **12** Yo, k3tog, [yo, k2tog] twice, k13, k next st tog with 1 st from shawl. **13** K3, yo k2tog, k2, [yo, k2tog] twice, k9. **14** Yo, k3tog, [yo, k2tog] twice, k12, k next st tog with 1 st from shawl. **15** K3, yo, k2tog, k3, [yo, k2tog] twice, k7. **16** Yo, k3tog, [yo, k2tog] twice, k11, k next st tog with 1 st from shawl. **17** K3, yo, k2tog, k4, [yo, k2tog] twice, k5. **18** Yo, k2tog, k15, k next st tog with 1 st from shawl. Rep Rows 1–18 for Raphael Stinson's Lace Border.

Stinson's Lace Border Chart

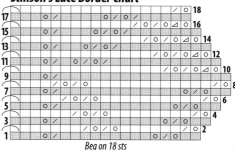

17
15
13
11
9
7
5
3
1

18
16
14
12
10
8
6
4
2

Beg on 18 sts

Double Circle Edging Chart *Beg on 15 sts*

Row 1 K2, yo, k3, yo, k2tog, k3, k2tog, yo, k2, k next st tog with 1 st from shawl. **2 and all even-numbered rows** K, working (k1, p1, k1) into any double yo of previous row. **3** K2, yo, k5, yo, k2tog, k1, k2tog, yo, k3, k next st tog with 1 st from shawl. **5** K2, yo, k1, k2tog, yo twice, k3tog, k1, yo, k3tog, yo, k4, k next st tog with 1 st from shawl. **7** K2, yo, k2tog, k3, k2tog, yo, k3, yo, k2tog, k2, k next st tog with 1 st from shawl. **9** K1, k2tog, yo, k2tog, k1, k2tog, yo, k5, yo, k2tog, k1, k next st tog with 1 st from shawl. **11** K1, k2tog, yo, k3tog, yo, k1, k2tog, yo twice, k3tog, k1, yo, k2, k next st tog with 1 st from shawl. Rep rows 1–12 for Double Circle Edging Chart.

Double Circle Edging Chart

11
9
7
5
3
1

Beg on 15 sts

"Now, about lace shawls!!! I have had a long fascination for lace; in particular, lace shawls! Sara Don's book *The Art of Shetland Lace* was a great inspiration to me as it was the first really worthwhile book I found available on fine lace knitting. I read about how the Shetland Islanders knitted their shawls and thought that there must be an easier way other than all the grafting together of the lace sides onto the main part. I admire them immensely but thought I would take advantage of circular needles. "

Barbara George

snowdrops & snowflakes

Once in a while a piece of knitting appears in our pages that we know you will not be able to fully appreciate— unless you are here to touch it. That's good; it reminds us that knitting, after all, is not about words and pictures. They are simply the means we use to convey knitting ideas and are essential. Words and images highlight, analyze, associate, evoke; but only knitting is knitting. Often these textiles that must be felt use materials unfamiliar to most knitters: a beaded bag, a qiviut hood, and these handspun shawls.

It is pointless to present shawls from handspun yarns as projects and to pretend that they are easily duplicated. There certainly are commercial yarns as fine as these, but we know of none with their softness and elasticity. If you are a skilled handspinner, you can aspire to such. But if you are not, there's much to learn from Barbara George's very straightforward method for knitting all the borders simultaneously, round-and-round. And, perhaps more important is her example of an isolated knitter using traditional lace patterns (available to us all through those words and pictures we must use) to create her own beautiful shawls—Shetland in spirit, if not in fact.

Barbara's basic method

1 Knit a center piece either by casting on a number of stitches (for example, 60 stitches) and then knitting twice the number of rows of pattern (120 rows) or by casting on 2 stitches as one corner and increasing 1 stitch at the beginning of each row to the desired number of stitches, then decreasing to form a square diamond.
2 Then pick up the stitches around the square (1 stitch for every second row) or the loops around the diamond onto a circular needle. I usually do a couple of patterns of lace holes around the ordinary square before beginning my lace border pattern. Count the stitches on each side to make sure they are even, and place a marker for the beginning and three markers of a different color for each of the other three corners. I choose a stitch pattern (or number of stitch patterns) to be used for the lace edge. To keep a balanced edge, it is best to choose stitch patterns of the same multiple of stitches. Sometimes I mull over my design for days!! A beginner would best do just one stitch pattern, such as feather and fan, to get the hang of this process. If there are not enough stitches for a pattern you want to do, increase evenly across each side to adjust.
3 If the shawl is to be all-lace garter stitch, purl every alternate round. Increase one stitch each side of the four corner stitches: yarn over, knit into back of corner stitch, yarn over. (I knit into the back of each corner stitch to give it a twist.) Do this increase every second row; this makes the shawl square. Of course, you have to adjust the pattern to suit the increases. If the pattern is complicated, I sometimes make these increases in plain knitting. This segment then makes its own pattern shape. But this only happens if I'm changing stitch patterns, say every 10 or 20 rows. If you had only, say feather and fan stitch, then you would include the increases in the pattern, but if I were doing a spider webs pattern, then I would make the increases in plain knitting.
4 When the lace border is completed, then do not break the yarn but at the beginning of the next round cast on the desired number of stitches for the lace edge with a short needle. That is, after choosing a suitable lace edge pattern.
On the rows of lace edge knitted towards the shawl, *knit the last edge stitch and*

one border stitch together. That is, on every second row knit (or purl) 2 together. This grafts the lace edge onto the lace border simultaneously. Again you must choose a lace edge not only to suit the shawl but also to suit the number of stitches on the border side (for example, a border of 480 stitches could use a lace edge with 12 or 24 pattern rows—it is the number of pattern rows that matters, not the number of stitches cast on—also remember that 24 pattern rows uses up half the number of border stitches (12 stitches). With experience you can adjust by decreasing 2 stitches off the lace border (knit 3 together) to fit in the required number of patterns but this must be done evenly at each end. I do not make a mitered corner. When all four sides of lace edge are completed, the only joining is to graft the two lace edge ends together.

Blocking

Wash the shawl gently, roll in towel to absorb excess moisture, then pin out, stretching gently to make a perfect square. This takes time, and a tape measure is essential to get a perfect square. The lace edge corners are not a perfect square but they do stretch. Allow to dry completely before lifting (12-24 hours). I do mine on towels or a sheet over towels on the carpet. This is the method I have devised for myself. A new pinned shawl is as exciting as a new born babe!! I keep tiptoeing back to see that it is still there!!!

Sources

I use Barbara Walker's two books, *Treasury of Knitting Patterns I and II*; Sarah Don's *The Art of Shetland Lace* (Unicorn)*; and Barbara Abbey's *Knitting Lace*.

The white shawl

The blocked shawl measures 54" square and weighs 4 ounces. Polwarth fleece was used. This shawl (photo, on baby and Meg Swansen), is the most recent one I made using simple designs to explain my technique. The center is knit from one corner to the opposite diamond corner. Yarn over loops were made at the beginning of each row and these then picked up on a circular needle for the border.

The center is worked in stockinette stitch with 3-over-3 cable crossings spaced 6 stitches and 12 rows apart and offset. The border is mostly Snowdrop lace and finishes with a few repeats of Bead. The edging is Lover's Knot edging.

The grey shawl

The blocked shawl measures 54" square and weighs 5 ounces. This shawl is natural-colored gray Polwarth. It is the first design I did entirely on my own. All the stitches are garter stitch lace from Sarah Don's book (Leaf for the center; Spider's Web, Lace Holes, Madeira and Diamond for the border). The edging pattern is Valenciennes from Barbara Abbey's book.

Here are several of the stitch patterns that I used. Please see the resources I listed for more stitch patterns.

knitter's pattern
· in other words ·

Bead Stitch *Multiple of 6 sts plus 1*
Row 1 (RS) K2, *yo, SK2P, yo, k3; rep from* to last 5 sts, yo, SK2P, yo, k2. **2** K1, k2tog, *yo, k1, yo, k2tog, k1, k2tog; rep from* to last 4 sts, yo, k1, yo, k2tog, k1. **3** K2tog, yo, *k3, yo, SK2P, yo; rep from* to last 5 sts, k3, yo, k2tog. **4** K1, yo, k2tog, k1, *k2tog, yo, k1, yo, k2tog, k1; rep from* to last 3 sts, k2tog, yo, k1. Rep rows 1–4 for Bead Stitch Chart.

Snowdrop Lace *Multiple of 8 sts plus 3*
Rows 1 and 3 (RS) *Yo, S2KP2, yo, k5; rep from* to last 3 sts, yo, SK2P2, yo. **2 and all WS rows** Purl. **5** *K3, yo, ssk, k1, k2tog, yo; rep from* to last 3 sts, k3. **7** *Yo, S2KP2, yo, k1; rep from* to last 3 sts, yo, S2KP2, yo. **8** Purl. Rep rows 1–8 for Snowdrop Lace Chart.

Lover's Knot Edging *Beg on 18 sts*
Cast on 18 sts. **Row 1** (RS) K2, yo, k2tog, yo, k1, [yo, k2tog] twice, yo, k1, [k2tog, yo] 3 times, k 1, k next st tog with 1 st from shawl. **2** K1, [k2tog, yo] 3 times, k1, p10, k2tog, yo. **3** K2, yo, k2tog, yo, k3, yo, k1, k2tog, yo, k2, [k2tog, yo] 3 times, k 1, k next st tog with 1 st from shawl. **4** K1, [k2tog, yo] 3 times, k1, p12, k2tog, yo. **5** K2, yo, k2tog, yo, k1, yo, SK2P, yo, k1, [yo, k2tog]

twice, yo, k1, [k2tog, yo] 3 times, k 1, k next st tog with 1 st from shawl. **6** K1, [k2tog, yo] 3 times, k1, p14, k2tog, yo. **7** K2, yo, k2tog, yo, k3, yo, k1, yo, k3, yo, k1, k2tog, yo, k2tog, [k2tog, yo] 3 times, k 1, k next st tog with 1 st from shawl. **8** K1, [k2tog, yo] 3 times, k1, p17, k2tog, yo. **9** K1, [k2tog, yo] twice, [SK2P] 3 times, yo, SK2P, yo, k2tog, [k2tog, yo] 3 times, k 1, k next st tog with 1 st from shawl. **10** K1, [k2tog, yo] 3 times, k1, p10, k2tog, yo. **11** K1, [k2tog, yo] twice, SK2P, yo, k1, k2tog, yo, k1, [k2tog, yo] 3 times, k 1, k next st tog with 1 st from shawl. **12** K1, [k2tog, yo] 3 times, k1, p9, k2tog, yo. **13** K1, [k2tog, yo] 3 times, SK2P, yo, k1, [k2tog, yo] 3 times, k 1, k next st tog with 1 st from shawl. **14** K1, [k2tog, yo] 3 times, k1, p8, k2tog, yo. Rep rows 1–14 for Lover's Knot Edging Chart.

Valenciennes Edging *Beg on 26 sts*
Cast on 26 sts. **Row 1** (WS) K1, k2tog, yo, k9, k2tog, yo, k2tog, k5, k2tog, yo, k1, k2tog. **2** K3, yo, k2tog, k3, k2tog, yo, k2, [k2tog, yo] twice, k2tog, k1, k2tog, yo, k2, k next st tog with 1 st from shawl. **3** K1, k2tog, yo, k11, yo, k2tog, k1, k2tog, yo, k4, yo. **4** K6, yo, SK2P, yo, k3, [k2tog, yo] twice, k3, k2tog, yo, k2, k next st tog with 1 st from shawl. **5** K1, k2tog, yo, k18, yo twice, k2tog, k1, yo. **6** K3, p1, k9, [k2tog, yo] twice, k4, k2tog, yo, k2, k next st tog with 1 st from shawl. **7** K1, k2tog, yo, k16, [k2tog, yo twice] twice, k2tog, k1. **8** [K2, p1] twice, k7, [k2tog, yo] twice, k5, k2tog, yo, k2, k next st tog with 1 st from shawl. **9** K1, k2tog, yo, k11, k2tog, yo, k1, yo, k3, k2tog, yo twice, k2tog, k1, k2tog. **10** K1, k2tog, p1, k3, k2tog, [yo, k3] twice, [yo, k2tog] twice, k3, k2tog, yo, k2, k next st tog with 1 st from shawl. **11** K1, k2tog, yo, k10, k2tog, yo, k5, yo, k2tog, k3, k2tog. **12** K2tog, k1, k2tog, yo, k7, yo, k3, [yo, k2tog] twice, k2, k2tog, yo, k2, k next st tog with 1 st from shawl. Rep rows 1–12 for Valenciennes Edging Chart.

Legend:
- ☐ K on RS, p on WS
- ▨ P on RS, k on WS
- ◯ Yo
- ╱ K2tog
- ╲ Ssk
- ◺ SK2P
- ▲ S2KP2
- ■ No stitch
- ⌒ K last st from chart tog with 1 st from shawl

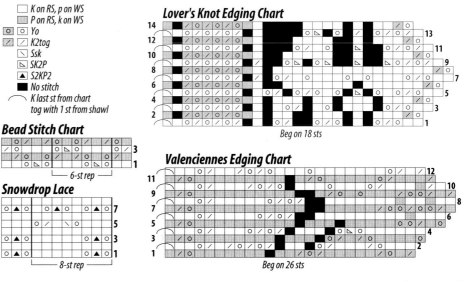

Lover's Knot Edging Chart
Beg on 18 sts

Bead Stitch Chart
6-st rep

Snowdrop Lace
8-st rep

Valenciennes Edging Chart
Beg on 26 sts

Chart Notes If working Bead and Snowdrop Lace Charts circularly, work every rnd as a RS row, reading chart rows from right to left.

Priscilla Gibson-Roberts

"The lace baby wraps of the Victorian era were based on the design of the traditional Shetland shawl, a seamless square with a center pattern encircled by a border and finished with a narrower edging. The principal difference between the shawl and the baby blanket was proportion—both had a center square of the same size (24-30"), with a large border for the shawl (finished, 54-60") and a smaller border for the blanket (finished, 42-48")."

christening chrysalis
designing a blanket or shawl

Knitters work with the tools available, and their construction techniques are adapted to those tools. In the 19th century, the seamless squares were worked in sections which involved painstaking grafting. Today's knitters, with the advantage of circular needles, can recreate the designs much more simply with a few stitches to graft at the very end.

Skill Level Intermediate
Finished Measurements 42" square (after blocking)
Yarns 9 oz (250g) 2-ply Tussah silk or fingering-weight wool with 30-32wpi
Needles Size 1 (2mm) circular, 29" (74cm) long, *or size to obtain gauge* Spare size 1 (2mm) straight needle
Extras Stitch markers • 7 yds ⅛" ribbon • waste yarn
Gauge (after blocking) 28 sts and 36 rows to 4" (10cm) over Center Panel chart

1 See *School,* pg.1 00 for ssk, SK2P, M1R, and M1L, invisible cast-on and garter stitch grafting. **2** Center panel is worked back and forth in rows on circular needle. When panel is completed, additional stitches are picked up along sides and bottom of panel and border is worked in rnds.

Shawl
Center Panel
Cast on 221 sts, using invisible cast-on. Work 16 rows of Center Panel chart 16 times, then work rows 1-7 once more. *Chart row 8* Work to 1 st before end of row, place marker (pm).

Border
K last st of center panel (first corner st of border), pick up and k220 sts down left side of panel, pm, pick up and k 1 st (2nd corner st), k220 cast-on sts, pm, k last cast-on st (3rd corner st), pick up and k220 sts along right side, pm, pick up and k 1 st (4th corner st), k to end—221 sts between markers. *Next rnd* *K corner st, k220 sts and inc 1 st; rep from* 3 times more—222 sts between markers. *Next rnd* Purl. *Beg Border chart: Rnd 1* *Work first 4 sts of chart, then work 36-st rep 6 times, work last 2 sts of chart; rep from* 3 times more. Cont in pat through chart rnd 29. Work 7 rnds in St st, AT SAME TIME, cont M1 incs every other rnd as established—256 sts between markers.

Edging
Do not cut yarn. Invisibly cast on 12 sts onto LH needle. With spare straight needle, work as foll: **Beg Edging chart: Row 1* (RS) Work 11 sts of chart, ssk (last edging st tog with 1 border st), turn. *Row 2* P1, work row 2 of chart. Cont in chart pat, joining last st of edging tog with 1 st from border every RS row, until 40 chart rows (and 20 border sts) have been worked. Cont in chart pat, work as foll: **Next row (RS) Work to last st of edging, ssk, turn. *Next row* P1, work chart to end. *Next row* Work to last st of edging, SK2P (last st of edging tog with 2 border sts), turn. *Next row* P1, work chart to end. Rep from** to 20 sts before marker. Resume joining 1 edging st with 1 border st every RS row over next 20 border sts. Rep from* 3 times more.

Finishing
Graft sts to cast-on sts. Wet block to size. Cut ribbon into 4 equal parts and lace through St st row immediately below purl rnd, using purl bumps as a guide. Tie a bow in each corner.

Designing a blanket or shawl
1. Center panel

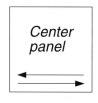

Center panel

Select a pattern (or combination of patterns) for the center. This pattern, worked back and forth, can be based on garter or stockinette stitch. The same base stitch is used for both the center and the border, but must be worked differently since the center is worked back and forth and the border is worked in rounds. For example, if the shawl is worked in garter stitch, you would knit every row of the center, and alternate knit and purl rounds in the border. If stockinette stitch is used, you must alternate knit and purl rows in the center, and knit every round of the border.

Since garter stitch is reversible, it works well for a shawl which is folded into a triangular shape when worn, thus exposing both sides, especially if the fold is off-center. Stockinette stitch is suitable for a baby's wrap since having a "wrong" side is not a problem.

Once the pattern has been selected, work a gauge swatch. Be sure to use an invisible cast-on and slip the final row of stitches onto waste yarn, rather than binding them off. The swatch must be blocked to determine the gauge, and regular cast-on and bound-off edges will not allow proper blocking. The best method for blocking is to wet the swatch and stretch it out to dry, just as with the final product.

With the gauge determined, begin the center panel. Invisibly cast on the number of stitches required for the pattern repeats, plus one selvage stitch on each edge. The extra stitches provide an edge for picking up border stitches. They should be worked in stockinette stitch even if garter stitch is being used in the main pattern. These stitches must not be slipped, but rather worked on every row to insure the same flexibility as the pattern itself.

Work the pattern to a length equal to its width. If necessary, add or subtract a few rows to complete a repeat of the pattern. Work the final row to the last stitch and place a marker before it (this will be the first corner stitch and the beginning of the round for the border).

2. Border To begin the border, knit the last stitch of the center panel, then pick up

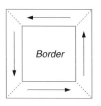

Border

and knit stitches down the left side of the panel, picking up the stitches through the center of the selvage stitch. Place the second corner marker and knit across the cast-on stitches to the last stitch. Place the third corner marker, then knit the last cast-on stitch and pick up and knit stitches along the right side, placing the

Knitter's choices: spin your own lace yarn

Lace knitting yarns can be spun from a variety of fibers—wool and luxury fibers being the most common.

Wool is the easiest to spin, least expensive, and most versatile for lace knitting. Using the fine wools, the yarn can be spun as a singles for a cobweb weight or plied for a more durable yarn. Among the more accomplished spinners (with good eyesight), two-ply cobweb yarns with as few as three to five fibers in the diameter of the singles are feasible. These are usually worsted (combed) yarns.

Silk, in a combed preparation, can be purchased in either bricks (a folded, compressed top) or as a loose roving, in either bombyx (a lustrous white silk from cultivated worms fed on a diet of mulberry leaves) or tussah (a rich, honey-colored silk from silk worms feeding on a diet of oak and other leaves). These yarns are spun worsted style with fairly high levels of twist. Rather than determining the number of twists per inch or measuring the angle of twist (difficult, if not impossible, in the very fine yarns), many spinners refer to inserting twist 'until you feel the beading.' *Beading* refers to building twist to the point that the spinner can *feel*

continues …

continued …

fourth corner marker. Knit to the end of the round. The same number of stitches must be picked up along the two side edges as at the two ends. Also, since the number of rows in the center panel is greater than the number of stitches, it will be necessary to calculate the number of rows that will need to be skipped, placing the skips evenly along the length of the piece. It may help to place a contrasting color marker at the first corner to mark the beginning of the round.

How the design merges in the corners must be considered when positioning it within the border. The border pattern should be centered along each edge so that the pattern builds identically in the corners. It can be moved up or down a few rounds or the beginning of the repeat can be shifted right or left to allow a visually pleasing merging of the design as the length of the rounds increases. This can best be determined by charting the corners out on graph paper.

If the pattern begins immediately, it is nice to work a round of eyelets (k1, k2tog around) as a demarcation from the center square. If a few rounds are to be worked before the pattern begins, the eyelets are not necessary. Immediately after the eyelet round or in the first round after the pick-up, the number of stitches may be adjusted to the number required for the border. The number of stitches in the border pattern will not include the corner stitch or stitches.

The corner increases can be worked in several ways. Usually, there is one corner stitch with increases worked on either side of it. To maintain the square shape, the increases must be worked on every other round. The simplest method is to work a yarn over on each side of the corner stitch, knitting through the back loop of the corner stitch to tighten it. This creates a line of small holes which may enhance the pat-

tern. If a solid join is desired, use a Make 1 (M1) increase. This type of increase must be paired, one leaning to the right and one to the left. If a distinct corner stitch is desired, the increases should lean out from the corner stitch. If a more invisible corner is desired, the increases should lean in toward the corner stitch.

When the border is complete, work a few rounds to allow a visual demarcation before starting the edging, increasing at the corners every other round as established.

3. Edging Do not cut the yarn. Use it to invisibly cast on the number of stitches

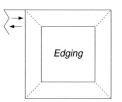

required for the edging. With a short straight needle of the same size, work the edging back and forth, joining with the border stitches as you work. Even if the shawl or blanket has been worked in stockinette stitch, the edging is best worked in garter stitch, both for the ease in knit-

ting and for the reversibility. The edging can be joined to the border in two ways. The first method is to join the last stitch of an incoming row (worked toward the center) with one border stitch; then on the next incoming row, join the last stitch of the edging with two border stitches. The second method is to join the last stitch of an incoming row with one border stitch and repeat this join on the next incoming row. On the third incoming row, join the last stitch of the edging with two border stitches. The first method, joining three border stitches to four edging rows, allows more horizontal stretching when blocking the edging. The second method, joining four border stitches to six edging rows, allows for greater vertical stretching when blocking the edging. For a less visible juncture, use a k2tog and k3tog; or for a distinctive

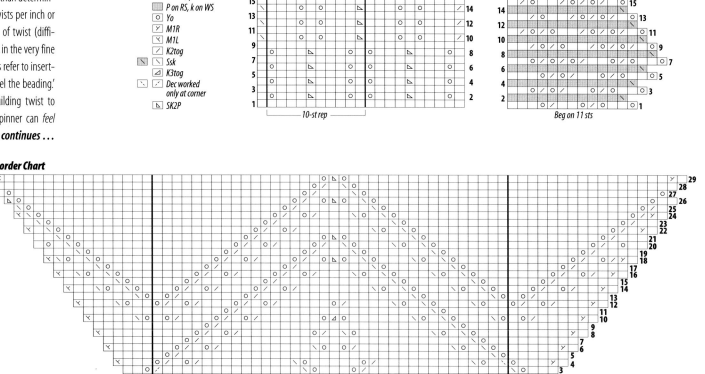

Center Panel Chart

10-st rep

	Kon RS, p on WS
	P on RS, k on WS
	Yo
	M1R
	M1L
	K2tog
	Ssk
	K3tog
	Dec worked only at corner
	SK2P

Edging Chart

Beg on 11 sts

Border Chart

36-st rep

line, join with an ssk and an SK2P (sl 1 knitwise, k2tog, psso). This joining stitch should be purled on the wrong-side rows.

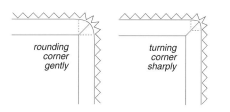

rounding corner gently

turning corner sharply

The corners of the edging can be gently rounded or sharply turned. To round the corner, the edging stitches are joined with the border stitches at the end of every incoming row throughout the corner section of border stitches. For a sharp turn, allow ease in about half of the corner section of the border. In this case, the edging is joined on every incoming row, ending several stitches before the corner stitch. Work the pattern centered over the corner stitch, joining at the end of every other incoming row, thereby crowding extra rows between each join. This is accomplished with short rows: work the last stitch of an incoming row, do not join, but turn and work back out. Then on the next incoming row, join as before. In both cases, blocking helps to ease the edging around the corner of the piece. When all the border stitches have been worked, the remaining edging stitches on the needle are grafted to those of the invisible cast-on.

Blocking

Blocking a shawl is often referred to as "dressing." The finished piece should be rinsed in warm water to thoroughly wet the entire piece. All the excess moisture should be squeezed out. The old-fashioned stretching frames are no longer available, but working on a rug or carpet (or large sheet of cardboard) covered with towels will suffice. With plenty of rust-proof pins, stretch out the center panel to the dimensions desired. It is best to stretch the center of each side first, then work out to the corners. After the center is stretched, again working from the center of each side, stretch out the points of each repeat of the edging to the desired size. When the edges have been securely pinned, remove all the pins around the center, smoothing out the line which otherwise is somewhat scalloped. Allow the piece to dry completely before removing the edge pins.

the twist as the yarn slides between the finger and thumb. If the beading becomes visible, too much twist has been inserted. Silk yarns must be plied for lace knitting.

Many other luxury fibers, principally the down fibers, are also used for lace knitting. Alpaca, camel down, qivuit, and cashmere are examples of suitable fibers for lace knitting. These come in various forms, both as raw fibers and carded or combed, plus many blends. Most of the raw fibers are hand carded by spinners (or prepared on specialty drum carders). Usually, the luxury fibers, even if carded, are spun worsted style, again at high levels of twist to hold them together as many are slick and/or short. Again, the yarns must by plied.

In all cases, lace yarns must be carefully finished. A simmer bath with a mild liquid dish detergent is highly recommended, both for thorough cleaning (some prepared fibers have oils added to ease spinning and control static electricity) and to set the twist. At the minimum, a good soaking in a warm bath with detergent is essential. This bath is followed by a thorough rinsing. White distilled vinegar added to the rinse water removes any film the detergent might leave behind. After rinsing, the yarn should have excess moisture squeezed out. Contrary to advice that knitting yarns should be left unblocked (dried without weighting), all lace knitting yarns should be lightly blocked. Adding weight to the skeins is sufficient for most of the wool and luxury fibers, but winding the silk skeins onto a blocker is recommended for silk lace knitting yarns. Blocking the *yarn* is recommended since the knitted piece requires blocking to enhance the lace stitches.

knitter's pattern · *in other words* ·

Center Panel Chart *Multiple of 10 sts, plus 1*

Row 1 and all WS rows Purl. *2, 4, 6, 8* (RS) *K1, yo, k3, SK2P, k3, yo; rep from*, end k1. *10, 12, 14, 16* K2tog, k3, yo, k1, yo, k3, *SK2P, k3, yo, k1, yo, k3; rep from*, end ssk. Rep rows 1-16 for Center Panel Chart.

Border Chart *Beg on 888 sts*

Rnd 1 Knit. *2* *K1, M1R, yo, ssk, k1, [yo, ssk, k13, k2tog, yo, k1, yo, ssk, k13, k2tog, yo, k1] 6 times, k2tog, yo, M1L; rep from*. *3* *K3, yo, ssk, [k14, k2tog, yo, k3, yo, ssk, k15] 5 times, k14, k2tog, yo, k3, yo, ssk, k14, k2tog, yo, k2; rep from*. *4* *K1, M1R, k3, yo, ssk, k1, yo, ssk, k9, k2tog, yo, k5, yo, ssk, k9, k2tog, yo, k1, k2tog, yo, [k2, yo, ssk, k9, k2tog, yo, k5, yo, ssk, k9, k2tog, yo, k1, k2tog, yo] 5 times, k3, M1L; rep from*. *5* *K6, [yo, ssk, k31, k2tog, yo, k1] 6 times, k4; rep from*. *6* *K1, M1R, k5, [k1, yo, ssk, k1, yo, ssk, k9, k2tog yo, k1, yo, ssk, k9, k2tog, yo, k1, k2tog yo, k2] 6 times, k4, M1L; rep from*. *7* *K7, [k2, yo, ssk, k27, k2tog, yo, k3] 6 times, k5; rep from*. *8* *K1, M1R, k6, [k3, yo, ssk, k1, yo, ssk, k7, yo, ssk, k1, k2tog, yo, k7, k2tog, yo, k1, k2tog, yo, k4] 6 times, k5, M1L; rep from*. *9* *K8, [k4, yo, ssk, k23, k2tog, yo, k5] 6 times, k6; rep from*. *10* *K1, M1R, k4, k2tog, yo, k1, [yo, ssk, k3, yo, ssk, k1, yo, ssk, k6, yo, k3tog, yo, k6, k2tog, yo, k1, k2tog, yo, k3, k2tog, yo, k1] 6 times, yo, ssk, k4, M1L; rep from*. *11* *K9, [k6, yo, ssk, k19, k2tog, yo, k7] 6 times, k7; rep from*. *12* *K1, M1R, k3, k2tog, yo, k1, k2tog, yo, [k2, yo, ssk, k3, yo, ssk, k1, yo, ssk, k4, k2tog yo, k5, k2tog, yo, k1, k2tog, yo, k3, k2tog yo, k1, k2tog, yo] 6 times, k2, yo, ssk, k3, M1L; rep from*. *13* *K7, k2tog, yo, k1, [yo, ssk, k6, yo, ssk, k15, k2tog, yo, k6, k2tog, yo, k1] 6 times, yo, ssk, k6; rep from*. *14* *K1, M1R, k2, k2tog, yo, k1, k2tog, yo, k2, [k1, yo, ssk, k1, yo, ssk, k3, yo, ssk, k1, yo, ssk, k7, k2tog, yo, k1, k2tog, yo, k3, k2tog, yo, k1, k2tog, yo, k2] 6 times, k1, yo, ssk, k1, yo, ssk, k2, M1L; rep from*. *15* *K6, k2tog, yo, k3, [k2, yo, ssk, k6, yo, ssk, k11, k2tog, yo, k6, k2tog, yo, k3] 6 times, k2, yo, ssk, k5; rep from*. *16* *K1, M1R, k1, k2tog, yo, k1, k2tog, yo, k4, [k3, yo, ssk, k1, yo, ssk, k3, yo, ssk, k1, yo, ssk, k3, k2tog, yo, k1, k2tog, yo, k3, k2tog, yo, k1, k2tog, yo, k4] 6 times, k3, yo, ssk, k1, yo, ssk, k1, M1L; rep from*. *17*

K5, k2tog, yo, k5, [k4, yo, ssk, k6, yo, ssk, k7, k2tog, yo, k6, k2tog, yo, k5] 6 times, k4, yo, ssk, k4; rep from. *18* *K1, M1R, k2tog, yo, k1, k2tog, yo, k6, [k5, yo, ssk, k1, yo, ssk, k3, yo, ssk, k1, yo, ssk, k1, yo, SK2P, yo, k1, k2tog, yo, k3, k2tog, yo, k1, k2tog, yo, k6] 6 times, k5, yo, ssk, k1, yo, ssk, M1L; rep from*. *19* *K4, k2tog, yo, k7, [k6, yo, ssk, k6, yo, ssk, k3, k2tog, yo, k6, k2tog, yo, k7] 6 times, k6, yo, ssk, k3; rep from*. *20* *K2, yo, k1, k2tog, yo, k8, [k7, yo, ssk, k1, yo, ssk, k3, yo, ssk, k1, k2tog, yo, k3, k2tog, yo, k1, yo, k2tog, yo, k8] 6 times, k7, yo, ssk, k1, yo, k1; rep from*. *21* *K3, k2tog, yo, k9, [k8, yo, ssk, k6, yo, SK2P, yo, k6, k2tog, yo, k9] 6 times, k8, yo, ssk, k2; rep from*. *22* *K1, M1R, k1, k2tog, yo, k10, [k9, yo, ssk, k1, yo, ssk, k7, k2tog, yo, k1, k2tog, yo, k10] 6 times, k9, yo, ssk, k1, M1L; rep from*. *23* *K2, k2tog, yo, k11, [k10, yo, ssk, k11, k2tog, yo, k11] 6 times, k10, yo, ssk, k1; rep from*. *24* *K1, M1R, k2tog, yo, k12, [k11, yo, ssk, k1, yo, ssk, k3, k2tog, yo, k1, k2tog, yo, k12] 6 times, k11, yo, ssk, M1L; rep from*. *25* *K1, k2tog, yo, k13, [k12, yo, ssk, k7, k2tog, yo, k13] 6 times, k12, yo, ssk; rep from*. *26* K2, *yo, k14, [k13, yo, ssk, k1, yo, SK2P, yo, k1, k2tog, yo, k14] 6 times, k13, yo, work *corner dec* as foll: sl1, remove marker, k corner st and next st tog, psso, sl corner st to LH needle and replace marker, return corner st to RH needle; rep from* (the final *corner dec* will incorporate the first 2 sts of rnd 27). *27* *Yo, k15, [k14, yo, ssk, k3, k2tog, yo, k15] 6 times, k14, yo, k1; rep from* to end of rnd, ending last rep with yo. *28* *K17, [k15, yo, ssk, k1, k2tog, yo, k16] 6 times, k15; rep from*. *29* *K1, M1R, k16, [k16, yo, SK2P, yo, k17] 6 times, k15, M1L; rep from*.

Edging Chart *Beg on 11 sts*

1 Yo, k2, yo, k2tog, yo, k2, k2tog, yo, k3. *Row 2 and all WS rows* K to last 2 sts, ssk. *3* Yo, k2, yo, k2tog, yo, k2 [k2tog, yo] twice, k2. *5* Yo, k2, yo, k2tog, yo, k2, [k2tog, yo] twice, k3. *7* Yo, k2, yo, k2tog, yo, k2, [k2tog, yo] 3 times, k2. *9* Yo, k1, [k2tog, yo] twice, k2tog, k2, [yo, k2tog] twice, k2. *11* Yo, k1, [k2tog, yo] twice, k2tog, k2, [yo, k2tog] twice, k1. *13* Yo, k1, [k2tog, yo] twice, k2tog, k2, yo, k2tog, k2. *15* Yo, k1, [k2tog, yo] twice, k2tog, k2, yo, k2tog, k1. *16* Rep row 2. Rep rows 1-16 for Edging Chart.

■

Sidna Farley

shetland shawl

By the time she reached the border, Sidna was ready for a challenge. Really four challenges—why not miter the border at each corner? So she did, and now you can, too. Perfectly beautiful shawls may be knit without mitered corners (indeed, many are), but the miter offers satisfaction for the geometrically consistent knitters among us.

Notes

1 See *School*, pg. 100 for ssk, SK2P, invisible cast-on, short rows, and garter stitch grafting. **2** Shawl is worked on a garter st background (k every row). **3** Do not break yarn throughout. **4** After shawl is made, edging is attached as it is worked.

Shawl

Center Square

Start at corner A of center square. Cast on 2 sts. *Inc row* K1, yo, k to end. Rep Inc row to 116 sts (B–C). Mark each end of this row. *Dec row* K1, yo, k2tog, k to last 4 sts, k2tog, k2. Rep Dec row until 6 sts rem. *Next row* K1, yo, k3tog, k2—5 sts. *Next row* K1, yo, k3tog, k1— 4 sts. *Next row* K1, yo, k3tog—3 sts. *Next row* K3tog—1 st (D). Do not break yarn—center square complete.

Borders

First Border *Beg Border Chart: Row 1* Along the side of the center square to the left of the rem st, pick up and k76 more sts (approx 2 sts for every 3 rows)—77 sts total. *Rows 2-4* K1, yo, k to end. 80 sts at end of row 4. Cont foll chart until 79 rows complete—155 sts. Do not fasten off. Place sts on yarn for holder.

Second Border With RS facing, pick up and k1 st per ridge along angle of border just made—39 sts. Place marker (pm), pick up and k77 sts along the next edge of the center square. Work as for first border, except, on each WS row knit the last st worked tog with the next picked up st past marker. This attaches the 2nd border to the first.

Third Border Repeat 2nd border.

Fourth Border Rep 2nd border, and at same time, knit the last st of RS rows tog with a loop picked up from each ridge of first border, attaching both sides. Leave sts on the needle.

Sideways lace edging

Continuing with the same needle and the attached yarn, invisibly cast on 13 sts, turn. *Beg Lace Edging Chart: Row 1 and all WS rows* K to last edging st, work the last edging st and a border st (from E-H) tog as ssk. This attaches the lace edging to the shawl. Turn leaving rem sts

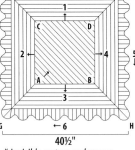

40½"

* invisible cast on and weave together line

Cast on A, increase to B-C, decrease to D. Pick up D-C, work side 1, pick up F-C. Pick up C-A, work side 2, pick up G-A. Pick up A-B, work side 3, pick up H-B. Pick up B-D, work side 4. Cast on edging sts, work side 5, miter corner H. Work side 6, miter corner G. Work side 7, miter corner F. Work side 8, miter corner E, weave end to cast on.

unworked. Cont foll chart, working last edging st tog with border st every WS row, and sl first st of every RS row as if to p with yarn in front (wyif). Work 28-row rep 11 times to corner. *Beg mitered corner chart* Mitered corner is worked in short rows. Only work sts indicated according to chart. When 28 chart rows complete, replace sts from next side onto needle. Rep edging and mitered corner on each side. Garter stitch graft end of edging to beg.

Finishing

Dampen and block severely, pinning out each point of lace edging.

knitter's pattern
· in other words ·

Border Chart *Beg on 77 sts*

Notes 1 When working 2nd and 3rd borders, knit last worked st tog with next picked up st past marker. **2** When working 4th border, work as for 2nd and 3rd and knit the last worked st of RS rows tog with a picked up loop from diagonal edge of first border.

Row 1 Pick up 2 sts for every 3 rows along center square edge—77 sts. *2-4 and all WS rows* K1, yo, k to end. *5* K1, yo, k8, *k2tog, yo, k1, yo, ssk, k9; rep from*, end k10. *7* K1, yo, k8, *k2tog, yo, k3, yo, ssk, k7; rep from*, end k10. *9* K1, yo, k9, *ssk, yo, k3, yo, k2tog, k7; rep from*, end k11. *11* K1, yo, k12, *yo, S2KP2, yo, k11; rep from*, end k14. *13* K1, yo, k to end. *15* K1, yo, k6, *k2tog, yo, k1, yo, ssk, k9; rep from*, end k8. *17* K1, yo, k6, *k2tog, yo, k3, yo, ssk, k7; rep from*, end k8. *19* K1, yo, k7, *ssk, yo, k3, yo, k2tog, k7; rep from*, end k9. *21* K1, yo, k10, *yo, S2KP2, yo, k11; rep from*, end k12. *23* Rep row 13. *25* K1, yo, k4, *k2tog, yo, k1, yo, ssk, k9; rep from*, end k6. *27* K1, yo, k4, *k2tog, yo, k3, yo, ssk, k7; rep from*, end k6. *29* K1, yo, k5, *ssk, yo, k3, yo, k2tog, k7; rep from*. *31* K1, yo, k8, *yo, S2KP2, yo, k11; rep from*, end k10. *33* Rep row 13. *35* K1, yo, k2, *k2tog, yo, k1, yo, ssk, k9; rep from*, end k4. *37* K1, yo, k2, *k2tog, yo, k3, yo, ssk, k7; rep from*, end k4. *39* K1, yo, k3, *ssk, yo, k3, yo, k2tog, k7; rep from*, end k5. *41* K1, yo, k6, *yo, S2KP2, yo, k11; rep from*, end k8. *43* Rep row 13. *45* K1, yo, *k2tog, yo, k1, yo, ssk, k9; rep from*, end k2. *47* K1, yo, *k2tog, yo, k3, yo, ssk, k7; rep from*, end k2. *49* K1, yo, k1, *ssk, yo, k3, yo, k2tog, k7; rep from*, end k3. *51* K1, yo, k4, *yo, S2KP2, yo, k11; rep from*, end k6. *53* Rep row 13. *55* K1, yo, k12, *k2tog, yo, k1, yo, ssk, k9; rep from*, end k14. *57* K1, yo, k12, *k2tog, yo, k3, yo, ssk, k7; rep from*, end k14. *59* K1, yo, k13, *ssk, yo, k3, yo, k2tog, k7; rep from*, end k15. *61* K1, yo, k16, *yo, S2KP2, yo, k11; rep from*, end k18. *63* Rep row 13. *65* K1, yo, k10,

Skill Level Intermediate

Finished Measurements 54" square blocked (40½" square unblocked)

Yarn 1,575 yds (1,413m) of fingering-weight yarn

Needles Size 8 (5mm) circular needle, 24" or 29" (60cm or 74cm) long, *or size to obtain gauge*
Double-pointed needles (dpn) useful for border

Extras Lengths of yarn for st holders · stitch markers · T-pins

Gauge 18½ sts to 4" (10cm) over garter st (unblocked)
(Any gauge between 18 and 19 sts to 4" (10 cm) is fine)

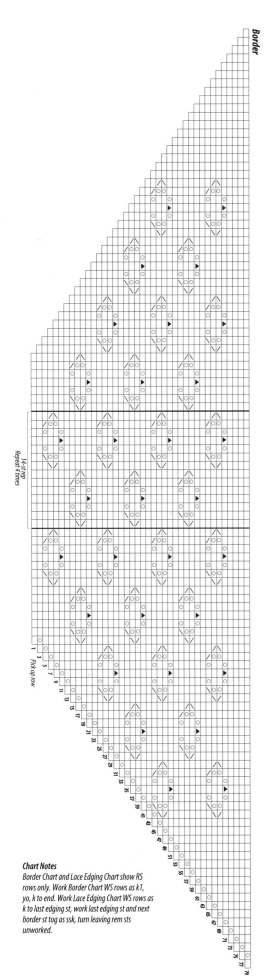

k2tog, yo, k1, yo, ssk, k9; rep from, end k12. **67** K1, yo, k10, *k2tog, yo, k3, yo, ssk, k7; rep from*, end k12. **69** K1, yo, k11, *ssk, yo, k3, yo, k2tog, k7; rep from*, end k13. **71** K1, yo, k14, *yo, S2KP2, yo, k11; rep from*, end k16. **73-79** Rep row 13.

Lace Edging Chart *Beg on 13 sts*

Row 1 and all WS rows K to last edging st, work the last edging st and a border st tog as ssk. Turn. leaving rem sts unworked. **2** Sl 1 as if to p wyif, k1, [yo, k2tog] twice, k1, [yo, ssk] twice, yo, k2. **4** Sl 1 as if to p wyif, k1, [yo, k2tog] twice, k2, [yo, ssk] twice, yo, k2. **6** Sl 1 as if to p wyif, k1, [yo, k2tog] twice, k3, [yo, ssk] twice, yo, k2. **8** Sl 1 as if to p wyif, k1, [yo, k2tog] twice, k4, [yo, ssk] twice, yo, k2. **10** Sl 1 as if to p wyif, k1, [yo, k2tog] twice, k5, [yo, ssk] twice, yo, k2. **12** Sl 1 as if to p wyif, k1, [yo, k2tog] twice, k2, yo, k2tog, k2, [yo, ssk] twice, yo, k2. **14** Sl 1 as if to p wyif, k1, [yo, k2tog] twice, ssk, yo, k1, yo, k2tog, k2, [yo, ssk] twice, yo, k2. **16** Sl 1 as if to p wyif, k1, [yo, k2tog] twice, k2, yo, k2tog, k1, ssk, [yo, k2tog] 3 times, k1. **18** Sl 1 as if to p wyif, k1, [yo, k2tog] twice, k4, ssk, [yo, k2tog] 3 times, k1. **20** Sl 1 as if to p wyif, k1, [yo, k2tog] twice, k3, ssk, [yo, k2tog] 3 times, k1. **22** Sl 1 as if to p wyif, k1, [yo, k2tog] twice, k2, ssk, [yo, k2tog] 3 times, k1. **24** Sl 1 as if to p wyif, k1, [yo, k2tog] twice, k1, ssk, [yo, k2tog] 3 times, k1. **26** Sl 1 as if to p wyif, k1, [yo, k2tog] twice, ssk, [yo, k2tog] 3 times, k1. **28** Sl 1 as if to p wyif, k1, yo, k2tog, yo, SK2P, [yo, k2tog] 3 times, k1. Rep rows 1–28 for Lace Edging Chart.

Lace Edging

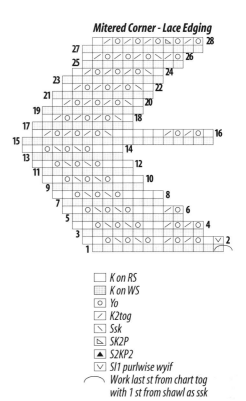

Mitered Corner - Lace Edging

- ☐ K on RS
- ▦ K on WS
- ⊙ Yo
- ╱ K2tog
- ╲ Ssk
- ◩ SK2P
- ▲ S2KP2
- ☑ Sl1 purlwise wyif
- ⌒ Work last st from chart tog with 1 st from shawl as ssk

Mitered Corner Chart *Beg on 13 sts*

Row 1 (WS) K to last edging st, work the last edging st and a border st tog as ssk. Turn, leaving rem sts unworked. **2** Sl 1 as if to p wyif, k1, [yo, k2tog] twice, k1 [yo, ssk] twice, yo, k2. **3** K12, turn. **4** [Yo, k2tog] twice, k2, [yo, ssk] twice, yo, k2. **5** K11, turn. **6** Yo, k2tog, k3, [yo, ssk] twice, yo, k2. **7** K10, turn. **8** K4, [yo, ssk] twice, yo, k2. **9, 11, 13** K9, turn. **10, 12, 14** K3, [yo, ssk] twice, yo, k2. **15** K19, turn. **16** K1, [yo, k2tog] twice, k5, ssk, [yo, k2tog] 3 times, k1. **17, 19, 21, 23** K10, turn. **18** K1, ssk, [yo, k2tog] 3 times, k1. **20** K1, ssk, [yo, k2tog] 3 times, k1. **22** K1, ssk [yo, k2tog] 3 times, k1. **24** K1, ssk, [yo, k2tog] 3 times, k1. **25** K11, turn. **26** Yo, k2tog, ssk, [yo, k2tog] 3 times, k1. **27** K12, turn. **28** Yo, k2tog, yo, SK2P, [yo, k2tog] 3 times, k1.

Chart Notes
Border Chart and Lace Edging Chart show RS rows only. Work Border Chart WS rows as k1, yo, k to end. Work Lace Edging Chart WS rows as k to last edging st, work last edging st and next border st tog as ssk, turn leaving rem sts unworked.

Marilyn van Keppel made news in the knitting world by translating a book of traditional shawls from the Faroe Islands. She says: "Traditional shawls from the Faroe Islands are distinguished from most North Atlantic shawls by having a center back gore and subtle shaping at the shoulders to make the shawl sit easily on the wearer without slipping. These shawls are still worn in the Faroes by women of all ages." Whether you make these shawls in the traditional manner from the lower edge up or from the top down in Myrna Stahman's variation, you'll want to make many.

faroese shawls

Meg Swansen

"My first attempt at a Faroese Shawl was just after we began to import the book from the Faroe Islands. With no hint of a translation of any kind, I ignored the enigmatic marks that I couldn't figure out and so missed one of the most unique features of Faroese Shawls: the shoulder shaping. Yes, I know, how can a shawl require anything like that. But, believe, me it makes a world of difference. The shawl stays put without clutching or constant adjusting. Since then, Marilyn van Keppel has translated the entire book into English. What follows and the shawls on pg. 38 were written for *Knitter's* Issue 9, Winter 1987."

Faroese shawls

The first Americans who wanted to make Faroese shawls used books in the Faroese language. Portions of these unique pieces were misunderstood even by the most diligent knitters. Meg 's insightful article and her 1999 update above explains all.

The ancient and traditional shawl of the Faroe Islands did not make itself known to me until about five years ago when we were sent a copy of a new book published in the Faroes. I had been to one of the islands several decades ago: an Icelandic school friend and I were on a freighter heading for Reykjavik, and the ship had to unload some goods in a Faroese port. We went ashore for a few hours and found a small country dance in progress in what seemed to be the town hall. We went in and listened to the music provided by a saxophone, violin, bass, and drums. Little did I know that the island was probably crawling with magnificent shawls!

The Faroese shawl is based on the three-decrease method (see Shawl silhouettes #2, pg. 40) except that instead of beginning at the top, you cast on the long lower edge, and work a single decrease at the beginning of each row, and a double decrease at the center every second row. This is psychologically more sound, as each succeeding row gets shorter and faster . . . but if you have a limited amount of wool, it is better to start at the top and increase.

Gussets

There are several unique and surprising tricks that separate the Faroese shawl from those of other cultures: all Faroe shawls have a center-back gusset. The center decreases are worked on each side of it, and the gusset itself gradually decreases as you head for the top of the shawl.

Sides and selvages

Next you may notice the side selvages: a narrow band of garter stitch (8-12 stitches wide) which remains undisturbed by working selvage decreases inside the narrow band. And, as with the gusset, the selvage band subtly narrows as you knit your way up the shawl.

Shoulder shaping

The most surprising detail to me was the shoulder shaping. In spite of the fact that knitting is so obliging, beautifully draping and conforming to whatever shape it is put on, the Faroese added this bit of perfectionism. This shaping is achieved near the end by a series of decreases in the main sections of the shawl.

Fringes

These are common, but not mandatory. I chose to eliminate them, as I find fringes tend to tangle and become a bit ratty-looking long before the rest of the shawl has begun to wear out. Perhaps their original purpose was—like the fringed buckskin jacket—to channel rain water off the garment before it had a chance to soak in. And, since these shawls were originally made (beginning about 150 years ago) as work garments, the fringes may have been a practical addition. The work shawls were knitted in rather coarse wool. Shawls for formal wear were knitted in a finer wool, and often lined by knitting another shawl in a contrasting color with no lace pattern, and sewing them together.

Lace patterns

Most of the shawls have a wide band of lace along the lower edge. Occasionally there is an allover lace motif; or a pattern that creeps seven eights of the way up the shawl; or no lace at all; or even a color pattern instead of lace. You have plenty of options. In choosing a lace pattern, pick one that has a repeat of between 20 and 35 stitches. To quote from a Faroese knitter: "Less than 20-25 eyelets for the center panels is not advisable. It makes the shawl strut, especially with age!" While you are knitting the lace, you may either continue the decreases each side of the gusset (eating up lace to left and right), or you may suspend the center decreasing until the lace is finished. The white and blue shawls have stopped the center shaping during the lace; the yellow version maintains the decreasing which minimally truncates the depth of the finished shawl.

Size

Most shawls have you cast on around 300-400 stitches, and it is not uncommon to see instructions asking you to cast on 500-600 stitches! This garment is one of the few in which gauge is not critical—within reason. At 300-350 stitches, at a gauge of 3.5-4 sts to 1" (2.5cm), you will get a size equal to the white and yellow models (about 35" from center top to outer point). This enables you to tie a cross-and-tuck with the ends to keep the shawl in place, and your hands free. (Yes, you do know how; cross-and-tuck is English for the first stage of a bow tie.) The blue version measures about 46" from center to tip, and is sufficently large to allow the ends to criss-cross over your chest and tie behind your back (with the apex in or out). Or, toss one or both ends over your shoulder(s), or wear as a hood with ends tied or flung. A most versatile garment!

The blunt tip of the shawl is an obvious characteristic of this traditional Faroese garment. My blue shawl comes to a point because of two mistakes I made: The lace pattern I chose from Barbara Walker's *Charted Knitting Book* was photographed without showing the lower edge of the pattern, and I did not make a swatch first. It turned out that the pattern caused a scalloped edge, and this, combined with the fact that I began the lace too soon, resulted in a pointed tip. You may circumvent that pitfall by working at least 12-14 ridges of garter stitch before beginning the lace. Also, most instructions call for the lace to stop after the band has been completed, but I found myself unwilling to chop it off suddenly, and continued the lace in the center panel only.

For further information about triangle shawls in general, and Faroese shawls in particular, I recommend Vibeke Lind's splendid book: *Knitting in the Nordic Tradition* (Lark Books) and the Faroese book: *Bundnaturriklaedid: The Faroe Shawl Book* with complete English translation (Schoolhouse Press), which includes 19 magnificent shawls. The book together with English translations of three of the shawls as well as the introduction is available from Schoolhouse Press, 6899 Cary Bluff, Pittsville, WI 54466.

A tied shawl allows this Faroese woman to knit as she totes. The Faroe islands lie in the North Atlantic midway between Norway and Iceland.

Elsa Maria Baerentsen, the woman who collected and preserved the patterns for the traditional Faroese shawls.

Marilyn van Keppel

my Faroese adventure

Several years ago at Meg Swansen's knitting camp, I discovered Faroese shawls. For many years, Elizabeth Zimmermann had imported a book of patterns for traditional shawls from the Faroe Islands. It was written in Faroese, a language spoken only in the Faroe Islands and related most closely to Old Norse which has not been spoken since the Vikings. Meg had puzzled over the charts and schematics in the book and had created a version of the Faroese shawl. It was Meg's version that intrigued me. She then showed me the book, and I fell in love with the shawls. The book came with rough translations for three of the shawls, and I made all three.

When I turned to the other patterns, they seemed impenetrable. I asked friends at universities around the country—and even in Finland—if they knew of an expert in Scandinavian languages who could help me. No luck. Then Meg and I discovered that the maintenance man at the building where camp was held was from the Faroes! We cornered him and begged him to translate just a paragraph or two in one of the patterns. The next day, the book of shawls reappeared on Meg's desk—without a translation—but the Faroe man had vanished. We never saw him again.

Eventually, I found a Faroese-English dictionary in the library of the University of Kansas. I checked it out and set to work. With needles, pictures and charts from the shawl book, and my precious dictionary, I began to work my way through the book. About the time I'd finished four more shawls, the library wanted the book back. I was tempted to report that I'd lost it, but my conscience won out. I returned the dictionary.

There were still a dozen shawls I hadn't explored. Some of the text I could decipher, but most of it was impossible for me to read. So I went to the Faroe Islands to buy a dictionary! A year later, I had knitted every shawl in the book and had translated the rest of the text, too. Schoolhouse Press published my translations, and now these lovely traditional patterns are available to English-speaking knitters.

Below, these two "museum" sheep are all that remain of the indigenous feral sheep of the Islands. In the early 1600s, they were nearly wiped out by disease. New flocks were imported from Iceland, Shetland, and the Orkneys, but the native sheep would not interbreed with the newcomers, so the last of the old breed were rounded up and shot in 1844. Excavation of Viking settlements show that these sheep were similar to those of the Vikings, and they are thought to be the same strain as those brought to the islands by the original settlers. The modern breed of sheep that they most closely resemble is the Soay of St. Kilda in the Outer Hebrides.

This is the view from the back door of the house where Óluva grew up.

Left, Óluva Husgard for whom my shawl pattern is named. She is wearing a lined Faroese shawl, which shows off the lace pattern band.

Middle left, a spinning wheel in a traditional farmhouse, also showing the sleeping cabinets for the family. The wheel is mounted on the wall when in use, and the spindle mount is placed on the bench and weighted with rocks to keep it from moving. The sweater shows a typical fisherman's sweater, worked in natural sheep colors.

Lower left, Carl Johan Olsen, the owner of the only commercial spinning mill in the Faroes wears a traditional Faroese farmer's sweater.

Below, a view of the old harbor of Tórshavn.

Below, looking across the harbor to the peninsula called Tinganes. This is where the Vikings set up their first parliament on the islands in 825 A.D. The turf roofs are typical even today, and the black boats are like those used by the early fishermen.

"Traditional shawls from the Faroe Islands are distinguished from most North Atlantic shawls by having a center back gore and subtle shaping at the shoulders to make the shawl sit easily on the wearer without slipping. These shawls are still worn in the Faroes by women of all ages. The teenagers use them like mufflers with their ski jackets, and older women wear them draped over a coat or suit jacket to show off the lace bands.

"A shawl is often named for its creator or owner; I followed suit and call this shawl Óluva. Óluva Husgard is the chair of the managing committee of the Faroese Home Industries Council; without her help and encouragement, I would not have been able to pursue my interest in things Faroese."

Marilyn van Keppel

Faroese shawl

The Faroe Islands lie in the North Atlantic, midway between Norway and Iceland. Laceweight wool and subtle shaping are just two of the features that make their shawls so special. Read about Marilyn's translation of the book on Faroese shawls on pg. 31.

Skill Level Intermediate
Yarn 1,500 yd (1,350m) of laceweight wool
Original yarn Schoolhouse Press
• Icelandic Lace Weight
100% wool
3½oz (100g) 500yd (450m)
3 balls in Pale gray
Needles Size 8 (5mm) circular needle, 26" (66cm) or longer, *or size to obtain gauge*
Extras Stitch markers in four colors • 16 ring markers • size E/4 (3½mm) crochet hook • tapestry needle
Gauge 14 sts to 4" (10cm) in garter st using size 8 (5mm) needles (blocked)

Notes

1 See *School*, pg. 100 for ssk and garter stitch grafting. *2* Shawl is worked back and forth on circular needle. *3* Splice yarn instead of weaving in ends.

Shawl

With size 8 (5mm) needle, cast on 431 sts (placing ring marker after every 25 sts for ease in counting; remove markers after cast-on row). *Next row* (WS) K5, place marker (pm), k193 (side panel), pm, k35 (back panel), pm, k193 (side panel), pm, k5. K 6 rows. *Next row* K5, *k2tog, k to 2 sts before marker, ssk*, k35, rep from * to * once, k5. *Next row* Knit. Rep last 2 rows 7 times more—5 + 177 + 35 + 177 + 5 sts. *Beg Charts: Row 1* (RS) K5, *work Side Panel chart over 177 sts*, work Center Panel chart over 35 sts, rep from * to * once, k5. Cont pats as established through chart row 38—5 + 139 + 35 + 139 + 5 sts. K 24 rows, working 4 decs (at markers) every RS row as before—5 + 115 + 35 + 115 + 5 sts. Cont in garter st, and cont decs on side panels every RS row as before and shape center panel as foll: *Next row* (RS) K5, *k2tog, k to 2 sts before marker, ssk*, k7, k2tog, k8, k2tog, k7, k2tog, k7, rep from * to * once, k5—5 + 113 + 32 + 113 + 5 sts. Work until there are 5 + 93 + 32 + 93 + 5 sts, end with a WS row. *Next row* (RS) K5, *k2tog, [k7, k2tog] 9 times, k8, ssk*, k6, k2tog, [k7, k2tog] twice, k6, rep from * to * once, k5—5 + 82 + 29 + 82 + 5 sts. Cont until there are 5 + 58 + 29 + 58 + 5 sts, end with a WS row. *Next row* (RS) K5, *k2tog, [k5, k2tog] 7 times, k5, ssk*, k5, k2tog, k6, k2tog, k7, k2tog, k5, rep from * to * once, k5—5 + 49 + 26 + 49 + 5 sts. Work until there are 35 sts in each side panel, end with a WS row. *Next row* (RS) Dec on each side panel and dec 3 sts evenly spaced in center panel—5 + 33 + 23 + 33 + 5 sts. Work until there are 5 + 23 + 23 + 23 + 5 sts, end with a WS row. *Next row* (RS) K5, *k2tog, [k1, k2tog] 6 times, k1, ssk*, [k4, k2tog] 3 times, k5, rep from * to * once, k5—5 + 15 + 20 + 15 + 5

sts. When there are 5 + 11 + 20 + 11 + 5 sts, move markers on each side of center panel out one st and work decs on center panel side of marker. Cont with 4 decs until there are 5 + 1 + 4 + 1 + 5 sts. Then work as foll (removing markers): *Next row* (RS) K5, k2tog, k2, ssk, k5. K 1 row. *Next row* K5, k2tog, ssk, k5—12 sts. Graft first and last 6 sts tog.

Finishing

With crochet hook, work sc into each garter st bump on 2 edge strips. Wash shawl gently in a mild dishwashing liquid or wool wash. Rinse thoroughly, adding a splash of vinegar to last rinse. Wrap shawl in a towel and press to remove excess water. Spin on gentle cycle in washing machine. Lay shawl flat and pin to shape, placing pins close tog along edges. If space is a consideration, fold in half to block. When dry, steam fold line.

Center panel

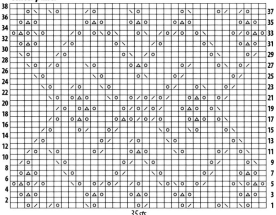

35 sts

□ K on RS, k on WS
☑ ☑ K2tog
◣ ◢ Ssk
◉ Yo
◫ SK2P

Side panel

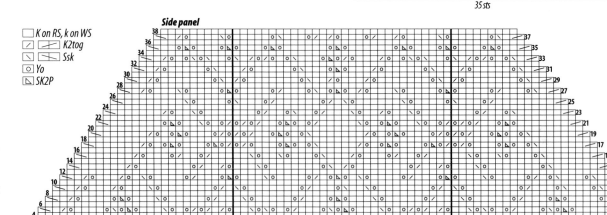

30-st rep

38"

38"

"This shawl I call "Catharina." It incorporates the splendid shaping typical of Faroese shawls, the beauty of lace, the simplicity of knitting from the neck down, the exquisite touch of merino/alpaca wools, and inspiration provided by many, many wonderful individuals.

"Knitting is a journey—designing is an evolutionary process. The evolution of these shawls began when I discovered Barbara G. Walker's *A Treasury of Knitting Patterns* and *Knitting from the Top Down*. Several years later at Meg Swansen's knitting camp, I purchased Foroys *Bindingarmynster,* a book I could not read, but loved. As a student in Cheryl Oberle's Faroese shawl class at Stitches West '95, I met Marilyn van Keppel. Thanks to Marilyn's inquisitive genius, the book I bought became *Faroese Knitting Patterns—Knitted Shawls*, now available as a set from Schoolhouse Press.

"After making Faroese shawls from Marilyn's translations in the traditional way with hundreds of stitches beginning at the lower edge, I decided to reverse the engineering and begin a shawl from the top. My love of lace induced me to switch from garter stitch to stockinette lace stitches. I've sometimes questioned whether I have sufficient yarn to finish my desired project. Knitting a shawl from the top down permits me to always be able to finish the shawl, although sometimes the recipient must be a short friend!"

Myrna A. I. Stahman

Faroese-style lace

Skill Level Intermediate

White shawl

Finished measurements 27½" long

Yarns 1,200yds (1,080m) of fingering-weight wool

Original yarn: Haneke • Merino Lace Weight

100% merino wool

2oz (56g) 300yds (270m)

4 balls in White

Needles Size 3 (3¼mm) circular needle, 26" (66cm) or longer, *or size to obtain gauge*

Gauge 18 sts to 4" (10cm) and 36 rows to 5" (12½cm) over Chart B (after dressing)

Gray shawl

Finished measurements 32" long

Yarns 1,350yds (1,215m) of fingering-weight wool

Original yarn: Haneke • Fingering Blend

75% merino wool, 25% alpaca

2oz (56g) 270yds (243m)

5 balls in Smoky gray

Needles Size 4 (3½mm) circular needle, 26" (66cm) or longer, *or size to obtain gauge*

Gauge 18 sts to 4" (10cm) and 36 rows to 6½" (16½cm) over Chart B (after dressing)

Extras for Both Stitch markers • small amount of waste yarn • dressing wires

Notes

1 See *School*, pg. 100 for ssk, SK2P, and chain cast-on. **2** Charts show RS rows only; work WS rows as indicated in instructions. **3** Sl st at beg of row purlwise with yarn in front.

Shawl

Cast on 7 sts, using chain cast-on. *Row 1* K2, p1, k1, p1, k2. *2* Sl 1, [k1, p1] twice, k2. Rep row 2 for 56 rows more. Do not turn work. Using needle that sts are on, pick up and p27 sts evenly along left side of band, then with free end of circular needle pick up the 7 cast-on sts, removing waste yarn. With these 7 sts on LH needle and 34 sts on RH needle, work across 7 cast-on sts as foll: K2tog, p1, k1, p1, k2—40 sts. Turn.

Beg Charts A and B: Row 1 (RS) Sl 1, [k1, p1] twice, k1, place marker (pm), work row 1 of Chart A over 3 sts, pm, row 1 of Chart B over 21 sts, pm, row 1 of Chart A over 3 sts, pm, k2tog, p1, k1, p1, k2. *2 and all WS rows* Sl 1, [k1, p1] twice, k1, p to last 6 sts, [k1, p1] twice, k2. *3* Sl 1, [k1, p1] twice, k1, work in chart pats as established between markers to last 6 sts, [k1, p1] twice, k2. Cont in pats as established, rep rows 53–70 of Chart A 6 times total (adding one lace motif with each rep) and rep rows 17–52 of Chart B 4 times total—443 sts, end with a WS row. Do not cut yarn.

Chart B

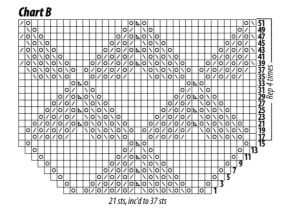

21 sts, inc'd to 37 sts

Chart A

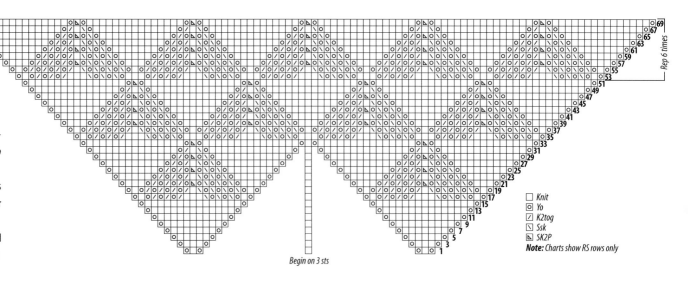

Begin on 3 sts

☐ Knit
◉ Yo
⟋ K2tog
⟍ Ssk
◣ SK2P

Note: *Charts show RS rows only*

So inspired by Faroese shawls, Myrna is getting ready to publish her first book on these shawls knit from the neck down. The one she gives us is versatile. In pure white, it's beautiful enough to be worn by a bride. In smoky gray, it's ideal for an evening on the town. Lush wool blends give them long-lasting, heirloom quality.

Lace Border
With RS facing and yarn from shawl, cast on 5 sts. Beg **Chart C: Row 1** (RS) K5, k2tog from shawl, turn leaving rem sts unworked. **2 and all WS rows** Sl 1, k to end, turn. Cont in pat as established through chart row 48, then rep rows 13–48 of Chart C 23 times more. Work chart rows 49–58, binding off sts on last (RS) row.

Finishing
For shawl dressing information, see pg. 37.

knitter's pattern
• in other words •

Chart A *Beg on 3 sts*
Row 1 [Yo, k1] 3 times, yo. **Row 2 and all WS rows** P all sts and yo's. **3** Yo, k3, yo, k1, yo, k3, yo. **5** Yo, k5, yo, k1, yo, k5, yo. **7** Yo, k7, yo, k1, yo, k7, yo. **9** Yo, k9, yo, k1, yo, k9, yo. **11** Yo, k11, yo, k1, yo, k11, yo. **13** Yo, k13, yo, k1, yo, k13, yo. **15** Yo, k15, yo, k1, yo, k15, yo. **17** *Yo, k1, [yo, ssk] 3 times, k3, [k2tog, yo] 3 times, k1, yo*, k1, rep from * to * once. **19** *Yo, k1, [yo, ssk] 4 times, k1, [k2tog, yo] 4 times, k1, yo*, k1, rep from * to * once. **21** *Yo, k3, [yo, ssk] 3 times, yo, SK2P, yo, [k2tog, yo] 3 times, k3, yo*, k1, rep from * to * once. **23** *Yo, k5, [yo, ssk] 3 times, k1, [k2tog, yo] 3 times, k5, yo*, k1, rep from * to * once. **25** *Yo, k7, [yo, ssk] twice, yo, SK2P, yo, [k2tog, yo] twice, k7, yo*, k1, rep from * to * once. **27** *Yo, k9, [yo, ssk] twice, k1, [k2tog, yo] twice, k9, yo*, k1, rep from * to * once. **29** *Yo, k11, yo, ssk, yo, SK2P, yo, k2tog, yo, k11, yo*, k1, rep from * to * once. **31** *Yo, k13, yo, ssk, k1, k2tog, yo, k13, yo*, k1, rep from * to * once. **33** *Yo, k15, yo, SK2P, yo, k15, yo*, k1, rep from * to * once. **35** Yo, k1, *[yo, ssk] 3 times, k3, [k2tog, yo] 3 times, k3; rep from* 3 times more, end last rep k1, yo. **37** Yo, *k1, [yo, ssk] 4 times, k1, [k2tog, yo] 4 times; rep from* 3 times more, k1, yo. **39** Yo, *k3, [yo, ssk] 3 times, yo, SK2P, yo, [k2tog, yo] 3 times; rep from* 3 times more, k3, yo. **41** Yo, *k5, [yo, ssk] 3 times, k1, [k2tog, yo] 3 times; rep from* 3 times more, k5, yo. **43** Yo, *k7, [yo, ssk] twice, yo, SK2P, yo, [k2tog, yo] twice; rep from* 3 times more, k7, yo. **45** Yo, *k9, [yo, ssk] twice, k1, [k2tog, yo] twice; rep from* 3 times more, k9, yo. **47** Yo, *k11, yo, ssk, yo, SK2P, yo, k2tog, yo; rep from* 3 times more, k11, yo. **49** Yo, *k13, yo, ssk, k1, k2tog, yo; rep from* 3 times more, k13, yo. **51** Yo, *k15, yo, SK2P, yo; rep from* 3 times more, k15, yo. **53-70** Rep rows 35-52 (rep from* 4 times more, instead of 3, on each RS row). Rep rows 53-70, adding one lace motif with each rep.

Chart B *21 sts inc'd to 37 sts*
Row 1 K1, yo, k1, [yo, ssk] 4 times, k1, [k2tog, yo] 4 times, k1, yo, k1. **2 and all WS rows** P all sts and yo's. **3** K1, yo, k3, [yo, ssk] 3 times,

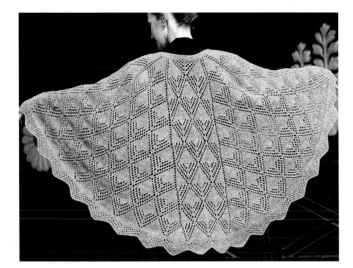

yo, SK2P, yo, [k2tog, yo] 3 times, k3, yo, k1. **5** K1, yo, k5, [yo, ssk] 3 times, k1, [k2tog, yo] 3 times, k5, yo, k1. **7** K1, yo, k7, [yo, ssk] twice, yo, SK2P, yo, [k2tog, yo] twice, k7, yo, k1. **9** K1, yo, k9, [yo, ssk] twice, k1, [k2tog, yo] twice, k9, yo, k1. **11** K1, yo, k11, yo, ssk, yo, SK2P, yo, k2tog, yo, k11, yo, k1. **13** K1, yo, k13, yo, ssk, k1, k2tog, yo, k13, yo, k1. **15** K1, yo, k15, yo, SK2P, yo, k15, yo, k1. **17** *K2, [yo, ssk] 3 times, k3, [k2tog, yo] 3 times, k1*, rep from * to * once, k1. **19** *K1, [yo, ssk] 4 times, k1, [k2tog, yo] 4 times*, rep from * to * once, k1. **21** *K2, [yo, ssk] 3 times, yo, SK2P, yo, [k2tog, yo] 3 times, k1*, rep from * to * once, k1. **23** *K3, [yo, ssk] 3 times, k1, [k2tog, yo] 3 times, k2*, rep from * to * once, k1. **25** *K4, [yo, ssk] twice, yo, SK2P, yo, [k2tog, yo] twice, k3*, rep from * to * once, k1. **27** *K5, [yo, ssk] twice, k1, [k2tog, yo] twice, k4*, rep from * to * once, k1. **29** *K6, yo, ssk, yo, SK2P, yo, k2tog, yo, k5*, rep from * to * once, k1. **31** *K7, yo, ssk, k1, k2tog, yo, k6*, rep from * to * once, k1. **33** *K8, yo, SK2P, yo, k7*, rep from * to * once, k1. **35** K2, [k2tog, yo] 3 times, k1, rep from * to * of row 17 once, k2, [yo, ssk] 3 times, k2. **37** K1, [k2tog, yo] 4 times, rep from * to * of row 19 once, k1, [yo, ssk] 4 times, k1. **39** Ssk, [yo, k2tog] 3 times, yo, k1, rep from * to * of row 21 once, k2, [yo, ssk] 3 times, yo, k2tog. **41** K1, [k2tog, yo] 3 times, k2, rep from * to * of row 23 once, k3, [yo, ssk] 3 times, k1. **43** Ssk, [yo, k2tog] twice, yo, k3, rep from * to * of row 25 once, k4, [yo, ssk] twice, yo, k2tog. **45** K1, [k2tog, yo] twice, k4, rep from * to * of row 27 once, k5, [yo, ssk] twice, k1. **47** Ssk, yo, k2tog, yo, k5, rep from * to * of row 29 once, k6, yo, ssk, yo, k2tog. **49** K1, k2tog, yo, k6, rep from * to * of row 31 once, k7, yo, ssk, k1. **51** Ssk, yo, k7, rep from * to * of row 33 once, k8, yo, k2tog. **52** Rep row 2. Rep rows 17-52.

Chart C *Beg on 5 sts*
Rows 1, 3, 5, 7, 9 K5, k2tog. **2 and all WS rows** Sl 1, k all sts and yo's. **11** K2, yo, k2tog, yo, k1, k2tog. **13** K2, yo, k2tog, yo, k2, k2tog. **15** K2, [yo, k2tog] twice, yo, k1, k2tog. **17** K2, [yo, k2tog] twice, yo, k2, k2tog. **19** K2, [yo, k2tog] twice, yo, k3, k2tog. **21** K2, [yo, k2tog] 3 times, yo, k2, k2tog. **23** K2, [yo, k2tog] 3 times, yo, k3, k2tog. **25** K2, [yo, k2tog] 3 times, yo, k4, k2tog. **27** K2, [yo, k2tog] 3 times, yo, k5, k2tog. **29** K2, [yo, k2tog] 3 times, yo, k6, k2tog. **31** K1, [k2tog, yo] 4 times, k2tog, k4, k2tog. **33** K1, [k2tog, yo] 4 times, k2tog, k3, k2tog. **35** K1, [k2tog, yo] 4 times, k2tog, k2, k2tog. **37** K1, [k2tog, yo] 4 times, k2tog, k1, k2tog. **39** K1, [k2tog, yo] 3 times, k2tog, k2, k2tog. **41** K1, [k2tog, yo] 3 times, k2tog, k1, k2tog. **43** K1, [k2tog, yo] 3 times, [k2tog] twice. **45** K1, [k2tog, yo] twice, k2tog, k1, k2tog. **47** K1, [k2tog, yo] twice, [k2tog] twice. Rep rows 13-48 as specified in shawl instructions. **49** K1, k2tog, k3, k2tog. **51-58** Rep rows 1 and 2.

Chart C
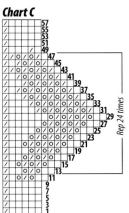

"Montse Stanley said, 'Handknitting often looks more homemade than handmade. The subtle difference hinges on an equally subtle choice of techniques that distinguish the outstanding from the mediocre.' In *Knitting Without Tears*, Elizabeth Zimmermann states, 'Properly practiced, knitting soothes the troubled spirit…[that is, when] executed in a relaxed manner, without anxiety, strain, or tension, but with confidence, inventiveness, pleasure, and ultimate pride.' To assist you in making your lace shawl a work of art, I offer the following tips for 'properly practicing' your knitting."

Myrna A. I. Stahman

lace shawl knitting tips

Gauge for knitting shawls?

My love of knitting began with a long "feather and fan" stitch scarf I knit more than forty years ago. I progressed from scarves to afghans to shawls, knitting a sweater, mittens, or socks only now and then. It was only recently that I came to understand why I have such a strong preference for the former—I am "gauge-impaired" and I don't do seams. Thankfully, neither gauge nor seams are of great importance when knitting wool lace shawls. If you have similar predilections, shawls may be just the projects for you.

Knitting a lace shawl with wool

Knitting a lace shawl with wool is very different from knitting lace with cotton or a similar non-stretch fiber or knitting a woolen garment using a pattern other than lace. The yarns I used for my shawls have a great deal of stretch, and when knit into a lace pattern they have even more stretch. Selecting the correct needle size to get the appropriate gauge is an interesting challenge. This challenge is off-set by these facts: a shawl does not require the exact fit of a sweater; its size can be varied by the "dressing process;" and when knit from the neck down, the knitter has control over length. Be aware that lace knit with fine wool grows approximately 25% to 30% when dressed.

Needle selection

I find that a circular needle with a nice point, rather than a rounded end, works best for lace. If you are a knitter who generally "knits to gauge," use the recommended needle size. But remember Elizabeth Zimmermann's great advice not to take needle size too seriously and to regard the given needle size as a suggestion.

Knit a swatch

It is most important that your hands feel comfortable when knitting and that you are happy with the fabric you produce. A good-sized swatch enables you to check both fabric and gauge. Be sure to "dress" your swatch before measuring it.

In my shawls, the most important aspect of gauge is the rows per inch, not stitches per inch. Both shawls pictured consist of 160 rows plus the knit-on border, but they vary by almost five inches in length.

Provisional cast-on

A provisional cast-on should be used for the beginning seven stitches. This cast-on assists in providing an outstanding rather than mediocre look. The chain cast-on (see *School*, pg. 100) is an easily mastered provisional cast-on.

Selvages

To give a nice "cable" look to the shawl's edges, slip the first stitch as if to purl with the yarn in front and knit the last stitch of the row. Work on developing an appropriate tension, as you do not want this stitch to be so loose that it is sloppy or so tight that it distorts your edge. Practice this selvage on your swatch.

Joining yarns for smooth sailing

When possible, avoid joining yarns by working from a cone. However, even with cones you'll sometimes encounter a knot which must be removed. When working with wool, I prefer to splice the ends of my yarn. Assuming that you're working with two-ply yarn, separate the last 10" length into two separate plys. Do the same for the first 10" length from the new yarn. Now overlap the two lengths right next to the last stitch knit and twist them together for about 6", making a two-ply fiber just like the yarn you are using. This leaves four "tails" hanging out. Resume work knitting up the spliced section. Later, carefully weave the four tails into the fabric for a few stitches, each in a different direction. Cut the tails.

Purling back backwards

Knitting on the lace border provides a wonderful opportunity to develop your purling-back-backwards skill (also called "left-handed" purling). Rather than constantly turning your work to knit the even-numbered rows, simply put your yarn to the front and purl your stitches from your right needle to your left needle.

Dressing your shawl

It is important to properly dress your shawl. I prefer the term "dressing" rather than "blocking" as blocking brings to mind a steam iron, lots of pins, and force. "Dressing" is a gentle process, such as the dressing of a new baby.

Your home washing machine, which you can control, is perfect for the first step of this process. You'll also need a bed sheet, floor space or a bed on which to lay your shawl while it is drying, and a set of "Zonta Dressing Wires". For more information, send a SASE to: Zonta Dressing Wires, PO Box 6823, Boise, ID 83707. Phone: 208-378-7757. Email: zontadw@aol.com.

Fill the washing machine with several inches of warm water and a capful or two of Lanocream Woolwash or a similar wool-friendly product. Turn the machine off and immerse your shawl, letting it soak for 10 to 15 minutes. Turn the machine to the last spin cycle and spin out the water. Do not let the machine go through the entire spin cycle. When you no longer hear water draining, stop the machine and remove your shawl.

A plaid or large-checked bed sheet spread on the floor is ideal for the final step in dressing your shawl. Thread the wires through the purl bumps of the front seed stitch border and through the stitches joining the lace border to the shawl. Lay the shawl on the sheet and gently pull it into the butterfly Faroese shape and the size from top to bottom that you desire, holding the wires in place with T-pins. Because of the shawl's shaping, the stitch gauge will vary greatly—there are more stitches to the inch closer to the neckline than around the lower edge. The row gauge will remain relatively constant. Pull out each point of the lace border and pin in place with a T-pin. Let your shawl dry overnight, permitting the pattern to "set."

Wearing a Faroese-style shawl

When you put on your shawl, place the "shoulder seam line" increases on your shoulders. Appreciate how nicely your shawl sits on your shoulders. Enjoy wearing the fruits of your knitting "properly practiced."

Purling backwards

1

1. With yarn in front, pass point of left needle from left to right through back of st on right needle.

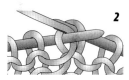

2

2. Wrap yarn counter-clockwise around left needle; draw under right needle and through loop to make st.

3

3. Drop st on right needle; new st is now on left needle.

37

Meg Swansen

Faroese shawls

Original Faroe charts were shown in a "terse" format that may at first appear unfamiliar. It becomes quite clear once you realize that each dark square represents a yarn over. The accompanying decrease is assumed. We chart in both formats on the following pages.

Skill level Intermediate
Yarn 800–900 yds (720–810m) of sport-weight yarn; approx 6–9 oz (168–252g)
Needle Size 8 (5mm) circular needle, 24" (60cm) or longer, *or size to obtain gauge*
Extras Stitch markers
Gauge 14 sts and 28 rows to 4" (10cm) in garter st

Yellow shawl

Notes

1 See *School* pg. 100 for ssk and I-cord cast-on. **2** An elastic cast on is essential for this shawl. So, choose your favorite method and think loose. Meg used I-cord cast on and I-cord selvages, but both require care (and extra I-cord rows) to be stretchy enough not to constrain the lace and should be attempted only if you are familiar with I-cord.

Shawl

Cast on 327 sts: 8 for each selvage band, 145 for each main section, and 21 for the gusset. K 1 row and place markers to mark off selvages and gusset. **Next row** (RS) K8 selvage sts (or, you may want to slip the first st and purl the last st of each row for a chain st edge); ssk next 2 sts, k to 2 sts before gusset, k2tog; k gusset sts; ssk, k to 2 sts before selvage, k2tog; k8 selvage sts—323 sts. **Next row** (WS) Knit. Cont alternating these 2 rows until 131 sts rem in each main section, ending with a WS row. **Beg Chart (Note** Chart shows right main section and gusset. Read chart rows from right to left, then read main section again from left to right reversing slant of decreases for left main section in all rows except rows 1 and 65. For example in Row 3, after the gusset you would: ssk, k10, k2tog, etc., for the left section, substituting k2tog for ssk and vice versa.) **Row 1** (RS) K8 selvage sts, work chart to end of gusset, then work chart in reverse across left main section to selvage, k8 selvage sts. **2 and all WS rows** Knit. Cont following the chart, working decs in left main section reverse of right main section (working ssk as k2tog and k2tog as ssk). The chart indicates the lace pattern and the shaping decreases. You will notice that the main section decreases along the gusset and selvage through Row 13 but then the decreases along the gusset are suspended until Row 35.

(**Note** The decreases along the gusset continue through the lace in the shawl photographed here, but the pattern is easier to work and a bit more elegant when worked as charted, and the shawl will be a bit longer.)

Additional shapings

As charted, the gusset is decreased by 2 sts on Rows 17, 73, 91, 105, and 115. Also dec each selvage band by 1 st on each of these rows.

Follow chart through Row 65—185 sts. Then cont working main sections in garter st, dec 1 st at beg and end of each main section every RS row, and working gusset according to chart, AT SAME TIME, work shoulder shapings on WS rows as foll: **Row 90** (WS) Work 6-st selvage, k3, [k2tog, k5] 7 times, k17, [k5, k2tog] 7 times, k3, work 6-st selvage—45 sts each main section. **104** (WS) Work selvage, k1, [k2tog, k3] 6 times, k15, [k3, k2tog] 6 times, k1, work selvage—25 sts each main

section. **114** (WS) Work 4-st selvage, [k1, k2tog] 5 times, k13, [k2tog, k1] 5 times, work 4-st selvage—10 sts each main section. On last chart row 123, work last 2 sts tog in main sections—19 sts total.

Work selvage sts as sideways border across gusset as foll: **Next row** (WS) K9, k2tog, k8—18 sts. **Next row** (RS) K2, ssk, k to last 4 sts, k2tog, k2. K1 row even. Rep last 2 rows until 6 sts rem—3 sts each selvage. Graft selvage sts tog. Block.

Lace knitting tips

If you are not familiar with working lace in a shaped piece of knitting, this chart will be quite instructive. See if you can notice places where the pattern was modified at either edge of the main section or of the gusset to accomplish the necessary shaping, usually by working a 3-to-1 dec instead of a 2-to-1 dec.

The blue shawl

Knit in Shetland wool (8 oz worth) at a gauge of 3½ stitches to 1" (2.5cm)

Cast on 391 stitches: 7 for each selvage band, 175 for each main section, and 27 for the gusset. Place markers for each section.

Work a dec at the beginning and end of every row (after and before the selvage band) and each side of gusset every other row: k2tog before and ssk after. Work about 2" in all garter st before beginning the Lobed Leaf Pattern from edge to edge. During the lace border you may either suspend the center decs (if it complicates the lace too much) or work the decs into the lace pattern. Complete as for yellow shawl.

The white shawl

This fringed piece comes directly from the Faroe Islands. It is relatively small, knitted at a gauge of 4½ sts to 1" (2.5cm), and begins with 353 stitches: 6 for each selvage band, 157 for each main section, and 27 for the gusset. When 109 sts rem in main section, k2tog twice in gusset, etc. Shoulder shapings are worked as indicated when 59, 40, and 23 sts rem in main section.

Lobed Leaf Pattern

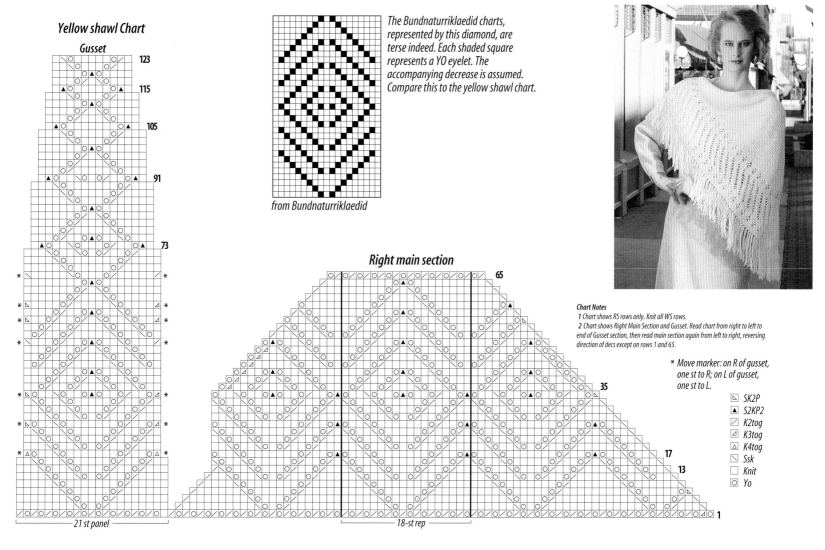

Yellow shawl Chart
Gusset

The Bundnaturriklaedid charts, represented by this diamond, are terse indeed. Each shaded square represents a YO eyelet. The accompanying decrease is assumed. Compare this to the yellow shawl chart.

from Bundnaturriklaedid

Right main section

Chart Notes
1 Chart shows RS rows only. Knit all WS rows.
2 Chart shows Right Main Section and Gusset. Read chart from right to left to end of Gusset section, then read main section again from left to right, reversing direction of decs except on rows 1 and 65.

* Move marker: on R of gusset, one st to R; on L of gusset, one st to L.

SK2P
S2KP2
K2tog
K3tog
K4tog
Ssk
Knit
Yo

Triangular shawl silhouettes

Knitted shawls come in many shapes and sizes: round, square, oblong, and triangular. Here, we are concerned with the triangle. There are several ways to achieve this silhouette, and it can be as simple or as complex as you choose.

1 Cast on a few stitches at one corner, increase to the apex, and decrease back down to a few stitches.

2 Begin with 3 stitches at the center top, increase one at the beginning of every row and increase 2 at the center every other row, until you run out of steam (or wool). (Or 2b: cast on long edge and decrease at 3 spots.)

3 Cast on 1 stitch at the apex, and increase at the beginning of each row until you reach wanted size. (Or 3b: cast on across long side and decrease at each side up to apex.)

Note By eliminating the center bit of shaping (as in 3), you will get horizontal rows of knitting. By adding the center shaping (as in 2), you will get what looks like two triangles of slanted knitting, forming one large triangle. By the way, all the versions listed below call for good old garter stitch.

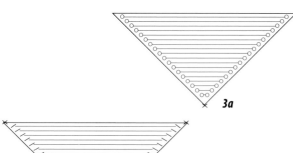

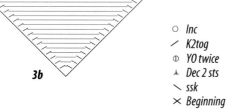

○ Inc
⟋ K2tog
⊕ YO twice
⊼ Dec 2 sts
⟍ ssk
✕ Beginning

A terse chart for white shawl

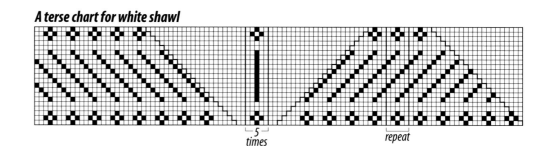

5 times

repeat

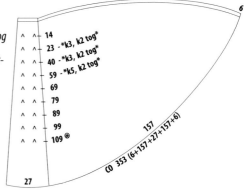

⊛ When 109 sts rem in main section, k2tog twice in gusset, etc.
Shoulder shapings are worked as indicated when 59, 40, and 23 sts rem in main section.

^ ^ 14
^ ^ 23 - *k3, k2 tog*
^ ^ 40 - *k3, k2 tog*
^ ^ 59 - *k5, k2 tog*
^ ^ 69
^ ^ 79
^ ^ 89
^ ^ 99
^ ^ 109 ⊛

6

157

CO 353 (6+157+27+157+6)

27

41

This chapter proves that there are many ways to create a circle. From Elizabeth Zimmermann we hear: "The shaping of a circular shawl, of course, is essential and can be no simpler." Circle improvements have successfully been tried by many designers. Elizabeth Zimmermann uses a mathmatical formula to create hers. JoAnne Besold makes a circular piece guaranteed to stay put on your shoulders. Meg Swansen makes her piece with a center hole for poncho-style wearing. These shawls are a wonderful introduction to both lace and shawl knitting. It's indeed fun to knit round and round in circles.

circular shawls

"While working to achieve my desired row gauge (and shawl radius), I enlarged my stitch gauge (and shawl circumference). The result was most wearable: it may not fit a table top as well, but folded in half, it certainly fit around human shoulders. This shawl in lightweight, non-bulky, relatively-slippery cotton folds up small enough to tuck into a knitting bag. When needed, it will hug active shoulders while the wearer knits or walks around with full hands?"

JoAnne Besold

more than circular

Observant knitters have wondered as they watched a be-shawled JoAnne Besold knit or walk around carrying bags of knitted goodies in each hand. Why doesn't that circular shawl (cotton, no less) begin to slide off her shoulders? Now JoAnne shares her secret: the 'circle' has more than 360°.

I recently knit a doily pattern from an out-of-print Coats and Clark book called *Old and New Favorites*. I began to convert 'Snow-on-the-Mountain' into a shawl using crochet cotton and size 5 (3¾mm) double-pointed needles (dpn) for the White Shawl. After working 21 rounds, I measured the radius and realized I'd have to switch to larger needles. (I had already done my calculations based on the finished doily which is 19" in diameter, and I hoped to achieve a 44 to 48" diameter for the shawl.)

I then worked for 18 rows with the next dpn, size 6 (4mm), changing to a 29" circular needle when I had enough stitches to go around. After measuring the radius again (each time stretching as if it were blocked), I used a size 8 (5mm) circular needle for 19 rows. Still not happy with the stretched radius I was getting, I finished the doily pattern with a size 10½ (6½mm) circular needle. I then stretched, pinned, steamed and blocked out the dampened shawl flat, and the shawl was beautiful.

After it dried, I removed the pins and saw that the shawl did ruffle and pucker a little. Unhappy, yet curious, I put the shawl around my shoulders, looked in a mirror and was given a very pleasant and wonderful surprise. The shawl hugged my neck and draped beautifully around and down my shoulders like a small cape. It would not and did not slip off my shoulders as other circular shawls have done. I then took the shawl off, folded it in half, and laid it on my dining room table only to discover that the 'half' filled almost two-thirds of a circle.

Eager to know if this technique really worked or was just a fluke, I knitted another shawl using a mohair/acrylic yarn and a different doily pattern (*Knitted Heirloom Lace II*, 'Snowflake'). Sure enough I got the same results. However, this time I side-knitted on an edging and enlarged the shawl even more. Since then I have continued experimenting and have come to the following conclusions:

Beginning

I have found that it's best to begin with size 5 (3¾mm) needles. Instead of working to a change in the lace pattern, you really must change to a second size needle (and size 6 (4mm) seems to be the best) after working a 3" radius in order for the shawl to wrap and lay neatly around the neck.

Changing up to two sizes seems to give a better drape and does not show a drastic change in gauge but a nice gradual spread of the pattern itself. Begin with size 5 (3¾mm) and work to 3" radius, then change to size 6 (4mm) and work until one-third of the doily is done; change to size 8 (5mm) and work another third; finish with a size 10 or 10½ (6 or 6½mm).

Sizes

If you want an elbow-length shawl, just do the doily pattern and, if it requires a crocheted edge, finish with I-cord using a needle two to three sizes larger than the last needle. If you want a larger shawl, you can knit an edging on sideways (again, using

a needle two to three sizes larger, leaving the shawl stitches on the circular needle and attaching the edging every other row while knitting the edging on), or you can incorporate what I call 'relief rounds' into the pattern. They are as follows: purl 1 rnd; knit 3 rnds; yo, k2tog for 1 rnd; knit 3 rnds; purl 1 rnd; knit 1 rnd. These 10 rnds can be used to enlarge your shawl by repeating them as many times as you wish and changing your needle size one to two sizes larger each time you repeat them. (On one shawl, I repeated these rounds eight times and used six sizes of needles; by doing this, a 14" diameter doily became a 62" diameter shawl.)

Yarn

This method applies with fingering, sport, and DK yarns. I enjoy using these yarns and find no necessary gauge is needed. I recommend at least 1,000 yards of yarn for an elbow-length shawl and 1,500 yards for a 62" diameter shawl. (You may want to use your yarn double if you use needles size 13 (9mm) and above.)

Patterns

I like to use patterns for 18" to 20"diameter doilies with at least 75 rows (90 is better) if I don't want to add an edge. Also the doily patterns that appear dense and not very lacy stand up much better to larger needles and yarns. The pattern and the chart are given for the White Shawl, and general guidelines are given for the Red Mohair Shawl and the Multi-colored Shawl.

White shawl

Skill level Intermediate

Finished Measurements Approx 44-48" diameter

Yarn 640yds (576m) of sportweight yarn
Original yarn: (No longer available)
Coats Patons • Opera
100% cotton
1¾oz (50g) 160 yds (144m)
4 balls in #503 White

Needles Size 6, 7, 8, 10½, and 11 (4, 4½, 5, 6½, and 8mm) circular needle, 24" or 29"(60 or 74cm) long
Optional: Size 5 (3¾mm) circular needle, 16" (40cm) long
Five size 5 (3¾mm) double-pointed needles (dpn)

Extras Size D/3 (3¾mm) crochet hook • stitch markers
Optional: We couldn't resist stitching on little shell mother-of-pearl beads to weight each point of the lace

White shawl

Note See *School*, pg. 100 for ssk and SK2P.

Shawl

Cast on 8 sts evenly distributed over 4 dpn (2 sts per dpn). Being careful not to twist sts, pm for beg of rnd.

Beg Chart Beg foll Chart A then B, working each Chart A row 8 times per rnd, then each Chart B row 16 times per rnd. At same time, change needle sizes as foll: change to size 6 on Rnd 22, size 8 in rnd 41, size 10½ on rnd 61, and size 11 on rnd 78. *Note* When changing from dpn to circular needle, place marker (pm) after each chart rep—8 markers evenly distributed. Work Chart A between each marker. When working first rnd of Chart B, pm after each chart rep—16 markers evenly distributed. Work Chart B between each marker. After Chart B is completed, work edging.

Edging

Bind off 3 sts, *k4, turn; p5, turn; ssk, k1, k2tog, turn; p3, turn; SK2P, slip the st from RH needle onto crochet hook; ch 1, with crochet hook sl st loosely along side edge to base of point, slip last st made back onto LH needle, bind off next 4 sts; rep from*, ending with sl st loosely along side edge to base of point. Break off and fasten.

Finishing

Weave in ends.

Block

Soak shawl in clear water for half an hour; roll in a towel to remove excess water. Pin out to shape. Remove pins when shawl still feels damp, then allow shawl to dry completely. Removing pins before it is completely dry allows shawl to pucker slightly and wrap better around shoulders—since we can't really block it to more than 360º. Unless we fold it in half and ….

Red mohair shawl

Skill level Advanced

Yarn 1,350yds (1,215m) of a fingering-weight yarn
Original yarn: A fine mohair blend
60% mohair, 40% acrylic
1¾oz (50 g) 250 yds (225m)
6 balls in Red

Needles 5, 6, 8, 10½, 13, and 15 (3¾, 4, 5, 6½, 9mm) Size 15 (10mm) for relief rounds with doubled yarn

Pattern The pattern was 'Snowflake' from *Knitted Heirloom Lace II*, compiled by Gloria Penning

Edging pattern 'Maidenhair' from the *Second Book of Modern Lace Knitting* by Marianne Kinzel (Unicorn)

Multi-colored shawl

This shawl which I fondly refer to as my odd-ball orphan shawl is a good project for all those leftovers lying around in baskets. Using fingering weight to DK-weight yarns, this shawl combined one strand of a dull shade (approximately 820 yards) with different brighter bits. If you want to incorporate colors and textured yarns in this way, lay out Devise a color plan and begin working.

The pattern used was 'The Knitted Doily,' from *Star Doily Book No. 104*. This shows the use of relief rounds to enlarge a shawl. It ends in I-cord worked with a double strand of the main yarn.

Red mohair shawl

Edging

Transfer shawl sts onto a size 8 (5mm) circular needle to do the purl rows and use a size 9 (5½mm) for the knit rows. *Note* Use markers of different colors to mark the rep in shawl pattern; the number of shawl sts that would be attached to one rep of edging (8 sts for the 16-row edge rep); and the heading sts, middle sts, and edge sts in the edging pattern. This was very helpful, saving a lot of time in recounting and finding mistakes. An added adventure: I ran out of yarn on the last section of the edging. I used some of the same yarn in white and overdyed the whole shawl, achieving this rich red.

CHART A

Starting at center, cast on 8 sts evenly distributed over 4 dpn (2 sts per dpn). Join, being careful not to twist sts. **Rnds 1, 2** K8. **3** [Yo, k1] 8 times—16 sts. **4, 5** Knit. **6** [Yo, k1] 16 times—32 sts. **7,8** Knit. (**Note** Stitch count will contiune to change and number given from here on will be for 1 rep. For ease in counting, after changing from dpn to circular needle, place marker after each chart rep—8 markers evenly distributed.) **9** [Yo, k2] twice—6 sts. **10, 11** Knit. **12** *[Yo, k3] twice—8 sts. **13, 14** Knit. **15** K1, yo, [k2, yo] 3 times, k1—12 sts. **16** K1; (k1, p1) in yo, [k2, (k1, p1) in yo] 3 times, k1—16 sts. **17** [Ssk, yo, k2tog] 4 times—12 sts. **18–21** Rep Rnds 16–17 twice. **22** K1; [(k1, p1, k1) in yo, k2] 3 times, (k1, p1, k1) in yo, k1—20 sts. **23** [Ssk, yo, k1, yo, k2tog] 4 times—20 sts. **24** Knit. **25-30** Rep Rnds 23–24 3 times. **31** Rep Rnd 23. **32** K2, [(k1, p1) in next st, k4] 3 times, (k1, p1) in next st, k2—24 sts. **33** [Ssk, yo, k2, yo, k2tog] 4 times—24 sts. **34** Knit. **35-38** Rep Rnds 33–34 twice. **39** K18, ssk, [yo, k1] twice, yo, k2tog—25 sts. **40** K21, (k1, p1) in next yo, k3—26 sts. **41** [K6, yo] twice, k6, [ssk, yo] twice, k2tog, yo, k2tog—27 sts. **42** K23, (k1, p1) in next yo, k3—28 sts. **43** K1, yo, k3, k2tog, yo, k1, yo, ssk, k2, k2tog, yo, k1, yo, ssk, k3, yo, k1, [ssk, yo] twice, k2tog, yo, k2tog—29 sts. **44, 46** K25, (k1, p1) in next yo, k3—30 sts. **45** K2, [yo, ssk, k2tog, yo, k3] twice, yo, ssk, k2tog, yo, k2 [ssk, yo] twice, k2tog, yo, k2tog—29 sts. **47** K3, [yo, k2tog, yo, k5] twice, yo, k2tog, yo, k3 [ssk, yo] twice, k2tog, yo, k2tog—32 sts. **48** K1, (k1, p1) in next st, k6, (k1, p1) in next st, k7, (k1, p1) in next st, k6, (k1, p1) in next st, k4, (k1, p1) in next yo, k3—37 sts. **49** K1, [yo, k9] 3 times, yo, k1, [ssk, yo] twice, k2tog, yo, k2tog—40 sts. **50** K36, (k1, p1) in next yo, k3—41 sts. **51** K2, [yo, ssk, k5, k2tog, yo, k1] 3 times, k1, ssk, [yo, k2] twice, yo, k2tog—42 sts. **52, 54, 56, 58** K37, (k1, p1) in next yo, k4—43 sts. **53** K3, [yo, ssk, k3, k2tog, yo, k3] 3 times, ssk, yo, k1, ssk, yo, k2tog, k1, yo, k2tog—42 sts. **55** K4, [yo, ssk, k1, k2tog, yo, k5] twice, yo, ssk, k1, k2tog, yo, k4, ssk, yo, k1, ssk, yo, k2tog, k1, yo, k2tog—42 sts. **57** K5, [yo, SK2P, yo, k7] twice, yo, SK2P, yo, k5, ssk, yo, k1, ssk, yo, k2tog, k1, yo, k2tog—42 sts. **59** K33, ssk, yo, k1, ssk, yo, k2tog, k1, yo, k2tog—42 sts. **60** K11, (k1, p1) in next st, k9, (k1, p1) in next st, k15, (k1, p1) in next yo, k4—45 sts. **61** K1, [yo, k11] 3times, [yo, k1, ssk] twice, yo, k2tog, k1, yo, k2tog—48 sts. **62** K43, (k1, p1, k1) in next yo, k4—50 sts. **63** K2, [yo, ssk, k7, k2tog, yo, k1] 3 times, [k1, ssk, yo] twice, [k1, yo, k2tog] twice—50 sts. **64, 66, 68, 70, 72** Knit. **65** [K3, yo, ssk, k5, k2tog, yo] 3 times, k3, yo, ssk, k2, yo, SK2P, yo, k2, yo, k2tog—50 sts. **67** K4, [yo, ssk, k3, k2tog, yo, k5] twice, yo, ssk, k3, k2tog, yo, k4, ssk, yo, k2, yo, SK2P, yo, k2, yo, k2tog—50 sts. **69** K5, [yo, ssk, k1, k2tog, yo, k7] twice, yo, ssk, k1, k2tog, yo, k5, ssk, yo, k2, yo, SK2P, yo, k2, yo, k2tog—50 sts. **71** K6, [yo, SK2P, yo, k9,] twice, yo, SK2P, yo, k6, ssk, yo, k2, yo, SK2P, yo, k2, yo, k2tog. **73** K18, yo, SK2P, yo, k18, ssk, yo, k2, yo, SK2P, yo, k2, yo, k2tog. **74** K7, (k1, p1) in next st, k23, (k1, p1) in next st, k18—52 sts. Break off and fasten. **Slip the next 8 sts to RH needle.** Attach thread to next st on LH needle, being careful not to drop the first yo where thread was attached. **75** Yo, k11, yo, SK2P, yo, k11, yo, ssk, k10, yo, SK2P, yo, k10, k2tog. **76** Knit.

CHART B *Work each rep 16 times*

Note Number given for stitch count is for 1 rep.
77 Yo, k1, yo, ssk, k9, yo, SK2P, yo, k9, k2tog—26 sts. **78 and rem even rnds except 94** Knit. **79** Yo, k3, yo, ssk, k19, k2tog. **81** Yo, k5, yo, ssk, k17, k2tog. **83** Yo, k7, yo, ssk, k15, k2tog. **85** Yo, k9, yo, ssk, k13, k2tog. **87** Yo, k11, yo, ssk, k11, k2tog. **89** Yo, k1, yo, k11, yo, k1, yo, ssk, k9, k2tog—28 sts. **91** *Yo, k3, yo, ssk, k7, k2tog, rep from*. **93** *Yo, k5, yo, ssk, k5, k2tog, rep from*. **94** *Yo, k7; rep from*—32 sts. **95** *(k1, p1, k1) in next yo ssk, k3, k2tog; rep from*—32 sts.

Originally published by Coats and Clark in Old and New Favorites. Reprinted with permission.

Chart B: Work each row 16 times

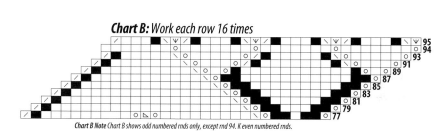

Chart B Note Chart B shows odd numbered rnds only, except rnd 94. K even numbered rnds.

Chart A: Work each row 8 times

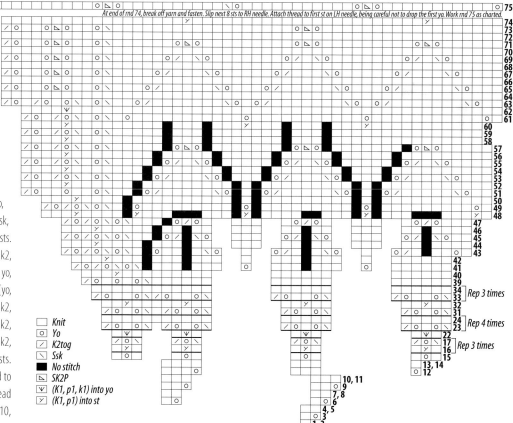

At end of rnd 74, break off yarn and fasten. Slip next 8 sts to RH needle. Attach thread to first st on LH needle, being careful not to drop the first yo. Work rnd 75 as charted.

Rep 3 times
Rep 4 times
Rep 3 times

☐ Knit
◉ Yo
⊘ K2tog
◹ Ssk
■ No stitch
◺ SK2P
Ⓥ (K1, p1, k1) into yo
Ⓨ (K1, p1) into st

"Though I dislike making two articles using the same pattern, this second was to be knitted in wool, so it became a different matter."

Emily Ocker

Patterns for fine lace doilies, antimacassars, and edgings abound. And, though these frills may not suit most modern tastes or tables, the patterns grow into beautiful shawls, afghans, and table-cloths when worked at a larger scale. There are knitting pleasures at both ends of the scale as Emily discovered when knitting two versions of one of her favorite patterns.

lace garland

Notes

1 See *School*, pg. 100 for Emily's circular beginning, ssk, SK2P, and blocking. **2** Use a fine contrasting thread (or the cast-on tail) to mark beg of rnd; at the end of one rnd, bring this thread to the front, and at the end of the next rnd, take the thread to the back. The thread weaves along the beg of rnd and can be removed when the knitting is finished. **3** For ease in working, mark each chart rep.

Shawl

Using crochet hook and Emily's circular beginning, cast on 6 sts evenly onto 3 dpn. K 1 rnd. **Next rnd** *Yo, k1; rep from* around—12 sts. K 1 rnd. **Next rnd** *P1, k1 through back lp (tbl); rep from* around. K 1 rnd. **Beg Chart A: Rnd 1** [Work rnd 1 of Chart A] 12 times—24 sts (2 sts in each rep). Cont in pat through chart rnd 70, end 1 st before rnd marker—26 sts in each rep. **Beg Chart B: Rnd 1** SM1R, [work rnd 1 of Chart B] 24 times—17 sts in each rep. Cont in pat through chart rnd 66—27 sts in each rep.

Crocheted edging

Rnd 1 Insert hook knitwise into first st, yo and pull lp through, dropping st from needle, *sl next 3 sts onto hook purlwise, yo and pull lp through all 3 sts, yo, pull lp through 2 lps on hook, ch 9, [sl next 4 sts to hook purlwise, yo and pull lp through all 4 sts, yo, pull lp through 2 lps on hook, ch 9] 6 times; rep from* around.

Finishing

Block piece.

knitter's pattern
· in other words ·

SM1R Sl 1, remove marker, sl st back to LH needle, replace marker (marker moved 1 st to right).

SM1L Remove marker, k1, replace marker (marker moved 1 st to left).

SM2L Remove marker, k2, replace marker (marker moved 2 sts to left).

Chart A *Beg on 12 sts*

Rnd 1 *Yo, k1 through back lp (tbl); rep from*—24 sts (2 sts in each rep). **2 and all even-numbered rnds** Knit. **3** *P1, k1 tbl; rep from*. **5** *Yo, p1, k1 tbl; rep from*. **7** *Yo, k1 tbl, p1, k1 tbl; rep from*. **9** *Yo, [p1, k1 tbl] twice; rep from*. **11** *Yo, [k1 tbl, p1] twice, k1 tbl; rep from*. **13** *Yo, [p1, k1 tbl] 3 times; rep from*. **15** *Yo, [k1 tbl, p1] 3 times, k1 tbl; rep from*. **17** *Yo, [p1, k1 tbl] 4 times; rep from*. **19** *Yo, [k1 tbl, p1] 4 times, k1 tbl; rep from*. **21** *Yo, [p1, k1 tbl] 5 times; rep from*. **23** *Yo, [k1 tbl, p1] 5 times, k1 tbl; rep from*. **25** *Yo, [p1, k1 tbl] 6 times; rep from*. **27** *Yo, [k1 tbl, p1] 6 times, k1 tbl; rep from*. **29** *Yo, [p1, k1 tbl] 7 times; rep from*. **31** *Yo, [k1 tbl,

Skill Level Advanced
Finished Measurements (after blocking)
13" diameter doily (shown)
21" diameter doily
54" diameter shawl (shown)
Yarns 13" diameter doily • 1 ball #100 crochet cotton
21" diameter doily • 1 ball #30 or #40 crochet cotton
Shawl • 1,000yds (900m) of sportweight yarn
Needles 13" diameter doily • Set of #18 steel lace needles
21" diameter doily • Size 0 (2mm) circular, 24" (60cm) long • Four size 0 (2mm) double-pointed needles (dpn)
Shawl •Size 7 (4½mm) circular, 29" (74cm) long • Four size 7 double-pointed needles (dpn)
Extras All • Stitch markers
13" diameter doily • Fine steel crochet hook
21" diameter doily • Size 8 steel crochet hook
Shawl • Size G/6 (4.50mm) crochet hook

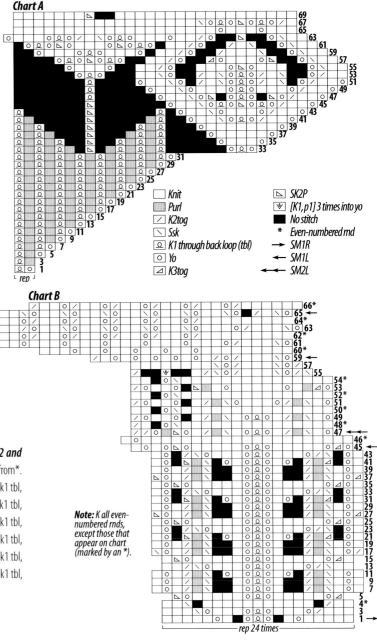

Chart A

Chart B

*Note: K all even-numbered rnds, except those that appear on chart (marked by an *).*

	Knit		SK2P
	Purl		[K1,p1] 3 times into yo
	K2tog		No stitch
	Ssk	*	Even-numbered rnd
	K1 through back loop (tbl)	→	SM1R
	Yo	←	SM1L
	K3tog	←	SM2L

rep 24 times

p1] 7 times, k1 tbl; rep from*—16 sts in each rep. **33** *Yo, k1 tbl, yo, [k1 tbl, p1] 3 times, SK2P, [p1, k1 tbl] 3 times; rep from*. **35** *Yo, k3, yo, [k1 tbl, p1] twice, k1 tbl, SK2P, [k1 tbl, p1] twice, k1 tbl; rep from*. **37** *Yo, k5, yo, [k1 tbl, p1] twice, SK2P, [p1, k1 tbl] twice; rep from*. **39** *Yo, k7, yo, k1 tbl, p1, k1 tbl, SK2P, k1 tbl, p1, k1 tbl; rep from*. **41** *Yo, k2, k2tog, yo, k1 tbl, yo, ssk, k2, yo, k1 tbl, p1, SK2P, p1, k1 tbl; rep from*. **43** *Yo, k2, k2tog, yo, k3, yo, ssk, k2, yo, k1 tbl, SK2P, k1 tbl; rep from*—16 sts in each rep. **45** *Yo, k2, k2tog, yo, k1 tbl, yo, SK2P, yo, k1 tbl, yo, ssk, k2, yo, SK2P; rep from*. **47** *Yo, k2, k2tog, yo, SK2P, yo, k1 tbl, yo, SK2P, yo, ssk, k2, yo, k1 tbl; rep from*. **49** *Yo, k2, k2tog, yo, k3, yo, k1 tbl, yo, k3, yo, ssk, k2, yo, k1 tbl; rep from*. **51** *Yo, k2, k2tog, yo, ssk, k1, k2tog, yo, k1 tbl, yo, ssk, k1, k2tog, yo, ssk, k2, yo, k1 tbl; rep from*. **53** *K2, k2tog, yo, ssk, k1, k2tog, yo, k1 tbl, yo, ssk, k1, k2tog, yo, ssk, k2, yo, k1 tbl, yo; rep from*. **55** *K2, ssk, yo, k3, yo, SK2P, yo, k3, yo, k2tog, k2, yo, k3, yo; rep from*—22 sts in each rep. **57** *K2, ssk, yo, SK2P, yo, k3, yo, k3tog, yo, k2tog, k2, yo, k1 tbl, yo, SK2P, yo, k1 tbl, yo; rep from*. **59** *K2, ssk, yo, ssk, k3, k2tog, yo, k2tog, k2, yo, k3, yo, k1 tbl, yo, k3, yo; rep from*. **61** *K2, ssk, yo, ssk, k1, k2tog, yo, k2tog, k2, yo, k1 tbl, yo, SK2P, yo, k3, yo, SK2P, yo, k1 tbl, yo; rep from*. **63** *K2, ssk, yo, SK2P, yo, k2tog, k2, yo, k3, yo, k1 tbl, yo, ssk, k1, k2tog, yo, k1 tbl, yo, k3, yo; rep from*. **65** *[K3, yo] twice, k20; rep from*—28 sts in each rep. **67** *K1, k2tog, yo, k1 tbl, yo, SK2P, yo, k1 tbl, yo, ssk, k18; rep from*. **69** *K18, SK2P, k7; rep from*—26 sts in each rep. **70** K to 1 st before rnd marker.

Chart B *Beg on 312 sts*

Rnd 1 SM1R, *k5, yo, k1, yo, k1 tbl, yo, k1, yo, k5; rep from*. ***2 and all even-numbered rnds except 4, 46, 48, 50, 52, 54, 60, 62, 64 and 66*** Knit. **3** *K3, k2tog, yo, k3, yo, k1 tbl, yo, k3, yo, ssk, k3; rep from*. **4** *K2, k2tog, k11, ssk, k2; rep from*. **5** *K3tog, yo, k5, yo, k1 tbl, yo, k5, yo, SK2P; rep from*. **7, 9** *K1, yo, k1, ssk, p1, k2tog, k1, yo, k1 tbl, yo, k1, ssk, p1, k2tog, k1, yo, k1; rep from*. **11** *K1, yo, k1, ssk, p1, k2tog, yo, k1, yo, k1 tbl, yo, k1, yo, ssk, p1, k2tog, k1, yo, k1; rep from*. **13** *K2, ssk, k2tog, yo, k3, yo, k1 tbl, yo, k3, yo, ssk, k2tog, k2; rep from*. **15** *K1, k3tog, yo, k5, yo, k1 tbl, yo, k5, yo, SK2P, k1; rep from*—19 sts in each rep. **17** *K2tog, yo, k1, ssk, p1, k2tog, k1, yo, k1 tbl, yo, k1, ssk, p1, k2tog, k1, yo, ssk; rep from*. **19** Rep row 7. **21** *K1, yo, k3tog, p1, k2tog, yo, k1, yo, k1 tbl, yo, k1, yo, ssk, p1, SK2P, yo, k1; rep from*. **23** *K1, yo, ssk, k2tog, yo, k3, yo, k1 tbl, yo, k3, yo, ssk, k2tog, yo, k1; rep from*. **25** *K1, yo, k3tog, yo, k5, yo, k1 tbl, yo, k5, yo, SK2P, yo, k1; rep from*. **27** *K3tog, yo, k1, ssk, p1, k2tog, k1, yo, k1 tbl, yo, k1, ssk, p1, k2tog, k1, yo, SK2P; rep from*. **29** Rep row 7. **31-39** Rep rows 21-29. **41-43** Rep rows 21-23. **45** SM1L, *yo, k3tog, yo, k5, yo, k1 tbl, yo, k5, yo, SK2P, [yo, k1] twice; rep from*. **46** *K21, yo, k1; rep from*—23 sts in each rep. **47** SM2L, *yo, k1, ssk, p1, k2tog, k1, yo, k1 tbl, yo, k1, ssk, p1, k2tog, k1, yo, SK2P, p1, yo, [k2tog] twice; rep from*. **48** *K15, ssk, yo, k1, k2tog; rep from*. **49** *Yo, k1, ssk, p1, k2tog, k1, yo, k1 tbl, yo, k1, ssk, p1, k2tog, k1, yo, k2, yo, k2tog; rep from*. **50, 52 and 54** *K15, ssk, yo, k2; rep from*. **51** *Yo, k1, ssk, p1, k2tog, yo, k3, yo, ssk, p1, k2tog, k1, yo, k2, yo, k2tog; rep from*. **53** *Yo, k3tog, p1, k1, yo, k5, yo, k1, p1, SK2P, yo, k2, yo, k2tog; rep from*. **55** *Ssk, k2tog, yo, ssk, k3, k2tog, yo, ssk, k2tog, k1, [k1, p1] 3 times into yo, k2tog; rep from*. **57** *K2tog, yo, ssk, k3, k2tog, yo, ssk, k8; rep from*. **59** SM1L, *yo, ssk, k3, k2tog, yo, k2tog, [k1, yo] 5 times, k1, k2tog; rep from*. **60** *K9, [yo, k2] 4 times, yo, k3; rep from*. **61** *Yo, ssk, k3, k2tog, [yo, k3] 6 times; rep from*. **62** *K8, [k2tog, yo, k2] 5 times, k2tog; rep from*. **63** *Yo, ssk, k3, k2tog, yo, k3, [yo, ssk, k2] 4 times, yo, k2tog, k1; rep from*. **64** *K8, [k2tog, yo, k2] 4 times, k2tog, yo, k3; rep from*. **65** SM1L, *yo, ssk, k1, k2tog, [yo, ssk, k2] 6 times; rep from*. **66** *K6, [k2tog, yo, k2] 5 times, k2tog; rep from*.

Emily is a lifelong knitted lace enthusiast and was given this pattern about forty years ago while a member of the Knitted Lace Division of the International Federation of Hand Arts.

Lace requires careful blocking, for advice, see Beginnings.

Elizabeth Zimmermann

Elizabeth explains

During the gestation of this design, my quite unmathematical brain was haunted by something called pi, and I applied it to my clever husband for an explanation of this illusion. "Sure," he said, "the circumference of a circle doubles itself as the radius doubles." Well!! What's a knitter to do with that piece of information? Put it to the test, of course. So I did, and it worked! I cast on 9 stitches (to fit not too comfortably on three needles), knitted one round, doubled the stitch to 18 by working k1, yo around (a slippery business), and knitted 2 rounds, doubled the stitches to 36 and knitted 4 rounds, slightly less slippery now, and slightly more encouraging. Again doubled the stitches, and again doubled the rounds. Needles still trying to slip out in all directions, but kept in their place by moi. Soon I got the stitches onto an 11½" needle, to be followed by a 16", then a mere 24" needle–on which the rest *continues ...*

Make it simple. For many knitters, this shawl has been an introduction to lace knitting and to the knitting of circular things. And a good choice it is. The lace patterns are not too difficult, and the circle's shaping is simpler yet. But all can be even simpler.

the pi shawl

Notes

1 See *School*, pg. 100 for ssk, SK2P, invisible cast-on, and garter stitch grafting. **2** To adjust size of shawl, use a smaller or larger needle. **3** After shawl is made, edging is attached as it is worked. **4** Edging is 'Pierrepoint Edging' from Barbara Abbey's *Knitting Lace*.

Inc rnd

Yo, k1; rep from—number of sts doubled.

Shawl

(**Note 1** Change from dpn to circular needle when number of sts permits. **2** When working Charts A and B, mark each rep, using markers a different color than beg of rnd marker.)

Cast on 9 sts evenly distributed over 3 dpn. Being careful not to twist sts, place marker (pm) for beg of rnd. K 1 rnd. *1st inc rnd* Work inc rnd—18 sts. K 3 rnds. *2nd inc rnd* Work inc rnd—36 sts. K 6 rnds. *3rd inc rnd* Work inc rnd—72 sts. K 12 rnds.

4th inc rnd Work inc rnd—144 sts. K24 rnds (or k 3 rnds, then work Chart A, then k 4 rnds). *5th inc rnd* Work inc rnd—288 sts. K 48 rnds (or k 3 rnds, work Chart B, then k 4 rnds). *6th inc rnd* Work inc rnd—576 sts. Knit until desired size (or move beg of rnd marker 6 sts to left, k 4 rnds, work Chart A, move marker 6 sts to right, work Chart A, then k 4 rnds). Do not bind off. Turn.

Edging

With same yarn, cast on 17 sts onto needle with shawl sts using invisible cast-on, turn. *Next row* K17 cast-on sts, turn leaving rem sts unworked. *Beg Edging Chart* (WS) Beg Edging Chart, working last chart st tog with next live shawl st every RS row until all shawl sts have been used. Remove the auxiliary thread from the invisible cast on and garter-stitch graft the end to the beginning. (Before grafting, you may want to rip back the first row of knitting.)

continues ...

Skill level Intermediate
Finished Measurements Approx 72" in diameter (blocked)
Yarn 9 oz fingering- (or 12oz sport-) weight Shetland wool
Needles Several sizes larger than normally would be used: Sizes 6–9 (4–5½mm) needles in double-pointed needles (dpn) and circular, 16" and 24" (41cm and 60cm) long, *or sized to obtain gauge*
Extras 48 Stitch markers
Gauge 12–14 sts to 4" (10cm) blocked

50

Pi shawl–a shawl for all

Make it simple The shaping of a circular shawl, of course, is essential and can be no simpler. The lace, though, can be eliminated entirely or made more basic: non-increase rounds of eyelet (*yo, k2tog*) worked, say, every 6th rnd.

Then there's the sideways border—it needn't be lace. Elizabeth also recommends a plain garter stitch border: Cast on 8 sts. *K7, k2tog (the 8th st plus a shawl st). Turn, k8. Turn. Rep from * until you have knitted off all the shawl stitches. (If you cast-on invisibly, graft ends together; if not, seam together.) Or, crocheters may finish with a chained edge as described in Lace Garland, pg. 48.

Make it together When it's your first round shawl, even the simplest pattern has a couple of scary moments: the beginning and the end. Often a friend or your shop person will help, or a solitary struggle may be brief and successful. Or, you could take a class.

Students of knitter/teacher Carol Anderson did more than sign up. Carol had no interest in shawl knitting and was really talked into teaching a class by the people who wanted to make one. She knit a pi shawl in preparation and became obsessed: "It was so much fun and a hit in the yarn shop."

Carol met with her students two hours at the beginning of the shawl and again a month later. A few students had completely finished their shawls, and now everyone has. Some are knitting another. "The shawl is so lovely that, even though it's not that difficult, you feel that you've arrived as a knitter."

Carol used Elizabeth Zimmermann's classic pi pattern, with some help of her own. Class guidelines list three prerequisites for the class: *1* You can accurately count up to 576! (Actually, as Carol's husband pointed out, you need only count to 12—48 stitch markers do the rest.) *2* You are willing, and have the knitting climate, to concentrate on counting stitches (12, that is) regularly throughout work. (Oh, to inhabit the temperate zone of the knitting world!) *3* You have had some experience with yarn overs in other pattern knitting. (We would cheat and say that the swatch would qualify as experience.)

Carol recommended working a swatch first. The shawl will be worked in rounds, but a swatch may be worked back and forth on 32 stitches. Cast on 32 sts. Knit 8 rows. *Pat Row 1* K4, repeat directions for Chart A, Rnd 1 following * twice, end k4. Continue following the pattern, knitting first and last 4 stitches, and purling 24 pat stitches every other row. After 1 repeat, cont in pattern if you need practice, or knit 8 rows and bind off.

This swatch is an opportunity to learn how the pattern works, to use the plain rows to check your accuracy (usually all that's necessary is to check that you still have 12 stitches between markers), and how to correct mistakes (the most common is omitting or losing a yarn over). There are almost no problems knitting simple lace, except not catching a mistake right away.

Carol's students made the shawl with Chart A and B; the only changes were in the borders. "They had such confidence when they finished the shawl, they wanted the edging to be just right" Carol says when they finished, "They felt they had an advanced degree in knitting." Not bad for four hours!

Between shawls, Carol runs Cottage Creations. She rounds out her life with very popular and entertaining patterns for knitted friends (OK, dolls), veiling their knitting skills with humor on every page plus a host of other patterns.

Isabella Kennedy, mother of Norman Kennedy

of the shawl may be easily completed. When it is big enough (about 72" in diameter, with roughly 576 stitches), choose a pretty lace edging for the sideways border. Cast on the necessary number of stitches, and work the lace pattern back and forth, knitting the last lace stitch together with one of the un-bound-off-stitches of the shawl.

This is a very saddening process, since each row of the border is a faint farewell to your beloved project, but there is nothing to stop your casting on its successor. It's nice always having an ongoing-shawl around. They make first-rate travel knitting, as the shawl and its circular instrument (no long needles to startle fellow travellers) may easily be rolled up and stuffed into a modestly-sized bag. The whole shawl takes only 8-9 oz of laceweight (or 12-13 oz of jumper-weight) wool. The ball from which you are knitting may be stored in the bag formed by the shawl in progress. Mathematical purists may have noticed the slight flaw in my understanding of the pi formula. The initial 9 stitches is an arbitrary number (one must begin somewhere), as the initial '1,' then '3' rounds. Perhaps my misinterpretation works because of the un-square-ness of an individual stockinette stitch . . .? Whatever the reason, it does work—for which I rejoice.

Isn't knitting wonderful?

■

continued . . .

SM1R (or 2R) Sl 1, remove marker, sl number of sts indicated to LH needle, replace marker on RH needle (marker moved 1 or 2 sts to right).

SM1L Sl 1, remove marker, sl 1, replace marker on LH needle, replace both slipped sts on LH needle (marker moved 1 st to left).

Chart A *Multiple of 12 sts*

Rnd 1 K5, *yo, k2tog, k10; rep from* ending last rep k5. *2 and all even rnds* Knit. *3* K3, *ssk, yo, k1, yo, k2tog, k7; rep from* ending last rep k4. *5* K2, *ssk, yo, k3, yo, k2tog, k5; rep from* ending last rep k3. *7* K1, *ssk, yo, k5, yo, k2tog, k3; rep from* ending last rep k2. *9* Ssk, *yo, k7, yo, k2tog, k1; rep from *. *11* K2, *yo, k2tog, k3, ssk, yo, k5; rep from* ending last rep k3. *13* K3, *yo, k2tog, k1, ssk, yo, k7; rep from* ending last rep k4. *15* K4, *yo, SK2P, yo, k9; rep from* ending last rep k5. *17* K5, *yo, k2tog, k10; rep from* ending last rep k5.

Chart B *Multiple of 24 sts*

Rnds 1-10 Rep Rnds 1-10 of Chart A. Rem pat is 24-st rep; remove unnecessary markers. *11* K2, *yo, k2tog, k3, ssk, yo, k2, ssk, yo, k9, yo, k2tog, k2; rep from* ending last rep k2tog. *13* K3, *yo, k2tog, k1, ssk, yo, k2, ssk, yo, k11, yo, k2tog, k2; rep from* ending last rep 1 st before marker, yo, SM1L, k2tog. *15* K3, *yo, SK2P, yo, k2, ssk, yo, k13, yo, k2tog, k2; rep from* ending last rep 1 st before marker, yo, SM1L, k2tog. *17* K3, *yo, k2tog, k1, ssk, yo, k7, yo, k2tog, k6, yo, k2tog, k2; rep from* ending last rep 1 st before marker, yo, SM1L, k2tog. *19.* K4, *ssk, yo, k6, ssk, yo, k1, yo, k2tog, k6, yo, k2tog, k3; rep from* ending last rep 1 st before marker, yo, SM1L, k2tog. *21* K2, *ssk, yo, k6, ssk, yo, k3, yo, k2tog, k6, yo, k2tog, k1; rep from* ending last rep 1 st before marker, yo, SM1L, k2tog. *23* Ssk, *yo, k6, ssk, yo, k5, yo, k2tog, k6, yo, SK2P; rep from* ending last rep 1 st before marker, yo, SM1L, k2tog. *25* K6, *ssk, yo, k7, yo, k2tog, k6, yo, k2tog, k5; rep from* ending last rep 1 st before marker, yo, SM1L, k2tog. *27* K4, *ssk, yo, k9, yo, k2tog, k11; rep from* ending last rep k7. *29* K3, *ssk, yo, k11, yo, k2tog, k9; rep from* ending last rep k6. *31* K2, *ssk, yo, k13, yo, k2tog, k7; rep from* ending last rep k5. *33* K1, *ssk, yo, k15, yo, k2tog, k5; rep from* ending last rep k4. *35* *Ssk, yo, k17, yo, k2tog, k3; rep from* ending last rep 1 st before marker, SM1R. *37* *Ssk, yo, k19, yo, k2tog, k1; rep from* ending last rep 1 st before marker, SM2R. *39* *SK2P, yo, k21, yo; rep from*. *41* *K2tog, k22, yo; rep from*.

Edging *Beg on 17 sts*

Cast on 17 sts. K17, turn, leaving rem shawl sts unworked. *Row 1* (WS) K3, k2tog, yo, k3, k2tog, yo, k5, yo twice, k2. *2* K7, k2tog, yo, k3, k2tog, yo, k2, yo, k2tog, k next st tog with 1 st from shawl. *3* K6, yo, k2tog, k3, yo, k2tog, k2, yo twice, k2tog, yo twice, k2. *4* K8, k2tog, yo, k3, k2tog, yo, k4, yo, k2tog, k next st tog with 1 st from shawl. *5* K8, [yo, k2tog, k3] twice, yo twice, k2tog twice. *6* K9, [yo, k2tog, k3] twice, yo, k2tog, k next st tog with 1 st from shawl. *7* K5, k2tog, yo, k3, yo, k10. *8* Bind off 5 sts, k5, yo, k2tog, k3, yo, k2tog, k1, yo, k2tog, k next st tog with 1 st from shawl. Rep rows 1-8 for Edging Chart.

Note for working Charts A & B
Charts A & B show odd numbered rnds only. Knit all even numbered rnds.

Chart A

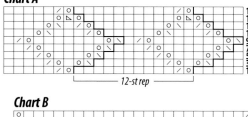

12-st rep

Chart B

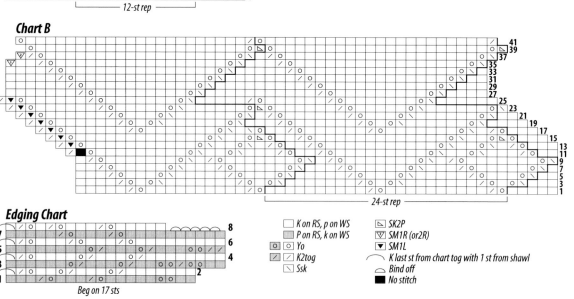

24-st rep

Edging Chart

Beg on 17 sts

☐ K on RS, p on WS	◩ SK2P
▨ P on RS, k on WS	▽ SM1R (or2R)
◎ Yo	▼ SM1L
⊘ K2tog	⌒ K last st from chart tog with 1 st from shawl
◹ Ssk	⌒ Bind off
	■ No stitch

Eugen Beugler

"When I saw Meg Swansen's "Icelandic Swirl Shawl," it occurred to me that one could insert any narrow lace pattern into that format and come up with a new design. I sat down with graph paper and pencil and came up with at least three new designs: Dayflower, Elm Leaf, and Trailing Vine. All worked splendidly in this construction. This shawl is the result of the Dayflower experiment. The pattern is adapted from Barbara G. Walker's Dayflower pattern. It is slightly different in that I added extra stitches in the flower itself, resulting in a wider pattern. This is just one example of how getting a pattern down on graph paper allows one to rework it to suit one's needs."

dayflower daydream

Using an idea from one shawl as a jumping-off point, Eugen has given us a distinctive circular shawl that takes lace knitting to new heights. A machine-washable baby wool makes this an adaptable piece that can be used for everything from a baby christening wrap to a stunning table topper.

Notes

1 See *School,* pg. 100 for ssk, M1, SK2P, and grafting. **2** Change from dpn to circular needle when necessary, placing marker for beg of rnd. **3** Shawl pat is divided into 8 sections. For ease in working, place marker between each section.

Shawl

Cast on 8 sts (1 st for each section) and divide evenly over 4 dpn. Join and k 3 rnds. *Beg Chart A* Rep Chart A 8 times per rnd (1 rep per section). Cont in pat through chart rnd 40—19 sts in each section. *Work Charts A and B* *Work rnd 1 of Chart A over 1 st, rnd 1 of Chart B over 18 sts; rep from * 7 times more. Cont in pat as established through chart rnd 40—37 sts in each section. *Next rnd* *Work rnd 1 of Chart A over 1 st, [rnd 1 of Chart B over 18 sts] twice; rep from * 7 times more. Cont in pat as established through chart rnd 40. Work chart rnds 1–40 once more, adding one rep of Chart B for each section and omit M1 at beg of rnd 39 on last rep—72 sts in each section. Do not cut yarn.

Edging

With spare needle and waste yarn, cast on 24 sts. With yarn from shawl, p across those 24 sts. Working back and forth, work rows 1-20 of Chart C until edging fits around shawl, end with chart row 20. Do not bind off. Undo waste yarn from cast-on sts and graft beg and end sts of edging tog.

Finishing

Darn in ends neatly. Block to size, stretching shawl to its limit.

Skill level Advanced
Finished Measurements 50" diameter (blocked)
Yarn 1,560 yds (1,404m) of laceweight yarn
Original yarn: Classic Elite/Sheperd • 4 Ply Baby Wool
100% machine-washable wool
¾oz (25g) 92yds (83m)
17 balls in #51 White
Needles Size 3 (3¼mm) circular needle, 24" and 42" (60 and 105cm), *or size to obtain gauge*
Extras Stitch markers • small amount of scrap yarn
Gauge 24 sts and 28 rows to 4" (10cm) over chart pat

Chart A

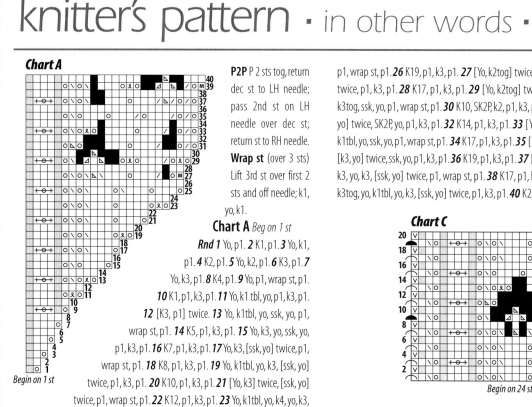

Begin on 1 st

P2P P 2 sts tog, return dec st to LH needle; pass 2nd st on LH needle over dec st; return st to RH needle.

Wrap st (over 3 sts) Lift 3rd st over first 2 sts and off needle; k1, yo, k1.

Chart A *Beg on 1 st*

Rnd 1 Yo, p1. *2* K1, p1. *3* Yo, k1, p1. *4* K2, p1. *5* Yo, k2, p1. *6* K3, p1. *7* Yo, k3, p1. *8* K4, p1. *9* Yo, p1, wrap st, p1. *10* K1, p1, k3, p1. *11* Yo, k1 tbl, yo, p1, k3, p1. *12* [K3, p1] twice. *13* Yo, k1tbl, yo, ssk, yo, p1, wrap st, p1. *14* K5, p1, k3, p1. *15* Yo, k3, yo, ssk, yo, p1, k3, p1. *16* K7, p1, k3, p1. *17* Yo, k3, [ssk, yo] twice, p1, wrap st, p1. *18* K8, p1, k3, p1. *19* Yo, k1tbl, yo, k3, [ssk, yo] twice, p1, k3, p1. *20* K10, p1, k3, p1. *21* [Yo, k3] twice, [ssk, yo] twice, p1, wrap st, p1. *22* K12, p1, k3, p1. *23* Yo, k1tbl, yo, k4, yo, k3, [ssk, yo] twice, p1, k3, p1. *24* K15, p1, k3, p1. *25* [Yo, k3] twice, ssk, yo, k3, [ssk, yo] twice, p1, wrap st, p1. *26* K17, p1, k3, p1. *27* M1, yo, k2tog, k3, yo, k3, ssk, SK2P, [ssk, yo] twice, p1, k3, p1. *28* K16, p1, k3, p1. *29* Yo, k1tbl, yo, k2tog, k3, yo, k1tbl, yo, SK2P, k1, k3tog, ssk, yo, p1, wrap st, p1. *30* K10, SK2P, k2, p1, k3, p1. *31* [Yo, k2tog] twice, [k3, yo] twice, SK2P, yo, p1, k3, p1. *32* K14, p1, k3, p1. *33* [Yo, k2tog] twice, k3, yo, k4, yo, k1tbl, yo, ssk, yo, p1, wrap st, p1. *34* K17, p1, k3, p1. *35* [Yo, k2tog] twice, k3, yo, k2tog, [k3, yo] twice, ssk, yo, p1, k3, p1. *36* K19, p1, k3, p1. *37* [Yo, k2tog] twice, SK2P, k2tog, k3, yo, k3, [ssk, yo] twice, p1, wrap st, p1. *38* K17, p1, k3, p1. *39* M1, yo, k2tog, SK2P, k1, k3tog, yo, k1tbl, yo, k3, [ssk, yo] twice, p1, k3, p1. *40* K3, SK2P, k10, p1, k3, p1.

Chart B *Beg on 18 sts*

Rnd 1 Yo, SK2P, [yo, k3] twice, [ssk, yo] twice, p1, wrap st, p1. *2* K14, p1, k3, p1. *3* Yo, k2tog, yo, k1tbl, yo, k4, yo, k3, [ssk, yo] twice, p1, k3, p1. *4* K17, p1, k3, p1. *5* Yo, k2tog, yo, k3, yo, [k3, ssk, yo] twice, ssk, yo, p1, wrap st, p1. *6* K19, p1, k3, p1. *7* [Yo, k2tog] twice, k3, yo, k3, ssk, SK2P, [ssk, yo] twice, p1, k3, p1. *8* K17, p1, k3, p1. *9* [Yo, k2tog] twice, k3, yo, k1tbl, yo, SK2P, k1, k3tog, ssk, yo, p1, wrap st, p1. *10* K10, SK2P, k2, p1, k3, p1. *11* [Yo, k2tog] twice, [k3, yo] twice, SK2P, yo, p1, k3, p1. *12* K14, p1, k3, p1. *13* [Yo, k2tog] twice, k3, yo, k4, yo, k1tbl, yo, ssk, yo, p1, wrap st, p1. *14* K17, p1, k3, p1. *15* [Yo, k2tog] twice, k3, yo, k2tog, [k3, yo] twice, ssk, yo, p1, k3, p1. *16* K19, p1, k3, p1. *17* [Yo, k2tog] twice, SK2P, k2tog, k3, yo, k3, [ssk, yo] twice, p1, wrap st, p1. *18* K17, p1, k3, p1. *19* Yo, k2tog, SK2P, k1, k3tog, yo, k1tbl, yo, k3, [ssk, yo] twice, p1, k3, p1. *20* K2, SK2P, k10, p1, k3, p1. *21* Yo, SK2P, [yo, k3] twice, [ssk, yo] twice, p1, wrap st, p1. *22* K14, p1, k3, p1. *23* Yo, k2tog, yo, k1tbl, yo, k4, yo, k3, [ssk, yo] twice, p1, k3, p1. *24* K17, p1, k3, p1. *25* Yo, k2tog, [yo, k3] twice, ssk, yo, k3, [ssk, yo] twice,

Chart B

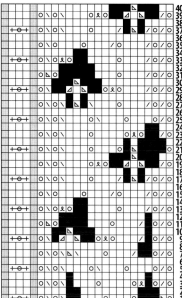

Begin on 18 sts

p1, wrap st, p1. *26* K19, p1, k3, p1. *27* [Yo, k2tog] twice, k3, yo, k3, ssk, SK2P, [ssk, yo] twice, p1, k3, p1. *28* K17, p1, k3, p1. *29* [Yo, k2tog] twice, k3, yo, k1tbl, yo, SK2P, k1, k3tog, ssk, yo, p1, wrap st, p1. *30* K10, SK2P, k2, p1, k3, p1. *31* [Yo, k2tog] twice, [k3, yo] twice, SK2P, yo, p1, k3, p1. *32* K14, p1, k3, p1. *33* [Yo, k2tog] twice, k3, yo, k4, yo, k1tbl, yo, ssk, yo, p1, wrap st, p1. *34* K17, p1, k3, p1. *35* [Yo, k2tog] twice, k3, yo, k2tog, [k3, yo] twice, ssk, yo, p1, k3, p1. *36* K19, p1, k3, p1. *37* [Yo, k2tog] twice, SK2P, k2tog, k3, yo, k3, [ssk, yo] twice, p1, wrap st, p1. *38* K17, p1, k3, p1. *39* Yo, k2tog, SK2P, k1, k3tog, yo, k1tbl, yo, k3, [ssk, yo] twice, p1, k3, p1. *40* K2, SK2P, k10, p1, k3, p1.

Chart C

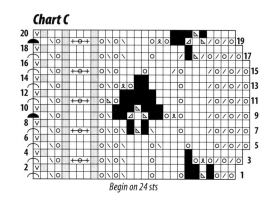

Begin on 24 sts

CHART C *Beg on 24 sts*

Row 1 (RS) Yo, k2tog, yo, SK2P, [yo, k3] twice, [ssk, yo] twice, p1, k3, p1, yo, ssk, k1, k next st tog with 1 st from shawl. *2* (WS) Sl 1 purlwise wyif, k1, p2, k1, p3, k1, p16. *3* [Yo, k2tog] twice, yo, k1tbl, yo, k4, yo, k3, [ssk, yo] twice, p1, wrap st, p1, yo, ssk, k1, k st tog with 1 st from shawl. *4* Sl 1, k1, p2, k1, p3, k1, p19. *5* [Yo, k2tog] twice, [yo, k3] twice, ssk, yo, k3, [ssk, yo] twice, p1, k3, p1, yo, ssk, k1, k st tog with 1 st from shawl. *6* Sl 1, k1, p2, k1, p3, k1, p21. *7* [Yo, k2tog] 3 times, k3, yo, k3, ssk, SK2P, [ssk, yo] twice, p1, wrap st, p1, yo, ssk, k1, k st tog with 1 st from shawl. *8* Sl 1, k1, p2, k1, p3, k1, p19. *9* [Yo, k2tog] 3 times, k3, yo, k1tbl, yo, SK2P, k1, k3tog, ssk, yo, p1, k3, p1, yo, ssk, k1, k next st tog with 2 sts from shawl. *10* Sl 1, k1, p2, k1, p3, k1, p2, P2P, p12. *11* [Yo, k2tog] 3 times, [k3, yo] twice, SK2P, yo, p1, wrap st, p1, yo, ssk, k1, k st tog with 1 st from shawl. *12* Sl 1, k1, p2, k1, p3, k1, p16. *13* [Yo, k2tog] 3 times, k3, yo, k4, yo, k1tbl, yo, ssk, yo, p1, k3, p1, yo, ssk, k1, k st tog with 1 st from shawl. *14* Sl 1, k1, p2, k1, p3, k1, p19. *15* [Yo, k2tog] 3 times, k3, yo, k2tog, [k3, yo] twice, ssk, yo, p1, wrap st, p1, yo, ssk, k1, k st tog with 1 st from shawl. *16* Sl 1, k1, p2, k1, p3, k1, p21. *17* [Yo, k2tog] 3 times, SK2P, k2tog, k3, yo, k3, [ssk, yo] twice, p1, k3, p1, yo, ssk, k1, k st tog with 1 st from shawl. *18* Sl 1, k1, p2, k1, p3, k1, p19. *19* [Yo, k2tog] twice, SK2P, k1, k3tog, yo, k1tbl, yo, k3, [ssk, yo] twice, p1, wrap st, p1, yo, ssk, k1, k st tog with 2 sts from shawl. *20* Sl 1, k1, p2, k1, p3, k1, p10, P2P, p4. Rep rows 1–20 for Chart C.

☐	K on RS, p on WS
▨	P on RS, k on WS
○	Yo
⅏	K1 tbl
╱	K2tog
╲	Ssk
◪	On RS rows, SK2P; on WS rows, P2P
◩	K3tog
⋁	Sl 1 purlwise wyif
M	M1
+○+	Wrap st
■	No stitch
⌒	K last st of chart tog with 1 st from shawl
⏜	K last st of chart tog with 2 sts from shawl

"Some days my sanity screams for safe, soothing stockinette stitch. Other times my adrenalin churns the urge for creative combinations of complicated configurations. Often circumstances dictate that simple knitting is the only recourse: meetings, riding in the car, etc. A shawl such as this one, with its plain center and patterned border, fulfills both needs. But the usual sequence of plain followed by fancy mandates that your moods also follow that order. Mine often don't."

Joan Schrouder

silk swirl

Notes 1 See *School, pg. 100* for ssk and grafting. **2** Godmother's edging is from Barbara G. Walker's *Second Treasury of Knitting Patterns.*

Shawl

With dpn, cast on 8 sts. Place marker (pm) for beg of rnd and join, being careful not to twist sts. K around. *Rnd 1* [K1, yo] 8 times—16 sts. *2 and all even rnd* Knit. *3* [K2, yo] 8 times—24 sts. *5* [K3, yo] 8 times—32 sts. *7* [K4, yo] 8 times—40 sts. *9* [K5, yo] 8 times—48 sts. *11 and all rem odd rnds* [K 1 more st than last odd rnd, yo] 8 times.

Cont working 1 more st between yo's every other rnd until 55 sts (or other multiple of 5) are in each section. Change to 16" and longer circular needle when possible. Finish with an even row of all knit. Do not bind off or fasten off.

Edging

Using 16" circular needle and waste yarn, cast on 20 sts. You will now be working back and forth across the edging sts only, working the last st of every even row tog with an unbound off st from the shawl body. Work as foll: *Beg Godmother's Edging: Row 1* With main yarn, work chart across 20 cast-on sts. *2* K to last edging st, work last edging st tog with 1 st from shawl as ssk. Cont working chart, working last st tog with 1 shawl st every even rnd. This attaches the edging to the shawl working L to R, not my usual R to L method, but aesthetically necessary so that slant of pattern in lace border goes in same direction as that of lace spirals. Work chart 11 times in each section (for a 55-st section), 88 times in all. On very last row, bind off 4 sts, graft rem edging sts with first row of edging, after removing waste yarn.

Blocking

Hand wash in lukewarm water with mild soap or detergent. Rinse with copious amounts of lukewarm water, adding a tablespoon or two of vinegar to the next to last rinse. Gently squeeze out excess water or run through the spin cycle of a washing machine. Pin out on a sheet over the carpet or a bed, using T-pins, one for every point, and stretching as much as possible. Let dry.

Notes about yarn

Joan's orginal shawl used a handspun silk called 'Silk for Life.' that was produced in Colombia, South America. It is no longer available in the United States.

The importer, Chery Kolander of Aurora Silk, has made it her mission to make silk more readily available by introducing its production into warmer climates in the United States (such as Hawaii) and the Carribean Islands.

The third edition of Cheryl's popular *The Silkworker's Notebook* is slated for publication in 1999. (Publisher "MAMA D.O.C." Inc. at address below).

If you cannot locate a suitable silk handspun yarn at your local shop , contact Cheryl Kolander of Aurora Silk. Let her know what you'll be making and she will pick skeins that best suit your use. Aurora Silk, 5806 N. Vancouver Ave., Portland, OR 97217, 503-286-4149.

• in other words •

Godmother's Edging

Row 1 Sl 1 (as if to purl), k3, [yo, k2tog] 7 times, yo, k2. *2, 4, 6, and 8* K across until 1 st left, ssk it tog with 1 st from shawl. *3* Sl 1, k6, [yo, k2tog] 6 times, yo, k2. *5* Sl 1, k9, [yo, k2tog] 5 times, yo, k2. *7* Sl 1, k12, [yo, k2tog] 4 times, yo, k2. *9* Sl 1, k across. *10* Bind off 4, k18. Purl it tog with 1 st from shawl. Rep rows 1-10 for chart.

This is probably the simplest of all circular shaping techniques: just increase one stitch by yarn overs at eight points every other round. The triangular sections between these increases just continue to enlarge to the finished dimensions that patience, desired measurements, and/or yarn supply dictate.

Skill Level Intermediate
Finished measurements 70" across after blocking • approx 60" across before blocking
Yarn 1,200yds (1,080m) of a sport-weight yarn
Original yarn: Aurora Silk • Silk for Life 100% silk, 4oz (112g)
2 skeins Natural
Substitution: Aurora Silk • Smooth Spun 2 ply Silk
12oz (336g)
Needles Size 9 (5½mm) 16" and 24," or 29" (40, 60, or 74cm) circular and double pointed needles, *or size to obtain gauge*
Extras Waste yarn
Gauge 12 sts to 4" (10cm) over St st, blocked

Godmother's Edging

| | K on RS | | K on WS | | K2tog | | P last st from chart tog with 1 st from shawl |
| Yo | | Sl 1 | | Bind off | | | |

Chart Note
Chart shows RS rows only, except for row 10. Knit all WS rows, working last chart st tog with 1 st from shawl as ssk. Work Row 10 as charted.

Joan Schrouder

Another way to attach a lace edging

EZ's pi shawl method

I usually add lace edgings at the end: knit shawl to desired diameter, then immediately cast on invisibly the edging stitches. I work back and forth over these stitches in pattern (but knit or purl, whichever looks better) the last stitch on the straight side of edging together with one of the unbound-off stitches from the shawl. I then slip-as-to-purl this same stitch at the beginning of the next row and repeat these two rows until all but one shawl stitch is bound off. Break yarn, leaving long enough length to graft the edging stitches to the cast on stitches. The last stitch of shawl is grafted into the join.

As you can see, only one stitch from the shawl is 'bound off' by each two rows of edging. Divide the number of rows per repeat for the edging you select by two to see how many shawl stitches will be bound off in each repeat. This number should divide evenly into the total number of shawl stitches. On the next-to-last round of shawl knitting, double check the number of stitches on the shawl body so that adjustments can be made (by increase or decrease) if you're off by a stitch or two.

But...

I often embark on projects with a limited supply of yarn. Since some of my shawls have needed one third or more of the total amount of yarn for the edging alone, estimating how much yarn to reserve for the edging is a struggle. I can't imagine anything more frustrating than finding myself a few inches shy of going full circle on a beautiful, intricate, time-consuming border—unless it would be to choose a spartan pattern only to discover lots of yarn left over.

Another dilemma I encounter is my vacillation between plain or patterned knitting. Some days my sanity screams for safe, soothing stockinette stitch. Other times my adrenaline churns the urge for creative combinations of complicated configurations. Often circumstances dictate that simple knitting is the only recourse—meetings, riding in the car, etc. A shawl such as this one, with its plain center and patterned border, fulfills both needs. But the usual sequence of plain followed by fancy mandates that your moods also follow that order. Mine often don't.

So...

These two problems, projecting yarn usage accurately and balancing plain versus fancy knitting, led me to the decision of knitting the two portions of the shawl separately. This way I could choose between simple and complex, depending on the circumstances and moods. Also, by working somewhat simultaneously, I could come closer to using up the available yarn without running out. For every additional round of eight increase stitches, I would have to knit 16 more rows of edging.

The merger

The crux of this whole idea revolves around the method of attaching the two pieces

together and hinges upon making a chain-stitch selvage along the straight edge of the lace border. This straight edge should contain at least one stitch at the end that is never involved in any patterning in any row. If necessary, add one stitch to serve as selvage (for example, change "cast on 11 stitches" to "cast on 12 stitches"). Always slip as to purl at the beginning of the row. If the next stitch is to be knit, then take the yarn to back between the needle tips. Always knit this stitch at the end of the row. Work all the rest of the stitches as directed in the pattern. You should end up with a chain stitch running straight along the edge. Each chain stitch equals two rows. When the number of chain stitches equals one less than the number of stitches on the shawl body to be bound off, stop knitting with yarn left hanging at the scalloped edge. Cut it, leaving about 20" to graft those stitches together with the cast on stitches (following the path of the waste cast-on stitches before removing them).

Now drop this chain stitch and help it run all the way back. Place the dropped loops onto a lengthy, large circular needle to keep them in order. Determine if there is a right side to the lace border. Godmother's edging is reversible. However, the pattern does slant so I chose as the 'right side' the side on which the pattern continues the swirl of the eyelets in the shawl. Arrange as photographed, right:

Using a suitable-sized crochet hook and working from right to left, pull a loop from the edging through a stitch from the shawl. *Leave loop on hook, insert hook into next shawl stitch and pull next edging loop through both loops on hook; repeat from*. The very last loop will be the end of the yarn; thread it through a blunt needle and duplicate stitch it to the very first chain stitch to complete the circle.

Using this method of attaching gives the exact same result as knitting or purling together the straight edge stitch with the shawl body stitch. It allows you the freedom of exchanging edges, removing and adding different ones if you should change your mind for any reason, and will work equally well on garments or anywhere else two pieces of knitting have been or are to be joined at right angles.

About knitting with handspun

Even in situations where I do have ample yarn, such as this one, the sometimes inherent discrepancies between skeins encourages me to be "wary" (the dictionary defined wary as "shrewd, wily"). The reason for these discrepancies is the very essence of handspun. An experienced handspinner easily turns out nearly identical skeins of yarn but her/his work may not match another spinner's work exactly. To eliminate a demarcation line where I changed from one skein to the next, I alternated rounds of the two yarns for an inch or three. (Actually, the whole center could be knit this way). A slightly different skein of yarn used for only the edging will not show because the different pattern stitch and the grain of the fabric going at right angles to the body will fool the eye.

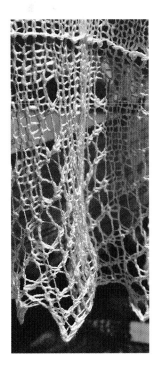

mañanita magic

What is it—a shawl, a poncho, or a unique canvas to show off your lacework? We think it's a knitter's delight and Meg tells us why. You'll definitely want to make more than one.

There are several advantages to choosing this shape for your first venture into lace knitting:

• It is enormously exciting.
• It takes only seven ounces of fine wool.
• It is quickly completed.
• It eliminates the trickiest part of knitting a circle from the center.
• It is elegant and dashing to wear—over an evening dress or with jeans and a T-shirt.

This beautiful pattern (which we call Peacock) is taken from a finely-knitted table center by Austrian lace designer Herbert Niebling. It had a crocheted border which we replaced with 'Very Narrow Eyelet Edging' from Barbara Abbey's *Knitting Lace* (Schoolhouse Press), which you may prefer to chart."

Notes

1 See *School*, pg. 100 for ssk, S2KP2, invisible cast-on, and garter stitch grafting. **2** To adjust size of shawl, use a smaller or larger needle. **3** After shawl is made, border is attached as it is worked.

Border pat *Beg with 5 sts*

Row 1 Sl 1, k1, k2tog, yo, k1. **2** K1, ([k1, p1] twice, k1) into yo, yo, k2tog, k2tog tbl (border st and shawl st). **3, 5, 7** Sl 1, k1, yo, k2tog, k5. **4, 6** K6, yo, k2tog, k2tog tbl. **8** Bind off 4, k1, yo, k2tog, k2tog tbl. Rep rows 1-8 for Border pat.

Shawl

Very loosely cast on 80 sts. K 1 rnd. ***Beg Chart*** Work in chart pat as foll: Knit every even numbered rnd (not shown on chart). For triple yo, wrap yarn around needle. On foll rnd work 18 sts into triple yo as foll: [kl,pl] 3 times into each yo (18 sts made). This is not shown on chart as it is an even numbered rnd. Rep each line 10 times per rnd—400 sts at end of rnd 65. K 1 rnd. Do not bind off.

Border

Cast on 5 sts onto needle with shawl sts using invisible cast-on, turn. *Next row* K5, working the last st tog with a shawl st as k2tog tbl, turn leaving rem sts unworked. ***Beg Border Pat: Row 1*** Work row 1 of Border pat, turn. *Row 2* Work row 2 of Border Pat, working last st of pat and next shawl st tog as k2tog tbl, turn leaving rem sts unworked. Cont in pat as established, working last pat st tog with next live shawl st every other row. With 400 sts and an 8-row rep, you will neatly fit in 100 units. Remove the auxiliary thread from the invisible cast-on and garter-stitch-graft the end to the beginning. (You may, or may not, want to rip back the first row you knitted before weaving.)

Finishing

The neck edge may easily be adjusted by the final I-Cord edging. Try it on — with the hope that it is either just right, or too large. If just right, work Elizabeth's Applied I-Cord edge on the same-size needle. If the opening is too large, work on smaller-sized needle.

Elizabeth's Applied I-cord

Pick up 1 st for each cast-on st around the neck edge. Cast on 2 sts (or 3 if you want a thicker edge). Sl the 2 sts to the pick-up needle and *k1, k2tog tbl (working last cast-on st with first picked-up st). Do not turn work. Sl the 2 sts to LH needle and rep from* around. Weave end to beginning.

Block

Wash the Mañanita in cool water. Wrap it in a bath towel to remove excess water. Pin out the shawl on a large, flat surface (I used my rug) — first in halves, then quarters, eighths, sixteenths, etc., until every scallop has a pin. You may stretch it quite severely, depending upon final desired length — the wool can take it. If knitted loosely on large needles, it will dry in a matter of hours.

• in other words •

Chart *beg on multiple of 8 sts*
Rnd 1 *K1 tbl, yo, k7, yo; rep from*. **2 and all even numbered rnds** Knit. **3** *K1 tbl, yo, k3, S2KP2, k3, yo; rep from*. **5** *(K1, p1) into st, k9; rep from*. **7** *K1 tbl, triple yo, k1 tbl, k3, S2KP2, k3; rep from*. **8** *K1, [kl, pl] 3 times into each yo (18 sts made), k8; rep from*. **9** *K20 tbl, k7; rep from*. **11** *K1 tbl, k18, k1 tbl, k2, S2KP2, k2; rep from*. **13** *K1 tbl, k18, k1 tbl, k5; rep from*. **15** *K1 tbl, [(ssk, yo) twice, k1 tbl, (yo, k2tog) twice] twice, k1 tbl, k1, S2KP2, k1; rep from*. **17** *K1 tbl, [(ssk, yo) twice, k1 tbl, (yo, k2tog) twice] twice, k1 tbl, S2KP2; rep from*. **19** *K1 tbl, ssk, yo, ssk, k1, k2tog, yo, k2tog, triple yo, ssk, yo, ssk, k1, k2tog, yo, k2tog, k2 tbl; rep from*. **20, 32, 44, 56** K across, working 18 sts into triple yo's. **21** *K1 tbl, ssk, yo, S2KP2, yo, k2tog, k18 tbl, ssk, yo, S2KP2, yo, k2tog k2 tbl; rep from*. **23** *K1 tbl, ssk, k1, k2tog, k18, ssk, k1, k2tog, k2 tbl; rep from*. **25** *K1 tbl, S2KP2, k18, S2KP2, k2 tbl; rep from*. **27** *K2tog, [(ssk, yo) twice, k1 tbl, (yo, k2tog) twice] twice, ssk, (k1, p1) into st; rep from*. **29** *K1 tbl, [(ssk, yo) twice, k1 tbl, (yo, k2tog) twice] twice, k3 tbl; rep from*. **31** *K1 tbl, ssk, yo, ssk, k1, k2tog, yo, k2tog, triple yo, ssk, yo, ssk, k1, k2tog, yo, k2tog k2 tbl, triple yo, k1 tbl; rep from*. **33** *K1 tbl, ssk, yo, S2KP2, yo, k2tog, k18 tbl, ssk, yo, S2KP2, yo, k2tog, k21 tbl; rep from*. **35** *K1 tbl, ssk, k1, k2tog, k18, ssk, k1, k2tog, k2 tbl, k18, k1 tbl; rep from*. **37** *K1 tbl, S2KP2, k18, S2KP2, k2 tbl, k18, k1 tbl; rep from*. **39** *K2tog, [(ssk, yo) twice, k1 tbl, (yo, k2tog) twice] twice, ssk, k1 tbl; rep between [ ]'s twice, k1 tbl; rep from*. **41** *K1 tbl, [(ssk, yo) twice, k1 tbl, (yo, k2tog) twice] twice, k1 tbl; rep from*. **43** *K1 tbl, ssk, yo, ssk, k1, k2tog, yo, k2tog, triple yo, ssk, yo, ssk, k1, k2tog, yo, k2tog, k1 tbl; rep from*. **45** *K1 tbl, ssk, yo, S2KP2, yo, k2tog, k18 tbl, ssk, yo, S2KP2, yo, k2tog; rep from*. **47** *K1 tbl, ssk, k1, k2tog, k18, ssk, k1, k2tog, k1 tbl; rep from*. **49** *K1 tbl, S2KP2, k18, S2KP2, k1 tbl; rep from*. **51** *K2tog, [(ssk, yo) twice, k1 tbl, (yo, k2tog) twice] twice, ssk; rep from*. **53-65** Rep rnds 41–53.

Skill level Intermediate
Finished Measurements approx 20" deep
Yarn 1,000yds (900m) of laceweight yarn
Original yarn: Schoolhouse Press • Spun Icelandic Laceweight 100% wool
1¾oz (50g) 250 yds (225m)
4 balls Off White
Needles Size 10 (6mm) circular needle, 24" (60cm) long, *or size to obtain gauge* (Size of shawl may be adjusted by needle size)
Extras Straight pins for blocking
Gauge 16 sts equal 4" (10cm) over St st (blocked)

Chart Note Chart shows odd numbered rnds only. K even numbered rnds, working 18 sts into each triple yo (k into front & back 3 times of each yo).

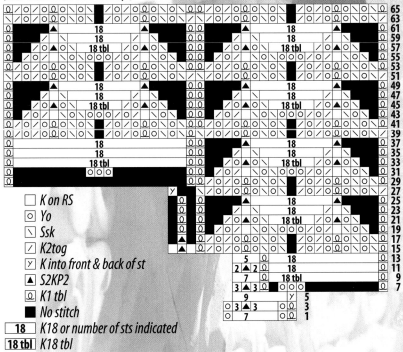

- ☐ K on RS
- ⊙ Yo
- ＼ Ssk
- ／ K2tog
- ⓨ K into front & back of st
- ▲ S2KP2
- Ⓠ K1 tbl
- ■ No stitch
- 18 K18 or number of sts indicated
- 18 tbl K18 tbl

59

Meg Swansen gives us this advice:
"If lace knitting is new to you, this
triangular shawl may be a good place to
begin." You can work from the top down
or the lower edge upwards. Again from
Meg: "If, psychologically, the thought of
beginning with a few stitches and having each succeeding pair of rows get
longer and slower bogs you down, you
have the option of casting on (invisibly)
hundreds and hundreds of stitches from
corner to corner, and decreasing four
stitches every ridge." Add lace stitches
to this shape and a lace edge to the finished triangle and you have a perfect
shawl for all occasions!

triangular shawls

Meg Swansen

If lace knitting is new to you, this triangular shawl may be a good place to begin. Ninety percent of the shawl is simply smooth knitting back and forth, producing reversible garter stitch, which, when knitted very loosely, gives the illusion of an openwork stitch pattern. Then, as a reward for patiently plowing through that rather slow-growing stitch, you have an opportunity to knit an elegant lace border on the thing. Even though the actual amount of lace is small, the impact is great, and you may choose your "lace edging degree of difficulty" from one of the books available on the subject, or use the one shown here.

garter and lace

Notes 1 See *School*, pg. 100 for knitting-on. **2** After shawl is made, border is attached as it is worked. **3** Border pat is "Faggoting with Double Ladder and 3-drop triangle" (from Hazel Carter's book: *Shetland Lace Knitting from Charts* (Schoolhouse Press): Edging #2).

Shawl
Cast on 3 sts. *Row 1* Knit. *2* [K1, yo] twice, k1. *3 and all odd numbered rows* Knit. *4* [K1, yo] 4 times, k1. *6* [K1, yo, k3, yo] twice, k1. *8* [K1, yo, k5, yo] twice, k1. *10* [K1, yo, k7, yo] twice, k1. *12* [K1, yo, k9, yo] twice, k1. Cont inc as established every other row to 433 sts or desired size (total number of sts must be a multiple of 12 plus 1), end with a k row. If working a different border than given, total number of sts must equal multiple of rows in pat used plus 1 (center st). Do not bind off. Mark center st.

Border
Notes 1 A small fill-in triangle is worked before beg border pat and after, to keep triangular shape of shawl at top corners. Without this, the corner will fall away at an angle (see illustration). This triangle may be worked in a lace pat, but garter st is easier and ties in nicely with main body of the shawl. **2** If triangle is omitted, cast on 12 sts, k same sts, then turn, leaving rem sts unworked, to beg chart at correct place. Cast on 12 sts onto needle with shawl sts using knitting on cast-on.

Small fill-in triangle to set up border pat (optional)
Row 1 K2, turn leaving rem sts unworked, k back. *2* K4, turn, k back. *3* K6, turn, k back.

knitter's pattern
· in other words ·

Chart *Beg on 12 sts*
Row 1 K3, yo, k2tog, k1, [k2tog, yo] twice, k2. *2* K2, yo, k2tog, yo k5, yo, k2tog, k next st tog with 1 st from shawl. *3* K3, yo, k2tog, k4, yo, k2tog, yo, k2. *4* K2, yo, k2tog, yo, k7, yo, k2tog, k next st tog with 1 st from shawl. *5* K3, yo, [k2tog] twice, [yo] twice, [k2tog, yo] 3 times, k2. **Short row** [K2, turn] twice. *6* K2, yo, k2tog, yo, k5, p1, k3, yo, k2tog, k next st tog with 1 st from shawl. *7* K3, yo, k2tog, k2, k2tog, [yo] twice, [k2tog] twice, yo, k2tog, yo, k2. *8* K1, [k2tog, yo] twice, k2tog, k1, p1, k5, yo, k2tog, k next st tog with 1 st from shawl. *9* K3, yo, [k2tog] twice, [yo] twice, [k2tog] twice, [yo, k2tog] twice, k1. **Short row** [K2, turn] twice. *10* K1, [k2tog, yo] twice, k2tog, k1, p1, k3, yo, k2tog, k next st tog with 1 st from shawl. *11* K3, yo, k2tog, k2, [k2tog, yo] twice, k2tog, k1. *12* K1, [k2tog, yo] twice, k2tog, k3, yo, k2tog, k next st tog with 1 st from shawl. Rep rows 1–12 for chart.

Skill Level Intermediate
Finished Measurements
36" from center top to point
Yarn 750yds (675m) worsted-weight, looped mohair or other textured yarn—Approx 12 oz (336g)
Needles Size 10 (6mm) circular, 24" (60cm) long, *or size to obtain gauge*
Gauge 10 sts to 4" (10cm) in garter st

"Shetland knitters often 'lengthen the edge' by knitting two stitches in from the edge and then back again, each side of the point. The position of these 'lengthening short rows' is indicated by arrows."

—Hazel Carter

4 K8, turn, k back. *5* K10, turn, k back. *6* K12, turn, do not k back. *Beg Chart: Row 1* *Work 12 chart sts, turn. *2* Work 11 chart sts, k last chart st tog with first live shawl st, turn leaving rem sts unworked. Cont in pat as established, working last chart st tog with next live shawl st every other row to marked center st, end with Chart Row 12. K 2 rows, working last chart st and marked center st tog on last row. Rep from * to end, end with Chart Row 12—12 sts. Reverse small triangle shaping. Bind off loosely. Wash and block, pinning out each of the lace points for fuller definition.

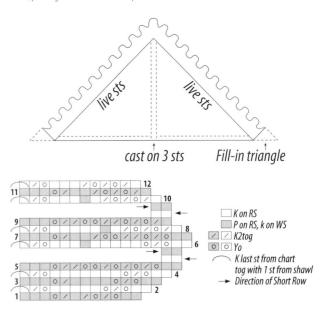

live sts   live sts

cast on 3 sts   *Fill-in triangle*

K on RS
P on RS, k on WS
K2tog
Yo
K last st from chart tog with 1 st from shawl
Direction of Short Row

"If, psychologically, the thought of beginning with a few stitches and having each succeeding pair of rows get longer and slower bogs you down, you have the option of casting on (invisibly) hundreds and hundreds of sts from corner to corner, and decreasing four stitches every ridge. This will cause the rows to become shorter and faster as you head for the three stitches at the top; then the auxiliary thread is removed from the invisible cast on, and you may add the lace border. Whichever method you choose, the object is to avoid a cast on or a bind off on the long edge, as both of these techniques produce a tight, unyielding selvage, and counter the elasticity achieved by a loosely-knitted openwork pattern. This is how I knit this particular version, and you may reverse it if you like."

nature scene shawl

An age-old technique with an update look is brought to us by a new-to-Knitter's-pages designer, Bridget Rorem. What a terrific introduction! The finest wool and a lovely pattern make for a special knitting experience.

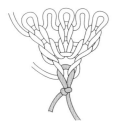

Skill Level Advanced
Finished Measurements 88" x 70" (blocked)
Yarn 2,570yds (2,476m) of fingering weight yarn.
Original yarn: JCA/Grignasco • Regina 100% wool
3½ oz (100g) 1375 yds (1238m) 2 balls in #162 Natural
Needles Size 0 (2mm) circular needle, 40" (102cm) long *or size to obtain gauge*
Extras Small amount of scrap yarn
Gauge 28 sts and 26 rows to 4"/10cm over St st (blocked)

Note: *Heavy line denotes area of Chart A.*

Notes

1 See School, pg. 100 for ssk and grafting. **2** Shawl is worked from lower point to top. **3** After shawl is made, border is attached as it is worked.

Shawl

Make a slip knot with scrap yarn and draw through a loop of shawl yarn, leaving an 8" tail. Tighten scrap yarn—1 st (see illustration). *Beg chart A: Row 1* (RS) (K1, yo, k1) into st. *2 and all WS rows* Purl. Work to top of chart, then work Charts B–F, working reps on each chart number of times indicated, end with WS row—449 sts. *Do not bind off.*

Edging

Note Edging around shawl is worked as foll: across top from right to left where first finger point is added, down left diagonal, around lower point, up right diagonal to top where 2nd finger point is added.

Top edging

Provisional cast-on Hold 2nd piece of scrap yarn against LH needle and wrap needle and scrap yarn tog with knitting yarn 12 times from back to front. Drop scrap yarn and bring up knitting yarn from behind scrap yarn. *Beg chart G: Row 1* (RS) Work row 1 to last chart st; attach edging to top of shawl by working ssk on last st tog with 1 st from shawl. *2 and all WS rows* Purl. Work through chart row 16, then rep rows 1-16 a total of 55 times more. Rep row 1—449 sts worked into edging, 12 edging sts rem. *Next row* Sl first st, purl across.

Finger point *Row 1* (RS) Ssk, yo, k2tog, k8. *2, 6, 10, 14, 18, 22, 26, 30, 34, 38* Wrap yarn firmly around RH needle from front to back, purl across. *3* Ssk, yo, k2tog, k7. *4, 8, 12, 16, 20, 24, 28, 32, 36, 40* Sl 1, purl across. *5* Ssk, yo, k2tog, k5. *7* Ssk, yo, k2tog, k4. *9* K1, yo, k5. *11, 13* K1, yo, k6. *15* K1, yo, k7. *17, 19* K1, yo, k2tog, k5. *21, 23* K1, yo, k2tog, k4. *25, 27* K1, yo, k2tog, k3. *29, 31* K1, yo, k2tog, k2. *33, 35* K1, yo, k2tog, k1. *37, 39* K1, yo, k2tog. Knitting now returns down the finger point; RS rows each incorporate 1 st from LH needle. *41* K1, yo, S2KP2. *42 and all even rows through row 80* Purl. *43* K1, yo, k2tog, k1. *45* K1, yo, k2tog, ssk. *47* K1, yo, k2tog, k2. *49* K1, yo, k2tog, k1, ssk. *51* K1, yo, k2tog, k3. *53* K1, yo, k2tog, k2, ssk. *55* K1, yo, k2tog, k4. *57* K1, yo, k2tog, k3, ssk. *59* K1, yo, k2tog, k5. *61* K1, yo, k2tog, k4, ssk. *63* K1, yo, k2tog, k6. *65* K1, yo, k2tog, k5, ssk. *67* Ssk, yo, k2tog, k6. *69* Ssk, yo, k2tog, k4, ssk. *71* Ssk, yo, k2tog, k5. *73* K1, yo, k2tog, k3, ssk. *75* K1, yo, k7. *77* K1, yo, k7, ssk. *79* K1, yo, k10.

Left diagonal edge Carefully remove slip knot and realign loose end. Join with a double half-hitch. This st will be the last st of left diagonal edge and the first st of right diagonal edge. Yarn end may be knitted in along last 7 or 8" of left edge. Diagonal edge has 37½ reps of Chart G between finger point and middle point, with 16 rows of edging for every 12 rows of shawl. Join edging to shawl by picking up the outer side of first st on shawl every other RS row, then work it tog with last st of rows 1, 3, 5, 9, 11, and 13 as ssk. Do not join rows 7 and 15, except where noted. Beg with row 1, work 37 reps of Chart G, joining as described, then rep chart rows 1-6. The rem st is held by the double half-hitch. Work chart row 7, joining last st of shawl edge to final st with ssk. Remove scrap yarn.

Middle point *Row 1* Ssk, yo, k2tog, k6. *2 and all even rows through row 46* Sl 1, p across. *3, 5, 7, 9* K1, yo, k7. *11* K1, yo, k2tog, k5. *13* K1, yo, k2tog, k4. *15* K1, yo, k2tog, k3. *17* K1, yo, k2tog, k2. *19* K1, yo, k2tog, k1. *21, 23, 25* K1, yo, k2tog. *27* K1, yo, k2tog, k1. *29* K1, yo, k2tog, k2. *31* K1, yo, k2tog, k3. *33* K1, yo, k2tog, k4. *35* K1, yo, k2tog, k5. *37* K1, yo, k2tog, k6. *39, 41, 43, 45* Ssk, yo, k2tog, k6.

Right diagonal edge Work edge as row 11 of Chart G, working ssk on last st with bottom st. Work chart rows 12-16, joining edge at rows 13 and 15. Work 37 reps of Chart G as on left diagonal and do not join on all rows three and 11 (instead of rows 7 and 15 as on left edge). Rep chart rows 1-2.

2nd finger point Work as for first finger point through row 78. Since provisional cast-on sts take the place of row 80, work row 79 as a grafting row, treating 2nd st as a yo.

Finishing

Wash gently in cool water. Block, carefully pinning out scalloped points.

• in other words •

Chart G *Beg on 2 sts*

Note Work last chart st tog with shawl st as ssk on rows indicated in instructions. *Row1* K1, yo, k11. *2 and all WS rows* Purl. *3* Ssk, yo, k2tog, k9. *5* Ssk, yo, k2tog, k8. *7* Ssk, yo, k2tog, k7. *9* Ssk, yo, k2tog, k6. *11* K1, yo, k8. *13* K1, yo, k9. *15* K1, yo, k10. *16* Purl. Rep rows 1-16 for Chart G.

G

Chart G note: *Work last chart st tog with shawl st as ssk on rows indicated in instructions.*

☐ K
◎ Yo
⊘ K2tog
◺ Ssk

Chart note:
*Charts show
RS rows only.
P all WS rows.*

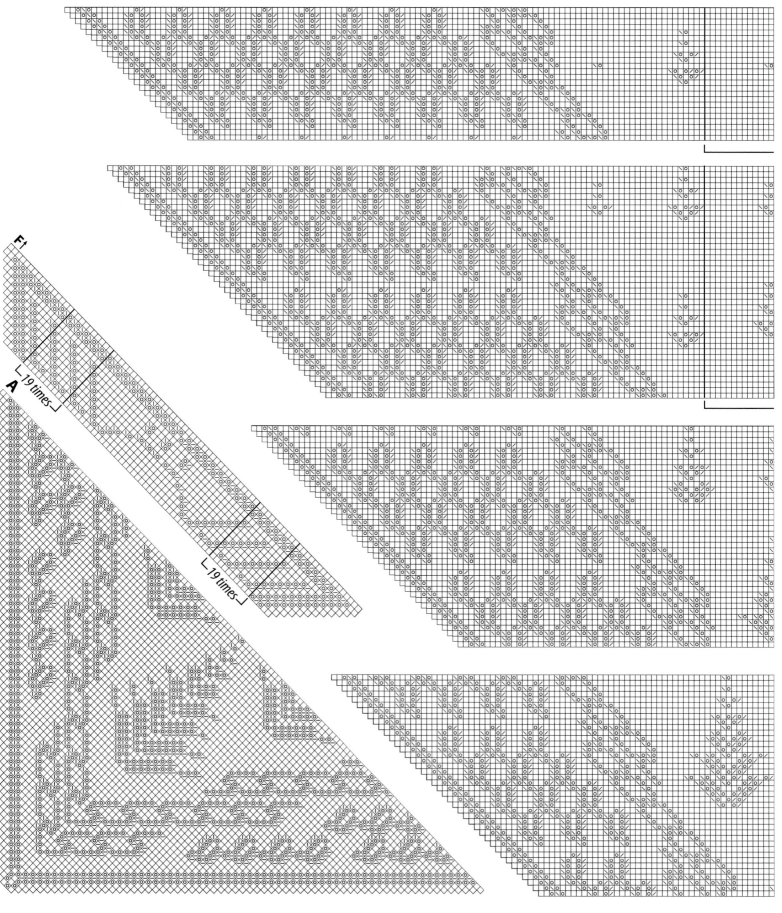

F↑

A

⌐ 19 times ⌐

⌐ 19 times ⌐

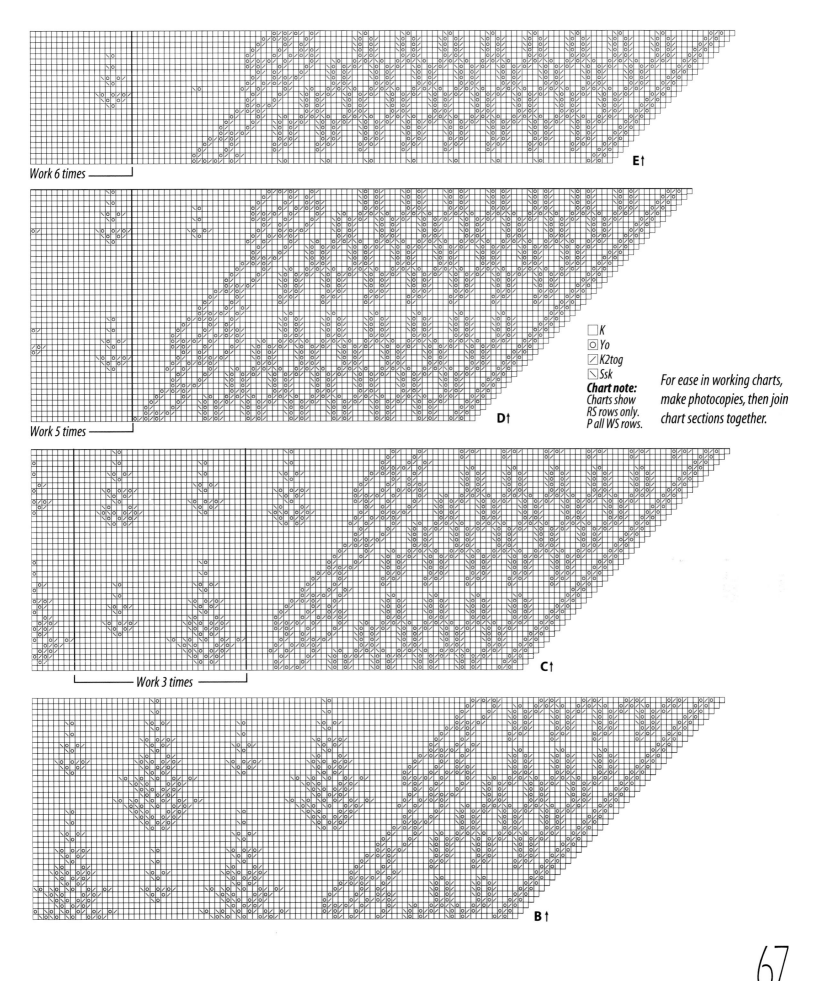

Work 6 times

E↑

☐ K
⊙ Yo
⊿ K2tog
◣ Ssk

Chart note:
Charts show
RS rows only.
P all WS rows.

*For ease in working charts,
make photocopies, then join
chart sections together.*

Work 5 times

D↑

Work 3 times

C↑

B↑

67

Joan Schrouder

"Several years ago I came across this lovely floral pattern, which I called 'Lotus Blossom', in a Burda magazine. I promptly knit up a triangular shawl and proved what I feared might happen—when the piece was wide enough to be a shawl, it was also quite l-o-n-g! This was due to the base stitch being stockinette instead of the square garter stitch. Fortunately, the intended wearer is a very tall woman so it didn't matter. But since then, I've been searching for a way to modify the triangle knit in stockinette to make a more wearable shape for us more 'altitudinally-challenged' folk! Here is one answer."

lotus blossom lace

One beautiful lotus flower motif multiplies to create a very special cotton and wool blend shawl. Joan uses her mastery for detail to make it the best fitting shawl you ever owned.

Skill level Advanced

Size Finished shawl measures approx 88" wide at widest point and 42" deep from top to point

Yarn 1,100yds (1,000m) of fingering-weight yarn
Original yarn:
Brown Sheep • Cotton Fine
80% cotton, 20% Merino wool
8oz (226g) 1,000yds (910m)
2 cones #375 Rue

Needles Size 5 (3¾mm) circular needle, 24" (60cm) long, *or size to obtain gauge*

Extras Stitch markers and holder
• blocking wires (optional)

Gauge 24 sts and 32 rows to 4"/10cm in St st (blocked)

Notes

1 See *School*, pg. 100 for ssk, yo before a k or p st, M1, SK2P, and S2KP2. **2** *To work yo at beg of a row* With yarn in front, insert RH needle into first st knitwise, then take yarn from front to back over the needle (forming the yo) in order to k the st. **3** Circular needle is used to accomodate large number of sts. Piece is worked back and forth as with straight needles.

Shawl

Back

Cast on 3 sts. *Row 1* Yo, k to end. Rep last row 12 times more—16 sts. *Beg Chart A* Work rows 1-18 of Chart A—34 sts. *Beg Chart B: Row 1* (RS) Work chart sts 1-8, then work 18-st rep once, work to end of chart. Cont in pat through chart row 18—52 sts. *Next row* (RS) Work chart sts 1-8, then work 18-st rep twice, work to end of chart. Cont in pat through chart row 18—70 sts. Cont to rep rows 1-18 of Chart B, working one more 18-st rep each time, 9 times more—232 sts. Work chart rows 1-16—248 sts. *Beg Chart C: Row 1* (RS) Work row 17 of Chart B until there are 97 sts on RH needle (ending with chart st 17), place marker (pm), work row 1 of Chart C over 54 sts, pm, work sts 18-26 of row 17 of Chart B, then cont Chart B to end. Cont in pat, working Chart C between markers, and rem sts in Chart B, through row 10 of Chart C and row 8 of Chart B—258 sts.

Right Front

Next row (RS) Work in pat to marker, work sts 1-19 of row 11 of Chart C and place rem sts on hold. Turn work. *Next row* Work right front sts of Chart C to marker, work in pat to end—122 sts. Work as established through row 20 of Chart C (remove marker), and row 18 of Chart B. *Next row* (RS) Work Chart B to last 9 sts of row, [k2tog] twice, k5. *Next row* Yo, k6, p1, work to end. Rep last 2 rows until 18 rows of Chart B have been worked a total of 15 times from beg, then work rows 1-16 once more. *Beg edge decs: Next row* (RS) Yo, k4, [ssk] twice, work in pat to end. *Next row* Work to last 7 sts, p1, k6. Rep last 2 rows until 16 sts rem, end with a WS row. *Beg Chart D* Work rows 1-13 of Chart D. Fasten off last st.

Left Front

Return sts on hold to needle, ready to work a RS row. *Next row* (RS) Attach yarn and bind off 17 sts, then work sts 38-54 of row 11 of Chart C, work in pat to end—121 sts. Work as established through row 20 of Chart C (remove marker), and row 18 of Chart B. *Next row* (RS) Yo, k4, [ssk] twice, then beg with chart st 12, work Chart B to end. *Next row* Work to last 7 sts, p1, k6. *Next row* Yo, k4, [ssk] twice, work to end. Rep last 2 rows until 18 rows of Chart B have been worked a total of 15 times from beg, then work

rows 1-16 once more. *Beg edge decs: Next row* (RS) Work to last 9 sts, [k2tog] twice, k5. *Next row* Yo, k6, p1, work to end. Rep last 2 rows until 16 sts rem, end with a WS row. *Beg Chart D* Work rows 1-13 of Chart D. Fasten off last st.

Finishing

Wash gently and block, running blocking wires through yo's at edges if desired.

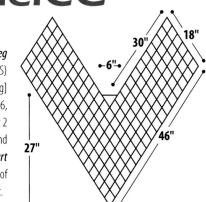

Chart A *Over 16 to 34 sts*

Row 1 (RS) Yo, k5, k2tog, yo, k1, yo, ssk, k6. **2, 4, 6, 8, 10, 12, 14** Yo, k6, p to last 6 sts, k6. **3** Yo, k5, k2tog, [k1, yo] twice, k1, ssk, k6. **5** Yo, k5, k2tog, k2, yo, k1, yo, k2, ssk, k6. **7** Yo, k5, k2tog, k3, yo, k1, yo, k3, ssk, k6. **9** Yo, k5, k2tog, k4, yo, k1, yo, k4, ssk, k6. **11** Yo, k5, k2tog, k5, yo, k1, yo, k5, ssk, k6. **13** Yo, k5, k2tog, k6, yo, k1, yo, k6, ssk, k6. **15** Yo, k5, p1, *k2, k2tog, yo, ssk, k2*, yo, k1, yo, rep from * to * once, p1, k6. **16** Yo, k7, p3, k1, p9, k1, p3, k7. **17** Yo, k6, p1, k1, *k2tog, yo, p1, yo, ssk*, k5, rep from * to * once, k1, p1, k7. **18** Yo, k6, p1, k1, p2, k3, p7, k3, p2, k1, p1, k6.

Chart B *Over a multiple of 18 sts, plus 16*

Row 1 (RS) Yo, k5, k2tog, yo, *k1, yo, ssk, p3, yo, ssk, k3, k2tog, yo, p3, k2tog, yo; rep from* to last 9 sts, k1, yo, ssk, k6. **2** Yo, k6, p3, *p2, k4, p5, k4, p3; rep from* to last 8 sts, p2, k6. **3** Yo, k5, k2tog, k1, yo, *k1, yo, k1, ssk, p3, yo, ssk, k1, k2tog, yo, p3, k2tog, k1, yo; rep from* to last 10 sts, k1, yo, k1, ssk, k6. **4** Yo, k6, p4, *[p3, k4] twice, p4; rep from* to last 9 sts, p3, k6. **5** Yo, k5, k2tog, k2, yo, *k1, yo, k2, ssk, p3, yo, SK2P, yo, p3, k2tog, k2, yo; rep from* to last 11 sts, k1, yo, k2, ssk, k6. **6** Yo, k6, p5, *p4, k9, p5; rep from* to last 10 sts, p4, k6. **7** Yo, k5, k2tog, k3, yo, *k1, yo, k3, ssk, p7, k2tog, k3, yo; rep from* to last 12 sts, k1, yo, k3, ssk, k6. **8** Yo, k6, p6, *p5, k7, p6; rep from* to last 11 sts, p5, k6. **9** Yo,

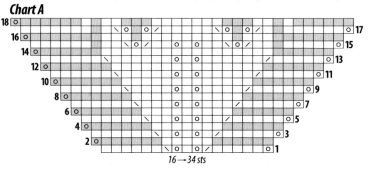

Chart A

16→34 sts

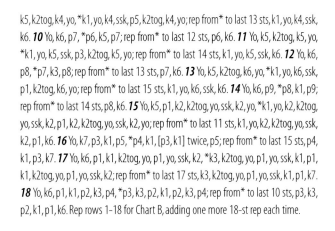

k5, k2tog, k4, yo, *k1, yo, k4, ssk, p5, k2tog, k4, yo; rep from* to last 13 sts, k1, yo, k4, ssk, k6. **10** Yo, k6, p7, *p6, k5, p7; rep from* to last 12 sts, p6, k6. **11** Yo, k5, k2tog, k5, yo, *k1, yo, k5, ssk, p3, k2tog, k5, yo; rep from* to last 14 sts, k1, yo, k5, ssk, k6. **12** Yo, k6, p8, *p7, k3, p8; rep from* to last 13 sts, p7, k6. **13** Yo, k5, k2tog, k6, yo, *k1, yo, k6, ssk, p1, k2tog, k6, yo; rep from* to last 15 sts, k1, yo, k6, ssk, k6. **14** Yo, k6, p9, *p8, k1, p9; rep from* to last 14 sts, p8, k6. **15** Yo, k5, p1, k2, k2tog, yo, ssk, k2, yo, *k1, yo, k2, k2tog, yo, ssk, k2, p1, k2, k2tog, yo, ssk, k2, yo; rep from* to last 11 sts, k1, yo, k2, k2tog, yo, ssk, k2, p1, k6. **16** Yo, k7, p3, k1, p5, *p4, k1, [p3, k1] twice, p5; rep from* to last 15 sts, p4, k1, p3, k7. **17** Yo, k6, p1, k1, k2tog, yo, p1, yo, ssk, k2, *k3, k2tog, yo, p1, yo, ssk, k1, p1, k1, k2tog, yo, p1, yo, ssk, k2; rep from* to last 17 sts, k3, k2tog, yo, p1, yo, ssk, k1, p1, k7. **18** Yo, k6, p1, k1, p2, k3, p4, *p3, k3, p2, k1, p2, k3, p4; rep from* to last 10 sts, p3, k3, p2, k1, p1, k6. Rep rows 1-18 for Chart B, adding one more 18-st rep each time.

Chart C *Over center 54 sts*

Row 1 (RS) *P1, k1, k2tog, yo, p1, yo, ssk, k5, k2tog, yo, p1, yo, ssk, k1*, p1, k1, k2tog, yo, k1, yo, ssk, k5, k2tog, yo, k1, yo, ssk, k1, rep from * to * once. **2** *P2, k3, p7, k3, p2*,

k6, p7, k6, rep from * to * once, k1. **3** K1, yo, *ssk, p3, yo, ssk, k3, k2tog, yo, p3, k2tog*, M1, k6, yo, ssk, k3, k2tog, yo, k6, M1, rep from * to * once, yo. **4** P2, k4, p5, k4, p1, k8, p5, k8, p1, k4, p5, k4, p3. **5** K1, yo, k1, *ssk, p3, yo, ssk, k1, k2tog, yo, p3, k2tog*, M1, k8, yo, ssk, k1, k2tog, yo, k8, M1, rep from * to * once, k1, yo. **6** [P3, k4] twice, p1, k10, p3, k10, p1, k4, p3, k4, p4. **7** K1, yo, k2, *ssk, p3, yo, SK2P, yo, p3, k2tog*, M1, k10, yo, SK2P, yo, k10, M1, rep from * to * once, k2, yo. **8** P4, k9, p1, k25, p1, k9, p5. **9** K1, yo, k3, *ssk, p7, k2tog*, M1, k25, M1, rep from * to * once, k3, yo. **10** P5, k7, p1, k27, p1, k7, p6.

Right front: Row 11 K1, yo, k4, ssk, p5, k2tog, M1, k5, place rem sts on hold. **12** Yo, k6, p1, k5, p7. **13** K1, yo, k5, ssk, p3, [k2tog] twice, k5. **14** Yo, k6, p1, k3, p8. **15** K1, yo, k6, ssk, p1, [k2tog] twice, k5. **16** Yo, k6, p1, k1, p9. **17** K1, yo, k2, k2tog, yo, ssk, k2, [k2tog] twice, k5. **18** Yo, k6, p4, k1, p5. **19** K3, k2tog, yo, p1, yo, ssk, [k2tog] twice, k5. **20** Yo, k6, p2, k3, p4. ***Left front: Row 11*** Bind off 17 sts (1 st rem on RH needle is next st of chart), k4, M1, ssk, p5, k2tog, k4, yo. **12** P6, k5, p1, k6. **13** Yo, k4, [ssk] twice, p3, k2tog, k5, yo. **14** P7, k3, p1, k6. **15** Yo, k4, [ssk] twice, p1, k2tog, k6, yo. **16** P8, k1, p1, k6. **17** Yo, k4, [ssk] twice, k2, k2tog, yo, ssk, k2, yo. **18** P4, k1, p4, k6. **19** Yo, k4, [ssk] twice, k2tog, yo, p1, yo, ssk, k2. **20** P3, k3, p2, k6.

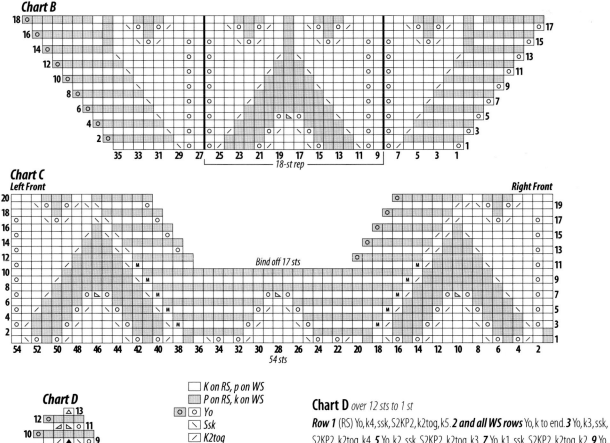

Chart B

18-st rep

Chart C

Left Front   Right Front

54 sts

Bind off 17 sts

Chart D

12 sts →1 st

Symbol	Meaning
☐	K on RS, p on WS
▨	P on RS, k on WS
◌	Yo
╲	Ssk
╱	K2tog
◢	K3tog
◿	SK2P
▲	S2KP2
M	M1
△	K4tog

Chart D *over 12 sts to 1 st*

Row 1 (RS) Yo, k4, ssk, S2KP2, k2tog, k5. **2 and all WS rows** Yo, k to end. **3** Yo, k3, ssk, S2KP2, k2tog, k4. **5** Yo, k2, ssk, S2KP2, k2tog, k3. **7** Yo, k1, ssk, S2KP2, k2tog, k2. **9** Yo, ssk, S2KP2, k2tog, k1. **11** Yo, SK2P, k3tog. **13** K4tog.

This would better be called the "Eugen Beugler Chapter" as the first four pieces come from his needles. He uses the same easy shape—what differs are the stitches, yarns, and approaches. Two of his shawls are worked on the diagonal. One is worked in two pieces to create perfectly identical ends. One begins and ends with a hemmed edge. If ease is your goal, give Karen Yaksick's checkerboard shawl on page 80 a try. Last but not least is Dawn Brocco's shawl on page 84, ideally made in a soft, luxurious, long-lasting fiber for years of wear.

rectangular shawls

Eugen Beugler

"After having worked lace patterns in black, white, and ecru for years, I have branched out into color—hence a very royal purple coloration! This particular version of feather and fan incorporates an open faggoted cable to offset the rather solid welts of the feather and fan. Although the pattern looks fairly complicated, I found that after a few repeats it is easily memorized."

theatrical lace

After a hard day's work, you'll be ready for a night on the town in Eugen's lively purple lace shawl. Using a trans-seasonal cotton and wool blend, and a version of the feather and fan stitch, Eugen has come up with another intriguing piece.

Skill level Intermediate
Finished Measurements 18" x 70" (blocked)
Yarn 1,000yds (910m) of fingering-weight yarn
Original yarn: Brown Sheep • Cotton Fine
80% cotton, 20% wool
8oz (226g) 1,000yds (910m)
1 cone in #710 Prosperous Plum
Needles Size 3 (3¼mm) needles, *or size to obtain gauge*
Extras Cable needle (cn) • stitch markers • small amount of scrap yarn
Gauge 25 sts and 24 rows to 3" (7.5cm) over chart pat

Notes
1 See *School* pg.100 for invisible cast-on and ssk. **2** Stole is worked from the middle to each end. **3** To adjust length, work fewer or more reps of 8-row chart pat.

Stole
First half
Invisibly cast on 78 sts. P 1 row. K 6 rows, working yo, k2tog at beg of each row. *Foundation: Row 1* (RS) Yo, k2tog, k4, place marker (pm), **p2, [k into front and back of next st] twice, p2*, k9**; rep from ** to ** 3 times more, work from ** to * once, pm, k6—88 sts. *Row 2* Yo, k2tog, k4, *k2, p4, k2, p9; rep from* 3 times more, end k2, p4, k8. *Beg chart: Row 1* (RS) Yo, k2tog, k4, work 17-st rep of chart 4 times, work last 8 sts of chart, k6. Working first and last 6 sts as in foundation rows 1-2, cont in chart pat as established until 8 rows of chart have been worked 31 times.

End piece: Row 1 (RS) Yo, k2tog, k4, *p2, 2/2yoLC, p2, k9; rep from* 3 times more, p2, 2/2yoLC, p2, k6. *Row 2* Yo, k2tog, k4, *k2, [k2tog] twice, k11; rep from* 4 times more, end last rep k8—78 sts. K 10 rows, working yo, k2tog at beg of each row. Bind off loosely.

Second half
Removing scrap yarn, sl 78 original cast-on sts to needle ready to beg a RS row. K 6 rows, working yo, k2tog at beg of each row. Work to correspond to first half, beg with foundation row 1.

Finishing
Weave in ends and block piece to measurements.

knitter's pattern
• in other words •

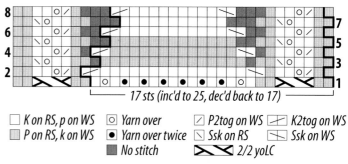

17 sts (inc'd to 25, dec'd back to 17)

□ K on RS, p on WS   ⊙ *Yarn over*   ☑ *P2tog on WS*   ⧄ *K2tog on WS*
▨ P on RS, k on WS   ● *Yarn over twice*   ◩ *Ssk on RS*   ⧅ *Ssk on WS*
■ *No stitch*   ⧄⧅ *2/2 yoLC*

2/2yoLC (2/2 yo Left Cross) Sl 2 sts to cn, hold to front, k2, then yo, ssk from cn.
Chart *Beg on multiple of 17 sts plus 8*
Note On row 2 of chart pat, work double yarn overs as foll: drop the first yo and p the 2nd. *Row 1* (RS) *P2, 2/2yoLC, p2, k1, yo, [k1, yo twice] 6 times, k1, yo, k1; rep from* to last 8 sts, p2, 2/2yoLC, p2. *2* K2, p2, yo, p2tog, k1, *k2tog, p15, ssk, k1, p2, yo, p2tog, k1; rep from*, end last rep k2. *3* *P2, k2, yo, ssk, p17; rep from* to last 8 sts, p2, k2, yo, ssk, p2. *4* K2, p2, yo, p2tog, k1, *k2tog, k13, ssk, k1, p2, yo, p2tog, k1; rep from*, end last rep k2. *5* *P2, k2, yo, ssk, p15; rep from* to last 8 sts, p2, k2, yo, ssk, p2. *6* K2, p2, yo, p2tog, k1,*k2tog, p11, ssk, k1, p2, yo, p2tog, k1; rep from*, end last rep k2. *7* *P2, k2, yo, ssk, p2, k11; rep from* to last 8 sts, p2, k2, yo, ssk, p2. *8* K2, p2, yo, p2tog, k1, *k2tog, p9, ssk, k1, p2, yo, p2tog, k1; rep from*, end last rep k2. Rep rows 1-8 for chart pat.

"I came up with the idea for a stole in the Ostrich Plumes pattern after having thought about one in a variation of Feather and Fan. I was annoyed that with Feather and Fan patterns the scallops at either end of a stole were not mirror images of one another. After perusing Barbara Walker's books for countless times, I remembered Ostrich Plumes. Surely its offsetting of the increase and decrease units of Feather and Fan would overcome this problem. I made a sample piece, and sure enough, it worked. Adding three stockinette stitches at the sides of the stole helped overcome the slight tendency of the pattern to wave. The mohair/silk blend I used is an ideal yarn for a stole because it not only shows off the pattern, but it drapes exceedingly well."

Eugen Beugler

lace dream

Lace master Eugen Beugler

brings us a soft,

light-as-a-feather stole.

The easy-to-do hems create

an anchor for the simple

'Ostrich Plumes' lace pattern.

For dreamy knitting,

use a soft luxurious yarn

such as the mohair/silk yarn

used here. Our choice for

versatile wearing:

a pastel soft banana coloring.

Notes
1 See *School*, pg. 100 for ssk, SK2P, grafting, and blocking. **2** To shorten or lengthen stole, work fewer or more 32-row reps (each repeat adds approx 4"), ending with row 32 so that scallops at each end of stole mirror image each other.

Stole
With waste yarn, cast on 115 sts.

Work facing
With main yarn, beg with a k row, work 8 rows in St st. *Next (eyelet) row* (RS) K2, *yo, k2tog; rep from*, end k1. P 1 row. Work 8 rows more in St st. Sl open sts from cast-on row to spare needle; remove waste yarn. *Form hem: Next row* With RS facing, fold piece at eyelet with WS tog, *k first st from main needle tog with first st on spare needle; rep from* across until all sts are joined and the yo, k2tog sts form a 'sawtooth' border. P 1 row. *Beg Chart: Row 1* (RS) Yo, k2tog, ssk, yo, k2, place marker

(pm), beg chart and work to rep line, work 16-st rep 5 times, work to end of chart, pm, k2tog, yo, k4. **2 and all WS rows** Yo, k2tog, p2tog, yo, p2, p to last marker, p2tog, yo, p2, k2. Working 6 sts before and after markers as given in rows 1-2, work all other sts in chart pat as established and work through chart row 31. **32** Rep row 2. Work 18 more reps of rows 1-32.

Work facing
Work 8 rows in St st, marking first row. *Next (eyelet) row* (RS) K2, *yo, k2tog; rep from *, end k1. P 1 row. Work 8 rows more in St st. Graft last row to marked row to form hem.

Finishing
Block stole carefully to approx 22" x 80". Steam lightly using press cloth or cover with a damp cloth and let dry.

knitter's pattern · in other words ·

Skill Level Intermediate
Finished Measurements 22" x 80"
Yarns 1,150yds (1,050m) fingering-weight yarn (best in a lofty mohair blend to recreate effect)
Original yarn: Cascade/Madil · Kid Seta 70% mohair, 30% silk
.88 oz (25g) 230yds (210m)
5 balls in #464 Cream
Needles Size 4 (3½mm) circular, 24" (60cm) long, *or size to obtain gauge*
Extras Stitch markers · waste yarn
Gauge 22 sts and 30 rows to 4" (10cm) in St st

Chart *Multiple of 16 sts, plus 7*
Rows 1, 5, 9, 13 K3, [k2tog] 3 times, [yo, k1] 5 times, yo, [ssk] twice, *SK2P, [k2tog] twice, [yo, k1] 5 times, yo, [ssk] twice; rep from* 4 times more, ssk, k3. *2 and all WS rows* P all sts and yo's. *3, 7, 11, 15, 19, 23, 27, 31* Knit. *17, 21, 25, 29* K4, [yo, k1] twice, yo, [ssk] twice, SK2P, [k2tog] twice, [yo, k1] twice, yo, *[k1, yo] 3 times, [ssk] twice, SK2P, [k2tog] twice, [yo, k1] twice, yo; rep from* 4 times more, k4. *32* Rep row 2. Rep rows 1-32 for chart.

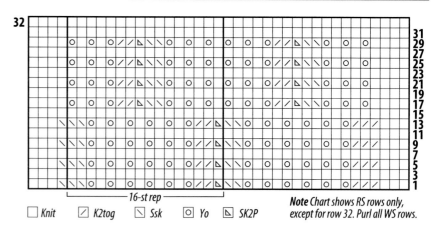

Note Chart shows RS rows only, except for row 32. Purl all WS rows.

☐ Knit   ☑ K2tog   ◩ Ssk   ○ Yo   ◪ SK2P

"I adapted this design from a square shawl in one of the Pingouin books—theirs had concentric squares and bands of garter stitch in uneven stripes. Since doing this stole, I have experimented with the idea and have come up with several other designs—mostly simple geometrics.

"I used the yarn-over increase in this stole. It makes for an elastic edge, which is highly desirable on a garter-stitch piece. As I work the odd-numbered rows, I mark the side facing me as the right side—at least until I become familiar with the pattern. Oh, yes, I mention using the 14" straight needles because so many people nowadays look upon them with scorn. Having learned to knit with them, I still love them. I stick the end of the right-hand needle into my waistband, and knit English style, throwing the yarn with my right hand."

Eugen Beugler

corner to corner shawl

This shawl is worked from corner to corner, on the diagonal, in garter stitch and a Shetland-type lace pattern. Using a lofty mohair blended yarn, you can create a "light-as-a-feather" piece that you'll wear for years to come.

Notes 1 See *School,* pg. 100 for ssk, and SK2P. **2** Shawl is worked on the diagonal from corner to corner on a garter st background (k every row).

Shawl

Cast on 1 st. *Beg Chart A: Row 1* Yo, k1. *2 and all Chart A WS rows* Yo, k to end. *3* Yo, k3. *5* Yo, k5. Cont in this way until there are 41 sts on needle (row 40, Chart A). Cont Chart A through row 136—137 sts. *Beg Chart B* Working all Chart B and C WS rows as yo, k3tog tbl, k to end; work rows 137-142 a total of 48 times, or until side is desired length, ending with row 142—137 sts. *Beg Chart C* Working yo, k3tog tbl, at beg of every row, work through row 560, k2tog. Fasten off.

Finishing

Weave in ends. Block lightly to measurements.

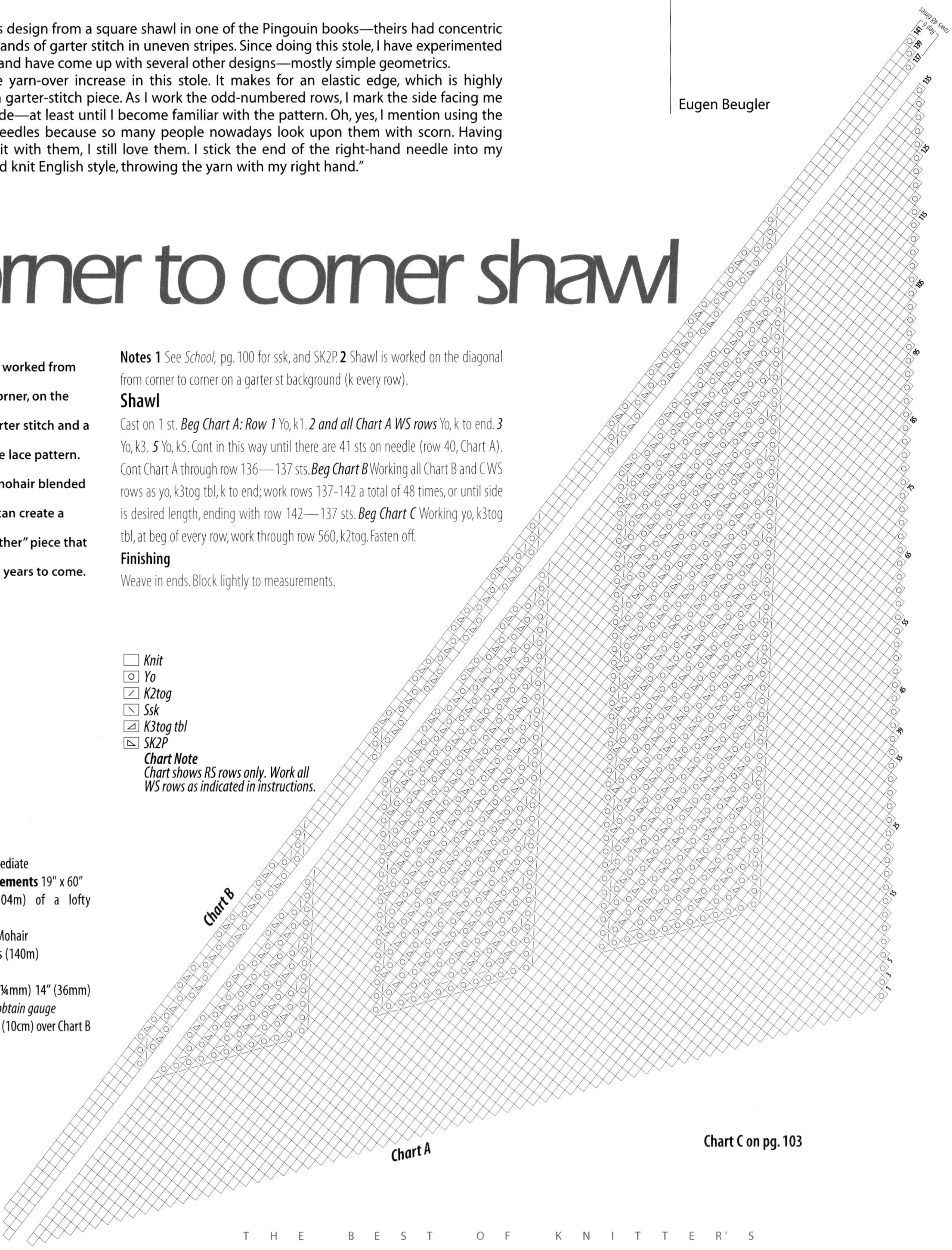

☐ Knit
⊡ Yo
⊘ K2tog
◻ Ssk
▨ K3tog tbl
◩ SK2P

Chart Note
Chart shows RS rows only. Work all WS rows as indicated in instructions.

Skill Level Intermediate
Finished Measurements 19" x 60"
Yarn 560yds (504m) of a lofty laceweight yarn
Original yarn: Kid Mohair
.70oz (20g) 154yds (140m)
4 balls in Yellow
Needles Size 3 (3¼mm) 14" (36mm) needles, *or size to obtain gauge*
Gauge 20 sts to 4" (10cm) over Chart B

Chart B

Chart A

Chart C on pg. 103

Eugen Beugler

symmetry in silk

Notes 1 See *School,* pg. 100 for backward loop cast-on, ssk, and SK2P. **2** Shawl is worked on the diagonal from corner to corner on a garter st background (k every row). **3** Work inc on first 3 rows as backward loop cast-on.

Shawl

Cast on 3 sts and knit. *Row 1* Sl 1 purlwise wyif, k1, inc 1, k1. *2* Sl 1 purlwise wyif, k1, inc 1, k2. *3* Sl 1 purlwise wyif, k1, inc 1, k3. *4* Sl 1 purlwise wyif, k2, yo, k3. *5* Sl 1 purlwise wyif, k2, yo, k4. *Beg Chart A: Row 1* (RS) Sl 1 purlwise wyif, k2, work chart across to last 3 sts, k3. *2 and all Chart A WS rows* Sl 1 purlwise wyif, k2, yo, k to end. Cont foll chart, working 3 sts before chart as sl 1 purlwise wyif, k2, and 3 sts after chart as k3—106 sts total at end of Row 96. *Beg Chart B* on WS rows, work all Chart B and C as sl 1 purlwise wyif, k2, yo, k3tog, k to end; and work first and last 3 sts of RS rows as for Chart A section. Work Chart B until piece measures 78" along longest side, or desired length, end with row 131—107 sts total. *Beg Chart C* Foll Chart C, cont working 3 sts before and after chart

as established—10 sts at end of last row. Cont to dec as foll: *Dec row 1* Sl 1 purlwise wyif, k2, yo, k3tog, k to end. *2-5* Sl 1 purlwise wyif, k2, k2tog, k to end. *6* Sl 1 purlwise wyif, k2, k2tog. *7* Sl 1 purlwise wyif, k1, k2tog. *8* Sl 1 purlwise wyif, k2tog. *9* K2tog. Fasten off.

Finishing

Block lightly to shape, and fringe if desired.

Even if you don't knit this scarf, the decrease used at the end of each motif deserves attention. Eugen uses a decrease that he found in an old German book: sl1, k2, psso (yes, pass the stitch over the 2 knit stitches). When flanked by 2 yo's and followed, in the next pattern row, by a k2tog, yo, ssk, it makes a beautifully centered single eyelet— silken symmetry.

Skill level Intermediate
Finished measurements 10½" x 78"
Yarn 1,200yds (1,080m) of laceweight tussah silk yarn (approx 3,750 yds per lb)
Needles Size 2 (2¾mm) needles, *or size to obtain gauge*
Gauge 22 sts to 4" (10cm) over garter st

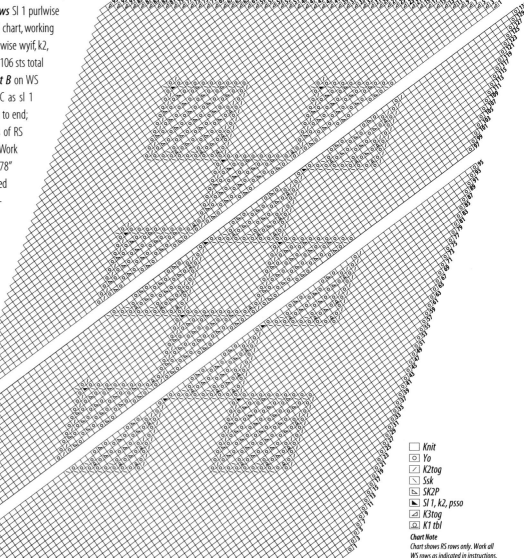

Chart C

Chart B

Chart A

☐ Knit
☑ Yo
☑ K2tog
☑ Ssk
☑ SK2P
☑ Sl 1, k2, psso
☑ K3tog
☑ K1 tbl

Chart Note
Chart shows RS rows only. Work all WS rows as indicated in instructions.

"What I have come up with is not only a shawl (like the original pattern) but a great scarf that takes only one ball of yarn. The variations are endless—make it long, short, wide, or square. Wear it in your hair, around your waist, with a fancy pin (an old brooch of your grandmother's), around your shoulders or around your baby. Start now. If lace is new to you, try the scarf; the investment in both yarn and time is small. The pleasure of wearing is great. Go for it!"

Karen Yaksick

grandma's checkerboard lace

This beautiful shawl has proven itself by being used over the years for many occasions. The fact that each side of the fabric is the same improves the wearability greatly because one never worries about it being wrong side out.

Notes
1 See *School*, pg. 100 for long-tail cast-on and fringe. **2** With yarn in front, sl first st of each row as if to p. **3** For scarf, cast on 24 sts and work as for shawl.

Shawl
Cast on 96 sts using the long tail method. (If the tail is long enough, it can be used to stitch the hem later.)

Form Eyelet hem
Beg with a p row, work 3 rows in St st (p 1 row, k 1 row). *Next (eyelet) row* (RS) *K1, yo, k2tog; rep from*. Beg with a p row, work 3 rows in St st. After the hem is folded at the eyelet row and sewn to the WS (you can do this after you're finished knitting), the scalloped edge that is created is very strong and neat. And the eyelets create a really good edge for fringe. After doing the eyelet hem, a fairly wide border is used to stabilize and frame the main lace pattern.

Border
Rows 1-8 Knit. *Rows 9-12* K4, *yo, p2tog; rep from*, end k4. *Rows 13-20* Knit.

Body
(RS) Work in Checkerboard Lace pat until piece measures 66" from eyelet row (or desired length). End with row 16. Checkerboard lace is easy to learn and fun to do. There is enough variety to keep your interest while you are knitting the length required.

Border and eyelet hem
Repeat Border. Then repeat Eyelet hem. (*Note* I reversed k and p rows so sewing is all on the same side.) Work as foll: Beg with a k row, work 3 rows in St st. *Next (eyelet) row* (RS) *P1, yo, p2tog; rep from*. Beg with a k row, work 3 rows in St st. Bind off in p.

Finishing
Fold each end at eyelet row and sew to WS. Using crochet hook, attach three 9" strands for fringe in each k2tog at eyelet fold.

Notes to a fledgling lace knitter
The knitting of this shawl should flow easily; there should be no struggling with the work. Whenever you are doing a p2tog you should always be presented with a stitch and then a yo. This sequence is easy to work. If a yo is the first stitch to the part of a p2tog then something is wrong. One reason may be an added yo. More likely, though, a yo has been left out. This can be caused by doing the sequence k-yo-p and ending up without the yo. After doing the k, bring the yarn to the front and wrap the yarn completely around the needle. It seems a little clumsy at first, but this is how it should be done. You will run into this situation on the pattern rows that are not just plain knit. They begin k4, yo, p2tog; be sure that after the k4 you bring the yarn forward and then bring it around the needle again to do the yo, before you p2tog, and you can be sure all is well.

knitter's pattern · *in other words* ·

Skill Level Easy
Finished Measurements
19" x 69½," excluding fringe
Yarn 1,000yds (900m) of sportweight yarn for shawl
200 yds (180m) for scarf
Needles Size 8 (5mm) needle, *or size to obtain gauge*
Extras Size D (3mm) crochet hook for attaching fringe
Gauge 20 sts and 28 rows to 4" (10cm) over chart

Checkerboard Lace Chart *Multiple of 12 sts*
Rows 1-4 K4, *yo, p2tog; rep from*, end k4. *5-8* K4, [yo, p2tog] twice, *k4, p4, [yo, p2tog] twice; rep from*, end k4. *9-12* K4, [yo, p2tog] twice, *p4, k4, [yo, p2tog] twice; rep from*, end k4. *13-16* K4, *yo, p2tog; rep from*, end k4. *17-20* Knit. Rep rows 1-20 for Checkerboard Lace Chart.

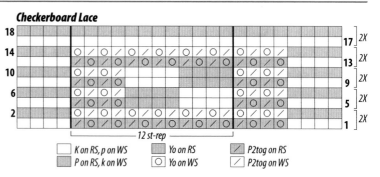

Checkerboard Lace

☐ K on RS, p on WS	▨ Yo on RS
▦ P on RS, k on WS	○ Yo on WS
▨ P2tog on RS	
╱ P2tog on WS	

My Grandma, Georgina Kearon, knitted. She also sang while doing housework and cooking dinner for our whole family. But mostly I remember her knitting: She always measured my body for the sweaters she knit for my cousins. I had to finally convince her not to string my mittens together. And I remember my panic thinking one of those mittens was lost!

Sweaters, mittens, booties, afghans, and lace— all sprang from her needles. She once knitted a magnificent lace tablecloth that stretched to the floor when it finally was put in place. I was thrilled because that dining room table now had walls of lace that my teddy bears and I could hide behind. However, my fortification was short-lived, as Grandma Kearon went back to work 'making it right.'

As a teenager, I was thrilled to discover that a lace shawl she had made was perfect with my prom dress. My excitement alone might have kept me warm—but in a strapless dress on a Michigan spring evening? I wore that shawl with grateful pride.

Grandma had made three of those shawls, and over the years they were used often. And when I learned to knit, I remembered that shawl pattern. I not only wanted a shawl to wear, I wanted a shawl to knit! The problem? My memory was vague. The shawls were missing! Finally when my favorite aunt moved the pattern surfaced (along with the shawls). I was thrilled, but my elation turned to dismay when I started knitting. The pattern (a 'Botany Model of the Month' circa 1953) was awkward and difficult to knit. I heard that voice from the past say, "Make it right." So I set about putting the pleasure of knitting back into this pattern. The look of the lace is essentially the same, but the 'knittability' is greatly improved. Now it feels as right as it looks.

81

"The blocks for this shawl were intriguing to design. The squares spiral out counterclockwise from the center. However, in the beginning, I did find myself getting lost. To avoid confusion, keep track of the right side and which square you are working on. After the first square or two, it should all make sense. After I put a marker on the right side and drew the diagram, it was easy to keep track of where I was."

"The two yarns held together throughout also have importance. The Fame gives it color and drape, the Cotton Sox gives it body and shape. The combined weight of these two yarns is what lets you drape this shawl and know that it will stay put."

a blue wrap

Constructed in blocks, this shawl makes for great portable knitting. Make it longer or shorter to suit your needs. It's a great signature piece to wear for dress, with jeans, or even as a swimsuit cover-up.

Skill Level Intermediate
Finished Measurements 24" x 60" (excluding fringe)
Each block is 12" square
Yarns 1,044yd (936m) of DK weight variegated yarn (A)
Original yarn: Classic Elite • Fame 75% rayon, 25% silk
1¾oz (50g 116yd (104m)
9 balls #1403 Glacier Blue
1,035yd (945m) of DK weight yarn (B)
Original yarn: Classic Elite • Cotton Sox 100% cotton
⅞oz (25g) 69yd (63m)
15 balls in #4916 Natural
Needles Size 10 (6mm), *or size to obtain gauge*
Extras Size J (6.00mm) crochet hook
Gauge 10 sts and 19 rows to 3" (7.5cm) over garter st (k every row)

Notes
1 See *School*, pg. 100 for fringe and overhand knot. **2** Work with 1 strand A and B held tog throughout. Do not cut yarn until all 16 squares of each block are completed.

Bind-off row (BOR)
Bind off sts knitwise, leaving last loop on needle.

Pick-up row (PUR)
Pick up and k first st, pass previous st over, then pick up and k9 more sts evenly spaced—10 sts.

Right-side join (RSJ)
Pick up st, going into the left of vertical bars of adjoining garter st square. Turn, and with yarn in back (wyib), pass picked-up st over next st on LH needle.

Wrong-side join (WSJ)
Pick up st, going into the left of vertical bars of bind-off chain of adjoining garter st square. Turn, and wyib, pass picked-up st over next st on LH needle.

Blocks *Make 10*
Square 1 Cast on 10 sts, leaving a 12" tail. K18 rows. Mark side facing as RS. Work BOR.

Square 2 Work PUR along left edge of square just completed. K17 rows. Work BOR.

Squares 3 and 4 Work as for square 2.

Square 5 Work PUR along right edge of Square 1. K17 rows. Work BOR.

Square 6 Work as for Square 2.

Square 7 Work PUR along left edge of square just completed. Work RSJ, work to end. K 16 rows more garter st, working RSJ at end of every RS row. Work BOR.

Square 8 Work PUR along right edge of Square 2. *Next row* (WS) K across, work

WSJ. Work to end of next RS row. K15 rows, working WSJ at end of every WS row. Work BOR.

Square 9 Work as for Square 2.

Square 10 Work as for Square 7.

Square 11 Work as for Square 8, picking up sts along right edge of Square 3.

Square 12 Work as for Square 2

Square 13 Work as for Square 7.

Square 14 Work as for Square 8, picking up sts along right edge of Square 4.

Square 15 Work as for Square 2.

Square 16 Work as for Square 7. Fasten off, leaving 12" tail.

Finishing
Using tails, sew seams between Squares 1 and 4, and 5 and 16. Block squares. Sew pieces tog as foll: 2 blocks wide by 5 blocks long.

Fringe
Cut 24" strands, 3 each of A and B. Fold strands in half. Work each fringe along a short side of shawl as foll: With RS facing, insert crochet hook into left corner, 1 row above bound-off edge. Pull up center of fringe, then pull tails through loop. Rep across, working 5 fringes for each square (40 total). *Make knots* Take first fringe and ½ strands from 2nd fringe, tie in an overhand knot approx ½" from edge. Take rem strands from 2nd fringe and ½ of strands from 3rd fringe and make a knot as before. Rep across, ending with a knot of ½ strands from 39th fringe and all strands from 40th (last) fringe. Rep for rem short side.

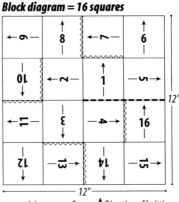

Block diagram = 16 squares

~~~ Join   --- Seam   ↑ Direction of knitting

Portable, practical, and pieced
are just three reasons to take
a second look at Linda's clever
shawl/wrap. Although the
blue and mauve pastel tones
are intended for a warm-
weather wardrobe, a simple
color change would make this
a year-round piece. It's made
of an ideal combination of a
rayon/silk blend for drape and
a cotton yarn for body.

> "I've made this shawl in handspun kid mohair, and cotton so I knew how nice the pattern stitch could look. The yarn I chose for *Knitter's* is perfect for pattern definition and yet fluffs up with wearing. I find it wonderful for cool summer nights, but it also works as a winter scarf or head wrap on the coldest days."

Dawn Brocco

featherweight fantasy

Luxury and lace go hand-in-hand in Dawn's quick-knitting shawl. A large gauge and entertaining lace pattern will have you finished with this season-spanning piece before you know it.

Notes

1 See *School*, pg. 100 for one-needle cast-on, ssk, SK2P, and fringe technique.

Shawl

Cast on 63 sts using one-needle cast-on. P 5 rows. **Beg Chart** Work chart as foll (purling all sts and yo's on WS rows): work rows 1-8 (section A), work rows 9-58 (section B) a total of 4 times, work rows 59-65 (section C). P 6 rows. Bind off knitwise.

Fringe

Cut a 9" piece of cardboard. Wrap yarn around it 104 times. Hold 4 strands tog and fold in half working fringe across approx 5 sts apart—approx 13 fringe at each end of shawl. Divide each fringe in half (4 strands each) and, with an adjoining 4-strand fringe group, work overhand knot fringe about 2½" from edge. Rep across. Form diamond shapes by tying another set of overhand knots near edge of fringe. Trim ends.

knitter's pattern · in other words ·

S2K2P2 Slip 2, k2tog, pass the slipped sts over the k2tog.

1/1 LT With RH needle behind LH needle, k 2nd st on LH needle through back loops, then k into first st; sl both sts off needle.

Row 1 Sl 1, p5, [ssk, yo] twice, k1 [yo, k2tog] 23 times, p5, sl 1. *2 and all WS rows* Purl. *3* Sl 1, p5, [ssk, yo] twice, k43, [yo, k2tog] twice, p5, sl 1. *5* Sl 1, p5, [ssk, yo] twice, [k3, k2tog, yo, k1tbl, yo, ssk] 5 times, k3, [yo, k2tog] twice, p5, sl 1. *7* Sl 1, p5 [ssk, yo] twice, k2, k2tog, [yo, SK2P, yo, ssk, k1, k2tog] twice, yo, k3, yo, [ssk, k1, k2tog, yo, SK2P, yo] twice, ssk, k2, [yo, k2tog] twice, p5, sl 1. *9* Sl 1, p5, [ssk, yo] twice, [SK2P, yo, k3, yo]

twice, SK2P, yo, k2tog, yo, k1tbl, yo, ssk, yo, [SK2P, yo, k3, yo] twice, SK2P, [yo, k2tog] twice, p5, sl 1. *11* Sl 1, p5, [ssk, yo] twice, k1tbl, yo, k5, yo, k1tbl, yo, k4, [k2tog, yo] twice, k1, k in front and back of st, k1, [yo, ssk] twice, k4, yo, k1tbl, yo, k5, yo, k1tbl, [yo, k2tog] twice, p5, sl 1. *13* Sl 1, p5, k1, yo, k2tog, [yo, SK2P, yo, ssk, k1, k2tog] twice, yo, k2tog, yo, k2, yo, 1/1LT, yo, k2, yo, ssk, yo, [ssk, k1, k2tog, yo, SK2P, yo] twice, ssk, yo, k1, p5, sl 1. *15* Sl 1, p5, k1, yo, k2tog, [yo, k3, yo, SK2P] twice, yo, k2tog, yo, k3, yo, [1/1LT] twice, yo, k3, yo, ssk, yo, [SK2P, yo, k3, yo] twice, ssk, yo, k1, p5, sl 1. *17* Sl 1, p5, k1, yo, k2tog, yo, k5, yo, k1tbl, yo, k4, [k2tog, yo] twice, k4, yo, [1/1LT] 3 times, yo, k4, [yo, ssk]

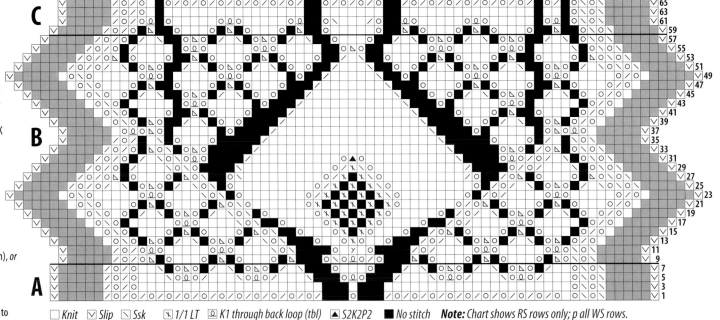

Skill Level Intermediate
Finished Measurements
18" x 60" (blocked), excluding fringe
Yarns 480yds (432m) of DK weight yarn
Original yarn: Fingerlakes Woolen Mills • Angora Luxury
50% wool, 50% handpucked angora
2 oz (56g) 160yds (144m)
3 balls in Satin
Needles Size 10½ *(6½mm), or size to obtain gauge*
Extras Crochet hook for attaching fringe
Gauge 16 sts and 20 rows to 4"(10cm) in St st

☐ Knit	☑ Slip	◩ Ssk	↗ 1/1 LT	⬚ K1 through back loop (tbl)	▲ S2K2P2	■ No stitch	**Note:** Chart shows RS rows only; p all WS rows.
▨ Purl	○ Yo	◿ K2tog	◺ SK2P	⊻ K in front and back of st		'Candlelight' adapted from First Book of Modern Lace Knitting by Marianne Kinzel (Dover).

twice, k4, yo, k1tbl, yo, k5, yo, ssk, yo, k1, p5, sl 1. **19** Sl 1, p5, k1, yo, k2tog, yo, k1, yo, ssk, k1, k2tog, yo, SK2P, yo, ssk, k1, [k2tog, yo] twice, k5, yo, [1/1LT] 4 times, yo, k5, [yo, ssk] twice, k1, k2tog, yo, SK2P, yo, ssk, k1, k2tog, yo, k1, yo, ssk, yo, k1, p5, sl 1. **21** Sl 1, p5, k1, yo, k2tog, [yo, k3, yo, SK2P] twice, yo, k2tog, yo, k6, yo, [1/1LT] 5 times, yo, k6, yo, ssk, yo, [SK2P, yo, k3, yo] twice, ssk, yo, k1, p5, sl 1. **23** Sl 1, p5, k1, yo, k2tog, yo, k5, yo, k1tbl, yo, k4, [k2tog, yo] twice, k7, yo, ssk, [1/1LT] 4 times, k2tog, yo, k7, [yo, ssk] twice, k4, yo, k1tbl, yo, k5, yo, ssk, yo, k1, p5, sl 1. **25** Sl 1, p5 [ssk, yo] twice, ssk, k1, k2tog, yo, SK2P, yo, ssk, k1, [k2tog, yo] twice, k9, yo, ssk, [1/1LT] 3 times, k2tog, yo, k9, [yo, ssk] twice, k1, k2tog, yo, SK2P, yo, ssk, k1, k2tog, [yo, k2tog] twice, p5, sl 1. **27** Sl 1, p5, [ssk, yo] twice, SK2P, yo, k3, yo, SK2P, [yo, k2tog] twice, k9, yo, ssk, [1/1LT] twice, k2tog, yo, k9, [ssk, yo] twice, SK2P, yo, k3, yo, SK2P, [yo, k2tog] twice, p5, sl 1. **29** Sl 1, p5, [ssk, yo] twice, ssk, k3, [k2tog, yo] twice, k2tog, k10, yo, ssk, 1/1LT, k2tog, yo, k10, [ssk, yo] twice, ssk, k3, k2tog, [yo, k2tog] twice, p5 sl 1. **31** Sl 1, p5, [ssk, yo] twice, ssk, k1, [k2tog, yo] twice, k1tbl, yo, ssk, k10, yo, S2K2P2, yo, k10, k2tog, yo, k1tbl, [yo, ssk] twice, k1, k2tog, [yo, k2tog] twice, p5, sl 1. **33** Sl 1, p5, [ssk, yo] twice, SK2P, yo, k2tog, yo, SK2P, yo, ssk, k21, k2tog, yo, SK2P, yo, ssk, yo, SK2P, [yo, k2tog] twice, p5, sl 1. **35** Sl 1, p5, ssk, yo, ssk, k1, k2tog, yo, k3, yo, ssk, k19, k2tog, yo, k3, yo, ssk, k1, k2tog, yo, k2tog, p5, sl 1. **37** Sl 1, p5, k1, yo, k1tbl, yo, SK2P, yo, k5, yo, ssk, k17, k2tog, yo, k5, yo, SK2P, yo, k1tbl, yo, k1, p5, sl 1. **39** Sl 1, p5, k1, yo, k2tog, yo, SK2P, yo, ssk, k1, k2tog, yo, k1, yo, ssk, k15, k2tog, yo, k1, yo, ssk, k1, k2tog, yo, SK2P, yo, ssk, yo, k1, p5, sl 1. **41** Sl 1, p5, k1, yo, k2tog, yo, k3, yo, SK2P, yo, k3, yo, ssk, k13, k2tog, yo, k3, yo, SK2P, yo, k3, yo, ssk, yo, k1, p5, sl 1. **43** Sl 1, p5, k1, yo, k2tog, yo, k5, yo, k1tbl, yo, k5, yo, ssk, k11, k2tog, yo, k5, yo, k1tbl, yo, k5, yo, ssk, yo, k1, p5, sl 1. **45** Sl 1, p5, k1, yo, k2tog, yo, k1, yo, ssk, k1, k2tog, yo, SK2P, yo, ssk, k1, k2tog, yo, k1, yo, ssk, k9, k2tog, yo, k1, yo, ssk, k1, k2tog, yo, SK2P, yo, ssk, k1, k2tog, yo, k1, yo, ssk, yo, k1, p5, sl 1. **47** Sl 1, p5, k1, yo, k2tog, yo, k3, yo, [SK2P, yo, k3, yo] twice, ssk, k7, k2tog, [yo, k3, yo, SK2P] twice, yo, k3, yo, ssk, yo, k1, p5, sl 1. **49** Sl 1, p5, k1, yo, k2tog, yo, k5, yo, [k1tbl, yo, k5, yo] twice, ssk, k5, k2tog, [yo, k5, yo, k1tbl] twice, yo, k5, yo, ssk, yo, k1, p5, sl 1. **51** Sl 1, p5, [ssk, yo] twice, [ssk, k1, k2tog, yo, SK2P, yo] twice, ssk, k1, k2tog, yo, k1, yo, ssk, k3, k2tog, yo, k1, yo, [ssk, k1, k2tog, yo, SK2P, yo] twice, ssk, k1, k2tog, [yo, k2tog] twice, p5, sl 1. **53** Sl 1, p5, [ssk, yo] twice, [SK2P, yo, k3, yo] 3 times, ssk, k1, k2tog, [yo, k3, yo, SK2P] 3 times, [yo, k2tog] twice, p5, sl 1. **55** Sl 1, p5, [ssk, yo] twice, ssk, k4, [yo, k1tbl, yo, k5] twice, yo, SK2P, yo, [k5, yo, k1tbl, yo] twice, k4, k2tog, [yo, k2tog] twice, p5, sl 1. **57** Sl 1, p5, [ssk, yo] twice, [ssk, k1, k2tog, yo, SK2P, yo] twice, ssk, k1, k2tog, yo, k3, yo, [ssk, k1, k2tog, yo, SK2P, yo] twice, ssk, k1, k2tog, [yo, k2tog] twice, p5, sl 1. **59** Sl 1, p5, [ssk, yo] twice, [SK2P, yo, k3, yo] twice, SK2P, yo, k5, yo, [SK2P, yo, k3, yo] twice, SK2P, [yo, k2tog] twice, p5, sl 1. **61** Sl 1, p5, ssk, yo, ssk, [yo, k1tbl, yo, k5] twice, yo, k1tbl, yo, k2tog, k3, ssk, [yo, k1tbl, yo, k5] twice, yo, k1tbl, [yo, k2tog] twice, p5, sl 1. **63** Sl 1, p5, [ssk, yo] twice, k41, [yo, k2tog] twice, p5, sl 1. **65** Sl 1, p5, [ssk, yo] twice, [k2tog, yo] 20 times, k1, [yo, k2tog] twice, p5, sl 1.

Reversible fabric, colorful pieces, woven looks, extra-long scarves and neck wraps are just a few non-traditional ways to create a shawl or a scarf. Take some of the ideas used in this chapter and create your own unique pieces. Use the formula for making a Graceful on page 88 and plug in your own gauge for a one-of-a-kind piece. Make a babushka as shown on page 98 and then scale it up to make a shawl. The Knitting Bee story tells you how to get some friends together to make a colorful shawl. Experiment with the possibilities.

taking it one step beyond

Karen Yaksick
Medrith Glover

"The inspiration for this exciting knitted garment, done entirely in garter stitch, was a marvelous handwoven piece that a dear friend, Grace Leonhardt, brought back from a trip to the southwest. Non-weavers, we shrieked, 'Aha! We can knit one.' We were so delighted with the inspiration that we dubbed ours 'The Graceful.' Our knitted version is truly a no-right-side-no-wrong-side-doesn't-matter-how-you-grab-it garment. And talk about a natural for unknown quantities of yarn—this is it! No one will slap your hand if you throw in different textures and thicknesses of yarn. Everything works!"

the graceful

Notes

1 See *School*, pg. 100 for long-tail cast-on, garter stitch grafting, and knotted fringe. **2** Always tie knot before you begin to knit to keep your tension even. **3** Fringe is made as you knit. Cut yarn at end of every row for fringe, even if not changing color. **4** Measure each fringe over some outside item; if you match each length to one next to it, fringes will gradually get longer or shorter. **5** Change colors after every row, or after every 3 rows for a woven looking fabric.

The Graceful

Loosely cast on 172 sts using variation of the long tail method as foll: Leaving 10-12" tails, knot 2 different yarns together. (Select unobtrusive colors for this.) Start casting on at knot. When all sts have been cast on, cut yarns, leaving an equal length for fringe. *Row 1* Select yet a different yarn, knot it to the tails, and k across. Cut it off, leaving fringe. Cont as for row 1 until you have 86 ridges.

Neck opening

K104 sts. Drop yarn and k the rem 68 sts with waste yarn. Do not turn. Replace the waste yarn sts onto LH needle, pick up original yarn and k the replaced sts as if nothing has happened. Cont k until you have completed 172 ridges.

Underarm join

In an unobtrusive color, k50 sts, bind off next 72 sts. Place last st back on LH needle. There will be 50 sts on each side of the bound off sts. Cut yarn, leaving a 72" tail. Thread end through tapestry needle. Hold 2 ends of needle parallel in LH with sts that have not yet been worked on front. Graft together the sides, starting with sts on back row next to bind off. Knot end in with fringe and cut to match.

Join other side

Thread 72" length of yarn through tapestry needle, leave fringe, and join cast on edges as foll: Hold folded fabric with cabled part of cast on to the outside. Starting at lower edge of join, lace through cabled parts only, first aiming tapestry needle toward you. Then, aiming needle away from you, go into very next cabled bit and out through space you came in through last time. Result should look almost like 2 garter st ridges on this side and almost like a valley between ridges on other. Cont until 72 sts or 20" of edge remains open. This is the only spot on the whole thing where you'll have an end to work in! Purists could always remove cast on (or plan ahead and begin with an invisible cast on) and finish exactly like first sleeve edge. No ends to work in.

Finishing neck and front opening

Gently remove waste yarn and place resulting sts onto your needle. Take a new strand of yarn, make fringe, and loosely bind off up one side and down the other. K into spot at center where those 2 last sts of incomplete row connect. (It'll make per-fect sense when you get to it.) You'll have a nice sturdy back-of-neck. Leave fringe-length end.

Fringe

Make knotted fringe and trim any uneven ends. We used 2 different methods of achieving an even bottom. Medrith laid a large index card on fringe and trimmed off what peeked out at the bottom. Karen used the 'groove in the dining room table' trick. If you have a table that 'expands,' you have a groove down the middle that makes a perfect guide for your scissors. If groove is not wide enough to guide scissors, open the table a bit. Lay 'Graceful' on table so that groove is positioned where you want to cut fringe. Use your non-cutting arm to hold fabric in place and cut up groove.

The Graceful Formula

Use whatever gauge pleases you in garter stitch!

Cast on whatever your gauge is, you'll need about 48" of it (or about 44" if you're really tiny):
_____ *"x* _____ *sts/1" =* _____ *sts to cast on. Following directions as in pattern, K every row until you have half as many ridges as sts on needle:* _____ *sts divided by 2 =* _____ *ridges.*

Neck opening

Next row k across until you've k halfway plus 5" worth of sts: halfway (_____ sts) plus (5" x _____ sts/1" = _____ sts) = _____ sts. (This 5" offset from center seems to work no matter what the overall dimensions of your 'Graceful.') Foll pattern directions and cont k every row until your total ridges = total sts. Subtract 20" worth of sts from total, divide what's left by 2 and k that number of sts: Total _____ sts less (20" x _____ sts/1" = _____ sts) = _____ sts divided by 2 = _____ sts (. . . k 'em).

Underarm join

Bind off loosely, next 20" worth of sts. Cont as in pattern, finishing second underarm join.

Knitter's Notes

• The 'Graceful' can be worn loosely draped, allowing those wonderful diagonals to form or the two fronts can be layered across your chest and the top one secured at the shoulder with a pin. It can also be worn with 'lapels' overlapping. As the day warms, just open and secure your pin into just one lapel—looks great and pin stays with you.

• The weight of the yarns and the fabric itself will affect the final dimensions of the garment. A 'Graceful' done in a loose gauge will grow as it drapes on the body; not a problem, it just seems to 'hug' you a little more than a firm-textured one. Longer fringe will make the garment appear larger.

• If a wonderful yarn strikes your fancy and you can't decide what color to get—buy all your favorites and combine them 'gracefully.' Variety in both color and texture makes it great fun. When using many different yarns, use an 'average' gauge.

We wanted reversible fabric because of the wonderful folding and draping it does on the body. All sorts of flattering diagonals occur on the front while the lines of color go straight up and down on the back. It's flattering to every figure from every angle!

Skill Level Easy
Finished Measurements 48" square
Yarn 1,600 to 1,800 yds (1,440 to 1,620m) of various DK-weight yarns (5-6 yds/m for each row)
Original yarn: Bryspun • Kid 'n' Ewe
50% kid mohair, 50% wool
1¾oz (50g) 120 yds (108m)
20 colors of choice
Needles Size 7 (4½ mm) 24-36" (60-90cm) circular needle, *or size to obtain gauge*
Extras Tapestry needle • small amount of waste yarn
Gauge 18 sts to 5" (12.5cm) in garter st (gauge does not have to be exact)

20"

Back

Neck trick

Front

48"

29"

← Cast on

"The basic premise of group knitting is that each knitter has her/his own ball of yarn, chair, and double pointed or circular needle. The knitters continue knitting without trading anything around—only the knitting moves slowly counterclockwise."

Joan Schrouder

knitting bee shawl

Joan calls this a "triangular shawl by committee," a description that fits the design process as well as the knitting process. The design consensus was — a triangular shawl knit from the center out. Instructions follow for a colorful shawl that can be knit by one or by many.

Notes

1 See *School* p.100 for ssk, grafting, and for large and small tassels. **2** Save 1¾ oz (50g) of yarn for border (or enough parts of skeins to make a multi-colored border). Also save extra yarn for tassels.

Shawl

Beg at the center with dpn, cast on 9 sts. Join and k 1 rnd. Mark 3rd, 6th, and 9th sts. (Actually place the marker into sts rather than on the needle between sts. Otherwise the yo inc shifts over the markers, and it's easy to lose track of the corner st.) *Inc rnd* Knit, working yo before and after each marked st; total of 6 sts inc on rnd. *Work 2 inc rnds, then 1 rnd plain. Rep from* until approx total of 600 sts, 200 on each side.

Changing colors

Change colors anywhere along a side away from a corner st to prevent losing a yo inc made with a tail of a new color. Introduce a new color by k 4-5 sts with both yarns tog, therefore minimizing the number of ends to be darned in later. Then drop old color (don't break yarn) and beg k new color. After you've k 1 rnd, drop 2nd color to the WS and cont with old color, without twisting yarns around each other. Cont to work alternate rnds of 2 colors for several rnds. To add in a 3rd color, either begin directly above other color change(s) or anywhere else along one of the sides; just join in as before. After that initial set-up rnd, *k to where the next color lies waiting, switch to it, and cont from.*

Border

Start away from a corner, cast on 6 sts and place them on the needle next to the live (un-bound off) shawl sts. *Row 1* Sl 1, k4, ssk (last edging st tog with shawl st). Turn. *Row 2* Sl 1, k5. Rep Rows 1 and 2 until the next shawl st to be worked off is a corner st.

Miter corner

Row 1 Sl 1, k4, turn. *2 and all even rows* Sl 1, k to end. *3* Sl 1, k3, turn. *5* Sl 1, k2, turn. *7* Sl 1, k1, turn. *9* Sl 1, k4, ssk (last st with corner st). *11* Sl 1, k1, turn. *13* Sl 1, k2, turn. *15* Sl 1, k3, turn. *17* Sl 1, k4, turn. *19* Sl 1, k4, ssk. Cont straight edges, attaching as before. Miter other 2 corners when you come to them. Weave, graft, or sew 6 rem sts to 6 cast on sts.

Tassels

Make 3 large tassels. Attach 1 to each corner. Make several small tassels and attach wherever whim dictates.

Knitter #1 uses ball A and ends of needles 1 and 2. Knitter #2 uses ball B and ends of needles 2 and 3. Knitter #3 uses ball C and ends of needles 3 and 1.

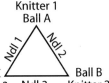

Knitter 1
Ball A
Ndl 1   Ndl 2
Ball C ———— Ball B
Knitter 3   Ndl 3   Knitter 2

Skill Level Easy
Yarn 1,560 yds (1,404m) of DK-weight yarn
Original yarn: 1 ball each of Cochineal, Plum Dusk, Teal, Midnight, Blue Indigo, Eldorado
100% alpaca
3½oz (100g) 260 yds (234m)
Needles Size 10 (6mm) double-pointed needles (dpn), 16" and 29" (40 and 74mm) circulars, *or size to obtain gauge* (If knitted by a group, various sizes such as 9, 10, and 10½ (5½, 6, 6½mm) can be used to obtain each knitter's gauge)
Extras Coiless pins, yarn, or open markers
Gauge Isn't crucial but should be loose, approximately 16 sts to 4" (10cm) unstretched, 12 sts to 4" (10cm) after blocking

The group approach

• Three or six knitters work best. When three are knitting, Knitters #1 and #2 always increase at each of the marked stitches while Knitter #3 works the plain round continuously. For six people, Knitters #1, #2, #4, and #5 increase while Knitters #3 and #6 knit even. We found it easier to actually mark the chairs to show who should or shouldn't increase. That way we didn't get confused when some knitters took breaks and were replaced or faster knitters traded places with slower knitters. See illustration below.

• Often we were asked if different gauges from different knitters would be a problem. Nope! Knitters could use different-sized needles; tight knitters chose size 10½ needles while size 9 needles went to the loose knitters. Just make sure that the correct size is in the knitter's right hand since that is the needle that forms the new stitches. It makes no difference what size needle is in the left hand unless you're knitting backwards (which you can't do here unless everybody does it.) The other reason gauge doesn't matter as much in this case is because each knitter only knits one round out of every three or six rounds, and then all the way around. Therefore the gauge is evenly dispersed around. An occasional loose round just looks like lacy, long stitches, while a slightly tight round makes shorter stitches.

talking about knitting bees

Alexis Xenakis

Jean We were trying to think of something we could do as a group to stimulate interest in our Professional Knitwear Designers' Guild (PKDG) booth at The National Needlework Association market (wholesale distributor show). Joan was the one who came up with the unique concept of starting with a circle—and ending up with a triangle! That is what we were so excited about—a technique in shawl making that hadn't been publicized before.

Joan We've been involved in groups that have knitted shawls from the center out and have heard of others doing it (usually Elizabeth Zimmermann's Pi shawl). We wanted to come up with a different shape, so I thought about what the mathematics would have to be . . . .

Obviously, we were familiar with 'circular' shawls ending up as a circle or square. When we were bantering about the idea at dinner one evening someone said 'triangle' as a joke. But it made sense that there should be a formula that would allow three points of increase—and the shawl would lie flat!

The problem was deciding on the rate of increase. Meg Swansen has written in the "Woolgathering" newsletter that in order for a piece to lie flat you have to have eight increases every other round (which computes to four increases every round). At that rate, it figures if you did 12 increases every three rounds, the increase proportion would be the same. A double increase at each of three points, which equals six increases: two increase rounds, then a round without increases would get it just right.

Sidna When you have three people knitting at the same time, it means two people increase every time they come to the increase point, and the third sails right on by. In other words, the third person just knits plain the whole way. And it works!

Joan We started with a big hole in the middle. We invisibly cast on 180 sts, (60 for

Knitting, six hands! Above, designers Jean Lampe, Sidna Farley, Joan Schrouder holding the alpaca used for the project; Here, group knitting attracting a crowd.

each side of the 'triangle' in order for each of the three of us to work a section with a circular needle . . . .

Jean And, at one time, we actually got up to six knitters!

Joan Two people can be on each side of the 'triangle': we split the stitches further by using 16" circular needles. It made sense to use six knitters. (It would be possible to have four or five, but then it would throw off the increasing: nobody would be sure who was the increase person and who wasn't!) So going from three people—two working increases every corner, one person not—to 6, you have two of them not doing increases—and they have to be across from each other, because as you work this in the round you build up concentric rounds!

You seemed to be having so much fun. How did you keep all of this straight?

Joan Jean held a whip!

Sidna Don't look at it too carefully! [Everyone laughs.]

Joan In the evening I knit the center triangle, increasing until I had 60 stitches on each side. Then Sidna laboriously grafted it to the center hole of the shawl, carefully lining up the points, and also mimicking the yarn overs at those points. It's impossible to tell where we started. It intrigued everybody and it was so much fun knitting it as a group.

Sidna People clustered around watching. Nothing that has to do with knitting draws a crowd like knitting in a group. People love to watch, trying to figure out what's happening.

Joan They're watching, trying to understand, and it takes a few minutes before it finally clicks in. They assume that at some point you have to stop and change places, or give your needle and yarn to the next person, as in a relay.

Sidna Or stop, and turn everything around!

Joan But it's not a relay: everybody gets to stay in the same place, each person with her own ball of yarn, holding two ends of two different needles. Each of us was knitting our own row—a concentric spiral really—passing stitches on to the next person, more or less at the same speed! We ended up with a barber-pole stripe, and the only time there was a jog was when a new color was introduced.

Sidna And we only changed places so the fastest knitter could knit some of the slowest knitter's stitches!

These knitters thought of everything—except perhaps who gets this beauty of a shawl. And . . . wait a minute; what about matching gauge?

Joan It didn't matter, because the spiral method of knitting evenly dispersed any variation around the whole shawl. Of course, a loose knitter could use a smaller working needle.

Sidna That could compensate somewhat, but it really didn't matter. The shawl is fine, and the bee was great.

We've heard of threshing bees, barn-building bees, quilting bees—have even taken part in a spelling bee or two. But this knitting bee was a first for us: there they were, Professional Knitwear Designers' Guild members Sidna Farley, Jean Lampe, Joan Schrouder, and others, yoked together by an invisible cast on and three circular needles!

Lily Chin

Borrowing techniques found in weaving, Lily creates a southwest-inspired shawl/table runner with surface slip-stitch patterning. She uses a mercerized cotton for the main yarn and cotton and rayon blend ribbon in an assortment of colors for the woven accents.

woven arrowheads

Notes

1 See *School* pg.100 for fringe. If fringe is not desired, do not leave tails of ribbon; weave in ends instead. **2** Slip first st of each row for selvage: RS, slip as if to knit; WS slip as if to purl. **3** Carry MC along side edge when not in use. **4** Piece is worked along long edge. To adjust finished length to any desired size, multiply inches by 5 sts, then round off to get pat st multiple of 4 plus 2. **5** To adjust finished width, just stop at any point after completing a MC row sequence.

Shawl/Table runner

With MC, loosely cast on 302 sts (or use needle 1 or 2 sizes larger for cast on). Do not join but work back and forth on circular needle. *Foundation row* (WS) Sl first st for selvage and k across. Drop MC. *Beg Chart: Row 1* Attach ribbon color A leaving 10" tail at beg as part of fringe and work rows 1-4 of chart while carrying MC along side edge, end ribbon leaving 10" tail. With MC work rows 5-8 of chart. Cont in chart as foll, leave ribbon tails at beg and end of each ribbon section: With B, work rows 9-12. With MC work rows 13-16. With C, work rows 1-4. With MC work rows 5-8. With D, work rows 9-12. With MC work rows 13-16. With E, work rows 1-4. Cont in chart pat, alternating every 4 rows MC with color sequence of A, B, C, D, and E. Work until shawl measures 16". End with the last row of a MC sequence. Bind off loosely with MC on RS.

Finishing

Apply fringe. Optional: Single crochet along cast-on and bind-off edges with cotton.

knitter's pattern · in other words ·

Chart *Multiple of 4 plus 2*

Note Rows 1-4 and 9-12 always worked with ribbon; Rows 5-8 and 13-16 always worked with MC. **Row 1** (RS) Sl first st for selvage, *k2, bring yarn to front and sl 2 as if to p (sl 2 wyif), bring yarn to back; rep from* across, k last st. **2** Sl first st, p1, *bring yarn to back and sl 2 as if to purl (sl 2 wyib), bring yarn to front and p2; rep from* across. **3** Sl first st, *sl 2 wyif, k2; rep from* across, k last st. **4** Sl first st, sl 1 wyib, p2, *sl 2 wyib, p2; rep from* across, end sl 1 wyib, p last st. Work Rows 5-8 with MC as foll: **5** Rep Row 1. **6** Rep row 4. **7** Rep row 3. **8** Rep row 2. **9-12** (worked with ribbon) Rep rows 5-8. **13-16** (worked with MC) Rep rows 1-4. Rep rows 1-16 for pat, changing color of ribbon for each 4-row section in A, B, C, D, and E sequence.

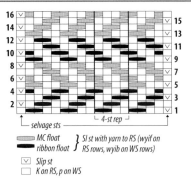

selvage sts — 4-st rep

MC float ⎱ Sl st with yarn to RS (wyif on
ribbon float ⎰ RS rows, wyib on WS rows)

☑ Slip st
☐ K on RS, p on WS

Skill level Intermediate
Finished measurements 60" x 16" without fringe
Yarn 558 yds (503m) worsted-weight cotton (MC)
206 yds (186m) each of 5 colors of cotton/rayon ribbon (colors A, B, C, D, and E)
Needle Size 8 (5mm) circular at least 29" (74cm) long, *or size to obtain gauge*
Extras Crochet hook for fringe and optional edging
Gauge 20 sts and 44 rows to 4" (10cm) in chart pat (Exact gauge is not important)

Lily Chin

on designing:
creating surface designs
with slip stitch floats

At times the search for verisimilitude motivates a design. In creating something 'Southwestern', I reflect the design elements used by the indigenous peoples in the area that is now New Mexico and Arizona. I look for desert colors and Indian motifs, but most importantly, I look to borrow from weaving techniques. (As with South American textiles, the traditional fabrics of the American Southwest are woven.) I ask myself, 'How can I make this look, or be, as close to the real thing as possible?' I analyze 'what's going on' and find ways of reproducing the same effects.

One method of creating woven-look fabric in knitting is through the use of slip stitches. When a stitch is slipped, the knitting yarn is carried in front of or behind the stitch. This horizontal strand resembles a weft float in weaving. And, as in weaving, these floats can be used to form patterns.

Machine knitters are no doubt familiar with this technique. However, on the machine, reverse stockinette stitch is the background on top of which the floats sit. Handknitters have the advantage of working floats atop smoother stockinette stitch.

Rules of the game

Since the row gauge is 'condensed', the stitch gauge can be loosened up a bit. Needles one or two sizes larger than usual are suggested, unless a stiff fabric is desired. As in two-color Fair Isle knitting, floats should never be very long. Since certain stitches will not be knit but slipped instead, these stitches will have fewer rows. Thus, the stitches to be slipped can never be the same ones over and over again. They have to be 'moved around' (unknit, slipped stitches have to be compensated for somewhere down the line). This aspect makes it akin to mosaic knitting, but in stockinette with the slipped floats to the right side as opposed to the wrong side. The patterning, because it is 'moved around' creates kinetic flow.

Arrowhead pattern

Barbara G. Walker refers to this pattern as a 'Woven Transverse Herringbone' in *A Treasury of Knitting Patterns* (Schoolhouse Press). The floats occur every two stitches and carry over two stitches. By moving the floats over by one stitch every row, and then reversing directions, a zigzag is formed.

I have Richard Bodack of Washington DC, to thank for this marvelous play of color and texture. This ingenious navigator of knit stitches figured out that with a change in color, the color from the previous row rides up at different stages depending on the slips. In this pattern, it takes four rows to complete the color change.

Take a look at the stitch chart: over the course of every four-row interval, each stitch gets knitted twice and slipped twice but at different times. With each color change, both old and new colors wind up in a diagonal. Add directional reversals and I arrive at Indian arrowheads.

Yarns

The contrast of cotton against shiny ribbon makes a fabric of intense textures. The palette not only imparts the mood of a desert oasis, it vibrates, it generates rhythm, it dances! The drape says 'caress me.' A versatile shawl is in order, doubling as a table runner when the parched air proves too oppressive. It helps that the fabric does not curl or roll at the edges as most stockinette stitch fabrics do. Fringes are 'released' from the main body and allowed to prance about.

Charting the way

These charts illustrate: **1** How these slip stitch 'weaves' work. **2** What kind of different directional patterns can be achieved. **3** How color infuses more syncopated interest in these same patterns.

Chart 2 reveals two directions the slip stitches progress in: to the right or to the left. Rows 1-4 make up a full right sequence. It's the combination of these four-row directional sequences that determines the path of your patterning.

The shawl/table runner is comprised of: right sequence, left sequence, left sequence, then right sequence. Repeat this and you'll find two rights, then two lefts alternating (Chart 1). The result is a zigzag repeat 16 rows in length. Omit color changes in Chart 1 to reveal the traverse clearly.

Chart 2 alternates one right and one left. The repeat length has been reduced to 8 rows. For this reason, this pattern doesn't read very well. However, throw in different colors every eight rows and arrowheads appear, all facing the same direction. The solid background color is more distinctive, continuous zigzag.

Chart 3 shows what happens when you go in one direction only. In this instance, it's always repeating the right sequence. Amazingly enough, there is no biasing and the fabric lies straight.

Don't just take my word for it. Try different directional combinations. Chart them first. Try three right alternating with three lefts for a 24-row repeat (and a very elongated zigzag). Or venture into split directions: one half going left, the other right and vice versa (separate them with a single garter stitch). Begin with one color, add more. Prepare to be surprised at the resulting dramatic shift.

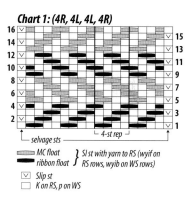

Chart 1: (4R, 4L, 4L, 4R)

selvage sts 4-st rep

MC float
ribbon float } Sl st with yarn to RS (wyif on RS rows, wyib on WS rows)

☑ Slip st
☐ K on RS, p on WS

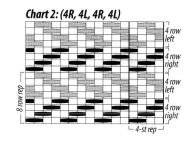

Chart 2: (4R, 4L, 4R, 4L)

4 row left
4 row right
8 row rep
4 row left
4 row right
4-st rep

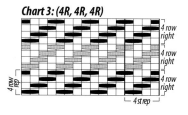

Chart 3: (4R, 4R, 4R)

4 row right
4 row right
4 row rep
4 row right
4 st rep

93

Susan Oldham

"With my graphics background, I like to use knitting to create motifs and designs that incorporate stitches into unusual formats. This tweedy yarn really showed off the lacy Celtic motifs."

amazing twining lace

Lace is an unexpected venue for Celtic motifs, but our trio of sophisticated accessories is both Celtic and lace. The *Knitter's* crew voted Susan's jaunty cap the most wearable knit hat in many seasons. The extra long scarf and hat both sport lush, full tassels. Mittens have warm, wide gauntlets. Tweedy Donegal wool gives this set pizzazz!

Skill Level Intermediate
Finished Measurements
Hat • 21¼" circumference
Scarf • 74" excluding tassels
Yarn 776yds (712m) worsted-weight yarn
Orginal yarn: Tahki • Donegal Tweed 100% wool
3½ oz (100g) 194 yds (178m)
4 balls in #844 dusty teal (1 ball each for hat and mittens, 2 ball for scarf)
Needles Size 7 (4½mm) needles for scarf, *or size to obtain gauge*
Size 7 (4½mm) circular, 16" (40cm) long for hat
Set of 5 size 7 (4½mm) double-pointed needles (dpn) for hat and mittens
Extras Cable needle (cn) • stitch markers and holders • tapestry needle
Gauge 20 sts and 26 rows equal 4" (10cm) in St st

Note See *School*, pg. 100 for ssk, SK2P, I-cord, M1R, M1L, tassel, and grafting.

Hat

With circular needle, cast on 100 sts. Place marker (pm) for beg of rnd and join, being careful not to twist sts. ****Rnd 1** (RS) Knit. **2** *K2tog, yo; rep from**. **3** Knit. **Beg Chart A** Work 10-st rep, k every even-numbered rnd through Rnd 29. K 1 rnd.****** **Next rnd** Purl. Knit 10 rnds. Turn work inside out. (WS becomes RS.) Knit for 3".
Shape Crown
Next rnd *K18, k2tog, pm; rep from**. **Next rnd** Knit. Cont dec every other rnd, working 1 less st between dec's until there are 11 knit sts between dec's; then dec every rnd until 5 sts rem. **Next rnd** K2tog, k1, k2tog. Place 3 rem sts on dpn for I-Cord. Work 3-st I-cord for 4." Bind off. Make a 4½" tassel, 80 strands thick and sew firmly to end of I-Cord.

Mittens
Left mitten
Cuff

Cast on 60 sts evenly distributed over 4 dpn. Being careful not to twist sts, pm for beg of rnd and work as for Hat from ** to **. **Next rnd** *K1, k2tog; rep from** — 40 sts. Knit 5 rnds.

Inc for thumb

Next rnd K2, M1R, k16, M1L, k4, M1R, k16, M1L, k2 — 44 sts. **Next rnd** Knit. **Next rnd** K3, M1R, k38, M1L, k3 — 46 sts. Knit 2 rnds. **Next rnd** K4, M1R, k38, M1L, k4 — 48 sts. Knit 2 rnds. **Beg Chart B: Rnd 1** K5, M1R, k2, pm, work Rnd 1 of Chart B over next 14 sts, pm, k22, M1L, k5 — 50 sts. **2** K to marker, work Chart B to next marker, k to end. Cont in pat as established, AT SAME TIME, on chart rnds 4 and 6, M1R before first marker and M1L 22 sts after 2nd marker—54 sts. Work even in pat to rnd 10.

Shape thumb opening

10 Break yarn. Place 6 sts on hold; rejoin yarn, k8, 1/1 RT, k2, 1/1 LT, k28; place 6 sts on hold, cast on 4 sts. Join —46 sts. Cont working even in pat through rnd 26. Knit 8 rnds.

Shape top of mitten

Next rnd *K2tog, k3; rep from**; end k1 — 37 sts. Knit 3 rnds. **Next rnd** *K2, k2tog; rep from**; end k1 — 28 sts. Knit 2 rnds. **Next rnd** *K1, k2tog; rep from**; end k1 — 19 sts. Knit 2 rnds. **Next rnd** *K2tog; rep from**; end k1 — 10 sts. Knit 1 rnd. **Next rnd** *K2tog; rep from** — 5 sts. Thread yarn through rem sts twice. Fasten off.

Thumb

Place 12 sts from holder on 3 dpn and knit them, then pick up 4 sts, by picking up loops from 4 cast on sts from mitten — 16 sts. Knit 14 rnds. **Next rnd** *K2tog; rep

Mittens have warm, wide gauntlets. Tweedy Donegal wool gives this set pizzazz!

from* — 8 sts. **Next rnd** *K2tog; rep from** — 4 sts. Thread yarn through rem sts. Fasten off .

Right mitten

Work as for left mitten to beg of Chart B. **Beg Chart B: Rnd 1** K5, M1R, k22, pm, work Rnd 1 of Chart B over next 14 sts, pm, k2, M1L, k5 — 50 sts. Cont as for left mitten.

Scarf

Note Scarf is worked in 2 sections then grafted tog.
Cast on 3 sts. Work Chart C, p every WS row, through Row 152. Rep rows 93-152 twice, end 2nd rep on row 131. P 1 row. Place sts on hold.

Second section

Work as for first section, end with 2nd rep on row 133. Graft open sts of 2 sections tog. Make 2 tassels as for hat. Attach to both ends of scarf.

1/1 RT K 2nd st on LH needle in front of first st, then k first st; sl both sts off needle.

1/1 LT With RH needle behind LH needle, k 2nd st on LH needle through back loop, then k into first st; sl both sts off needle.

YF-KTOG-K1 Place RH needle between 2nd and 3rd st on LH needle, pull yarn through to front and place loop on LH needle. K first st and loop tog, k1.

YA-KTOG-K1 Bring RH needle in front of and under LH needle, pull yarn around last 2 sts, place long loop on LH needle. K first st and loop tog, k1.

YF-KTOG-KTOG Place RH needle between 3rd and 4th st on LH needle, pull yarn through to front and place loop on LH needle. K first st and loop tog, k2tog.

YA-KTOG-KTOG Bring RH needle in front of and under LH needle, pull yarn around last 3 sts, place loop on LH needle. K first st and loop tog, k2tog.

CHART A *Multiple of 10 sts*

Rnd 1 *K4, yo, ssk, k4; rep from*. **2 and all even numbered rnds** Knit. **3** *K2, k2tog, yo, k1, yo, ssk, k3; rep from*. **5** *K1, k2tog, yo, k3, yo, ssk, k2; rep from*. **7** *K2tog, yo, k5, yo, ssk, k1; rep from*. **9** *Yo, k3, yo, ssk, k2, yo, k3tog; rep from*. **11** *K2, k2tog, yo, k1, yo, ssk, k1, k2tog, yo; rep from*. **13** *K1, k2tog, yo, k3, yo, k3tog, yo, k1; rep from*. **15** *K2tog, yo, k4, k2tog, yo, k2; rep from*. **17** *Yo, k1, yo, ssk, k1, k2tog, yo, k2, k2tog; rep from*. **19** *K3, yo, k3tog, yo, k2, k2tog, yo; rep from*. **21** *Yo, ssk, k1, k2tog, yo, k2, k2tog, yo, k1; rep from*. **23** *K1, yo, ssk, k3, k2tog, yo, k2; rep from*. **25** *K2, yo, ssk, k1, k2tog, yo, k3; rep from*. **27** *K3, yo, k3tog, yo, k4; rep from*. **29** *K3, k2tog, yo, k5; rep from*.

CHART B *Worked over 14 sts*

Rnd 1 K6, 1/1 LT, 6. **2** K5, 1/1 RT, 1/1 LT, k5. **3** K4, 1/1 RT, k2, 1/1 LT, k4. **4** K3, 1/1 RT, k4, 1/1 LT, k3. **5** K3, 1/1 LT, k4, 1/1 RT, k3. **6** K4, 1/1 LT, k2, 1/1 RT, k4. **7** K5, 1/1 LT, 1/1 RT, k5. **8** K6, 1/1 RT, k6. **9** K5, 1/1 RT, 1/1 LT, k5. **10** K4, 1/1 RT, k2, 1/1 LT, k4. **11** K3, 1/1 RT, k4, 1/1 LT, k3. **12** K2, 1/1 RT, k6, 1/1 LT, k2. **13** K1, 1/1 RT, k8, 1/1 LT, k1. **14** K1, 1/1 LT, k8, 1/1 RT, k1. **15** K2, 1/1 LT, k6, 1/1 RT, k2. **16** K3, 1/1 LT, k4, 1/1 RT, k3. **17** K4, 1/1 LT, k2, 1/1 RT, k4. **18** K5, 1/1 LT, 1/1 RT, k5. **19** K6, 1/1 RT, k6. **Rnds 20-26** Rep Rnds 2-8.

CHART C *Beg on 3 sts*

Row 1 K into front and back of st, k1, k into front and back of st— 5 sts. **2 and all WS rows** Purl. **Beg and end each RS Row 3-53** YF-ktog-k1, yo, …, yo, YA-ktog-k1. **Work center sts as follows: 3** K1 —7 sts. **5** K3 —9 sts. **7** K5 —11 sts. **9** K3, yo, ssk, k2—13 sts. **11** K2, k2tog, yo, k1, yo, ssk, k2—15 sts. **13** K2, k2tog, yo, k3, yo, ssk, k2—17 sts. **15** K2, k2tog, yo, k5, yo, ssk, k2—19 sts. **17** K2, k2tog, yo, k3, [yo, ssk, k2] twice—21 sts. **19** [K2, k2tog, yo] twice, k1, [yo, ssk, k2] twice—23 sts. **21** [K2, k2tog, yo] twice, k3, [yo, ssk, k2] twice—25 sts. **23** [K2, k2tog, yo] twice, k5, [yo, ssk, k2] twice— 27 sts. **25** [K2, k2tog, yo] twice, k7, [yo, ssk, k2] twice—29 sts. **27** [K2, k2tog, yo] twice, k9, [yo, ssk, k2] twice—31 sts. **29** [K2, k2tog, yo] twice, k5, yo, ssk, k4, [yo, ssk, k2] twice—33 sts. **31** [K2, k2tog, yo] twice, k4, k2tog, yo, k1, yo, ssk, k4, [yo, ssk, k2] twice—35 sts. **33** [K2, k2tog, yo] twice, k4, k2tog, yo, k3, yo, ssk, k4, [yo, ssk, k2] twice—37 sts. **35** K5, yo, ssk, k2, yo, ssk, k1, k2tog, yo, k5, yo, ssk, k1, k2tog, yo, k2, k2tog, yo, k5—39 sts. **37** K7, yo, ssk, k2, yo, k3tog, yo, k3, yo, ssk, k2, yo, k3tog, yo, k2, k2tog, yo,

k7—41 sts. **39** K3, yo, ssk, k4, yo, ssk, k1, k2tog, yo, k2, k2tog, yo, k1, yo, ssk, k1, k2tog, yo, k2, k2tog, yo, k4, k2tog, yo, k3— 43 sts. **41** K2, k2tog, yo, k1, yo, ssk, k4, yo, k3tog, yo, k2, k2tog, yo, k3, yo, k3tog, yo, k2, k2tog, yo, k4, k2tog, yo, k1, yo, ssk, k2—45 sts. **43** K2, k2tog, yo, k3, yo, ssk, k3, [k2tog, yo, k2, k2tog, yo, k4] twice, k2tog, yo, k3, yo, ssk, k2—47 sts. **45** K2, k2tog, yo, k5, yo, ssk, k1, [k2tog, yo, k2, k2tog, yo, k1, yo, ssk, k1] twice, k2tog, yo, k5, yo, ssk, k2— 49 sts. **47** K2, k2tog, yo, k3, yo, ssk, k2, yo, SK2P, yo, k2, k2tog, yo, k3, yo, SK2P, yo, k2, k2tog, yo, k3, yo, SK2P, yo, k3, [yo, ssk, k2] twice—51 sts. **49** K2, k2tog, yo, k2, [k2tog, yo, k1, yo, ssk, k2, yo, ssk, k1] 3 times, k2tog, yo, k1, [yo, ssk, k2] twice—53 sts. **51** K2, k2tog, yo, k2, k2tog, [yo, k3, yo, ssk, k2, yo, SK2P] 3 times, yo, k3, [yo, ssk, k2] twice—55 sts. **53** [K2, k2tog, yo] twice, k5, [yo, ssk, k2, yo, ssk, k4] 3 times, [yo, ssk, k2] twice—57 sts. **Beg and end each RS Row 55-155** YF-ktog-ktog, yo,…, yo, YA-ktog-ktog. **Work center sts as follows: 55** Ssk, k2, [yo, ssk, k2, yo, ssk, k1, k2tog, yo, k1] 3 times, yo, ssk, k2, yo, ssk, k1, k2tog, [yo, k2, k2tog] twice—55 sts. **57** Ssk, k2, yo, ssk, k2, yo, SK2P, yo, k3, [yo, ssk, k2, yo, k3tog, yo, k3] twice, yo, ssk, k2, yo, SK2P, [yo, k2, k2tog] twice—53 sts. **59** Ssk, k2, yo, ssk, k5, [k2tog, yo, k1, yo, ssk, k1, k2tog, yo, k2] twice, k2tog, yo, k1, yo, ssk, k2, yo, ssk, k1, k2tog, yo, k2, k2tog—51 sts. **61** Ssk, k2, yo, ssk, k3, [k2tog, yo, k3, yo, k3tog, yo, k2] twice, k2tog, yo, k3, yo, ssk, k2, yo, k3tog, yo, k2, k2tog—49 sts. **63** Ssk, k2, yo, ssk, k1, [k2tog, yo, k4, k2tog, yo, k2] twice, k2tog, yo, k5, yo, ssk, k1, k2tog, yo, k2, k2tog—47 sts. **65** Ssk, k2, yo, SK2P, yo, k4, k2tog, yo, k2, k2tog, yo, k1, yo, ssk, k1, k2tog, yo, k2, k2tog, yo, k1, yo, ssk, k4, yo, SK2P, yo, k2, k2tog—45 sts. **67** Ssk, k2, yo, ssk, k3, k2tog, yo, k2, k2tog, yo, k3, yo, SK2P, yo, k2, k2tog, yo, k3, yo, ssk, k4, yo, ssk, k1, k1tog—43 sts. **69** K7, k2tog, yo, k2, k2tog, yo, k1, yo, ssk, k5, k2tog, yo, k1, yo, ssk, k2, yo, ssk, k7. **71** K6, k2tog, yo, k2, k2tog, yo, k3, yo, ssk, k3, k2tog, yo, k3, yo, ssk, k2, yo, ssk, k6. **73** K5, k2tog, yo, k2, k2tog, yo, k5, yo, ssk, k1, k2tog, yo, k5, yo, ssk, k2, yo, ssk, k5. **75** K7, yo, ssk, k2, yo, ssk, k4, yo, SK2P, yo, k4, k2tog, yo, k2, k2tog, yo, k7. **77** K8, yo, ssk, k2, yo, ssk, k9, k2tog, yo, k2, k2tog, yo, k8. **79** K9, yo, ssk, k2, yo, ssk, k7, k2tog, yo, k2, k2tog, yo, k9. **81** K10, yo, ssk, k2, yo, ssk, k5, k2tog, yo, k2, k2tog, yo, k10. **83** K11, yo, ssk, k2, yo, ssk, k3, k2tog, yo, k2, k2tog, yo, k11. **85** K12, yo, ssk, k2, yo, ssk, k1, k2tog, yo, k2, k2tog, yo, k12. **87** K13, yo, ssk, k2, yo, SK2P, yo, k2, k2tog, yo, k13. **89** K14, yo, ssk, k2, yo, ssk, k1, k2tog, yo, k14. **91** K15, yo, ssk, k2, yo, SK2P, yo, k15. **93** K16, yo, ssk, k2, yo, ssk, k15. **95** K14, k2tog, yo, k1, yo, ssk, k2, yo, ssk, k14. **97** K13, k2tog, yo, k3, yo, ssk, k2, yo, ssk, k13. **99** K12, k2tog, yo, k2, k2tog, yo, k1, yo, ssk, k2, yo, ssk, k12. **101** K11, k2tog, yo, k2, k2tog, yo, k3, yo, ssk, k2, yo, ssk, k11. **103** K10, k2tog, yo, k2, k2tog, yo, k5, yo, ssk, k2, yo, ssk, k10. **105** K12, yo, ssk, k2, yo, ssk, k1, k2tog, yo, k2, k2tog, yo, k12. **107** K13, yo, ssk, k2, yo, SK2P, yo, k2, k2tog, yo, k13. **109** K14, yo, ssk, k2, yo, ssk, k1, k2tog, yo, k14. **111** K15, yo, ssk, k2, yo, SK2P, yo, k15. **113** K16, yo, ssk, k2, yo, ssk, k15. **115** K14, k2tog, yo, k1, yo, ssk, k2, yo, ssk, k14. **117** K13, k2tog, yo, k3, yo, ssk, k2, yo, ssk, k13. **119** K12, k2tog, yo, k2, k2tog, yo, k1, yo, ssk,

Chart A

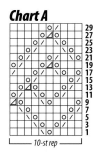

10-st rep

29 27 25 23 21 19 17 15 13 11 9 7 5 3 1

Chart B

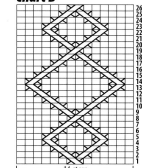

14-st rep

26 25 24 23 22 21 20 19 18 17 16 15 14 13 12 11 10 9 8 7 6 5 4 3 2 1

Notes Chart A & C
Charts show odd numbered rnds only. K even numbered rnds Chart A, p WS rows Chart C.

Chart C

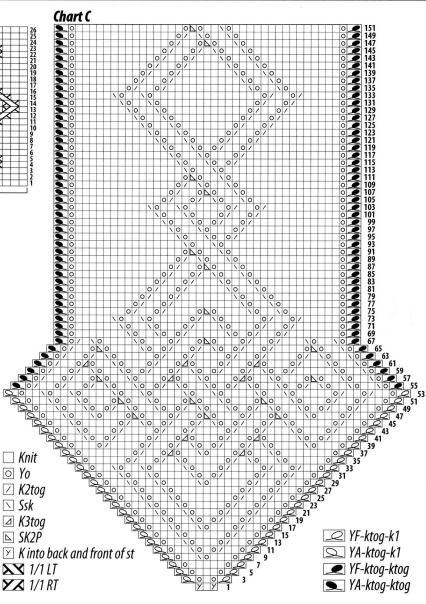

□ *Knit*
◉ *Yo*
╱ *K2tog*
╲ *Ssk*
◿ *K3tog*
⊠ *SK2P*
Y *K into back and front of st*
⟋⟍ *1/1 LT*
⟍⟋ *1/1 RT*

◿ *YF-ktog-k1*
◺ *YA-ktog-k1*
◖ *YF-ktog-ktog*
◗ *YA-ktog-ktog*

k2, yo, ssk, k12. **121** K11, k2tog, yo, k2, k2tog, yo, k3, yo, ssk, k2, yo, ssk, k11. **123** K10, k2tog, yo, k2, k2tog, yo, k5, yo, ssk, k2, yo, ssk, k10. **125** K9, k2tog, yo, k2, k2tog, yo, k7, yo, ssk, k2, yo, ssk, k9. **127** K8, k2tog, yo, k2, k2tog, yo, k9, yo, ssk, k2, yo, ssk, k8. **129** K7, k2tog, yo, k2, k2tog, yo, k11, yo, ssk, k2, yo, ssk, k7. **131** K6, k2tog, yo, k2, k2tog, yo, k13, yo, ssk, k2, yo, ssk, k6. **133** K5, k2tog, yo, k2, k2tog, yo, k15, yo, ssk, k2, yo, ssk, k5. **135** K7, yo, ssk, k2, yo, ssk, K11, k2tog, yo, k2, k2tog, yo, k7. **137** K8, yo, ssk, k2, yo, ssk, k9, k2tog, yo, k2, k2tog, yo, k8. **139** K9, yo, ssk, k2, yo, ssk, k7, k2tog, yo, k2, k2tog, yo, k9. **141** K10, yo, ssk, k2, yo, ssk, k5, k2tog, yo, k2, k2tog, yo, k10. **143** K11, yo, ssk, k2, yo, ssk, k3, k2tog, yo, k2, k2tog, yo, k11. **145** K12, yo, ssk, k2, yo, ssk, k1, k2tog, yo, k2, k2tog, yo, k12. **147** K13, yo, ssk, k2, yo, SK2P, yo, k2, k2tog, yo, k13. **149** K14, yo, ssk, k2, yo, ssk, k1, k2tog, yo, k14. **151** K15, yo, ssk, k2, yo, SK2P, yo, k15.

"I wear these scarves daily, and call mine by the colloquial expression babushka. It derives from the Russian word for grandmother, and that fits my feeling of comfort and security when wearing them."

Lizbeth Upitis

babushkas

This pair of scarves arrives at the same shape from different angles. The turquoise begins with the hypotenuse and works down to the point, while the magenta begins at the point and increases to the hypotenuse. Both could be enlarged easily to become a shawl.

Turquoise babushka

Notes

1 See *School* pg. 100 for invisible cast on and I-cord. **2** A row of eyelets can be worked 3 sts/ridges from edges of triangle. **3** Babushka is worked from hypotenuse (long edge) to point. Instead of decreasing sts, short rows are worked, leaving all sts on needle. **4** Both edgings are taken from an Australian book, *Classic Cotton Knitted Edgings.*

Cast-on hypotenuse

Invisibly cast on 99 sts. *Row 1* Knit. *2* Sl 1, place marker (pm), k to end, turn. *3* Sl 1, pm, k to marker, turn. *4* Remove marker, sl 1, pm, k to marker, turn. Rep row 4 until 1 st rem between markers (center point st). Break yarn and transfer all sts onto 1 needle, leaving markers on each side of center st—99 sts.

Side edging

Invisibly cast on 7 sts. K these sts and then k first st of the babushka. Turn, leaving rem sts unworked. *Beg Open Lace Edging Chart* Work chart until the next st of the babushka to be joined to the edging is the center point st, end with chart row 6. Turn.

Miter corner

Beg Mitered Corner Chart Foll chart, working 2 less sts each RS row as indicated through row 7. Rows 8 and 9 are worked across all 11 edging sts, joining edging to center point st at end of row 8. Beg with 3 sts, cont foll chart, working 2 more sts each RS row through row 18, joining edging to next babushka st. Cont working Open Lace Edging chart, joining edging to rem sts along other side of triangle—8 sts rem. Break yarn but do not bind off. On same needle as 8 rem sts, pick up 99 invisible cast-on babushka sts and 7 invisible cast-on edging sts—114 sts.

Ties and hypotenuse edging

With dpn, cast on 4 sts. Work I-cord for 5-6". Cast on 2 sts to the end of last row of I-cord, turn. *Beg Scalloped Edging Chart* Work chart, working last chart st tog with next invisible cast-on st of Open Lace Edging. Then cont as established across the hypotenuse and finally across the rem edging sts. On last chart row 5 when last st will be joined to edging, pass over only 2 sts

at beg of row so that 4 sts rem for the I-cord. Work I cord same length as beg. Pull yarn through sts and secure through center of cord.

Finishing

Weave in ends. Press with a damp cloth and stretch some to open lace and garter st.

Magenta babushka

Notes

1 See *School* pg. 100 for invisible cast on and grafting. **2** Beg at point and work to whatever size you would like.

Babushka

Beg Magenta Babushka Chart Cast on 2 sts and foll chart until babushka (or shawl) has reached desired length, or after 10 full diamonds from the center. Do not bind off.

Ties

Begin to work in St st and invisibly cast on 25 sts at each side of next 2 rows. Work 5 rows in St st. Fold to form hem with purl side out. Graft sts on the needle to the invisible cast on of one tie, weave live sts along the hypotenuse to the first row of St st on the scarf, and then cont grafting across the other tie. Sew in ends. Steam lightly and enjoy!

▪ in other words ▪

Magenta Babushka Chart *Beg on 2 sts*
Row1 Cast on 2 sts. *2* [K into front and back of st] twice—4 sts. *3 and all WS rows* Knit. *4* [K into front and back of st, k1] twice—6 sts. *6* K3, yo, k3. *8, 10, 12* K3, yo, *k1*, yo, k3. Knit 2 more sts between *'s each rep. *14* K3, yo, k2, k2tog, yo, k3, yo, k3. (**Note** The remainder of the scarf begins each even-numbered row with: k3, yo, k2, k2tog, yo and ends with the reverse: yo, k2tog, k2, yo, k3. All the following rows assume knitting those sts at the beg and end of the written row instructions.) *16, 18, 20* *K1*. Knit 2 more sts between *'s each rep. *22* K2, k2tog, yo, k3. *24* K2, k2tog, yo, k1, yo, k2tog, k2. *26* K2, [k2tog, yo] twice, k1, yo, k2tog, k2. *28* [K1, yo, k2tog, k1, k2tog, yo] twice, k1. *30* K3, yo, k2tog, k1, k2tog, yo, k2, k2tog, yo, k3. *32* K5, yo, k2tog, k3, k2tog, yo, k5. *34* K2, k2tog, yo, k3, yo, k2tog, k1,

Turquoise babushka
Skill level Advanced
Finished measurements The hypotenuse measures 19½" before edging—22½" after (Each side equals 14½" before added edging— 16" after)
Yarn 220yds (200m) fingering weight yarn
Original yarn: 1 ball Magenta in wool, camel hair blend
Needles Size 5 (3¾mm), *or size to obtain gauge*
Two size 3 (3¼mm) double pointed needles (dpn)
Extras Two stitch markers
Gauge 19 sts and 20 garter ridges (40 rows) to 4"(10cm) in garter st

Magenta babushka
Skill level Intermediate
Finished measurements The hypotenuse measures 29"—each side is 19"
Yarn 220yds (200m) fingering weight yarn
Original yarn: Froelich-Wolle • Camel 70% wool, 30% camel hair
1¾oz (50g) 220yds (200m)
1 skein in #6374 magenta
Needles Size 6 (4mm), *or size to obtain gauge*
Extras Tapestry needle
Gauge 22 sts and 44 rows to 4" (10 cm) in garter st

k2tog, yo, k2, k2tog, yo, k3. **36** K2, k2tog, yo, k1, yo, k2tog, k2, yo, k3tog, yo, k2, k2tog, yo, k1, yo, k2tog, k2. **38** K2, [k2tog, yo] twice, k1, yo, k2tog, k1, k2tog, yo, k2, k2tog, yo, k1, [yo, k2tog] twice, k2. **40** [K1, yo, k2tog, k1, k2tog, yo] 4 times, k1. **42** K3, yo, k2tog, k1, k2tog, yo, k2, k2tog, yo, *k3*, yo, k2tog, k2, yo, k2tog, k1, k2tog, yo, k3. **44** K5, yo, k2tog, k3, k2tog, yo, *k5*, yo, k2tog, k3, k2tog, yo, k5. **46** K2, k2tog, yo, k3, yo, k2tog, k1, k2tog, yo, *k7*, yo, k2tog, k1, k2tog, yo, k2, k2tog, yo, k3. **48** K2, k2tog, yo, k1, yo, k2tog, k2, yo, k3tog, yo, *k9*, yo, k3tog, yo, k2, k2tog, yo, k1, yo, k2tog, k2. **50** K2, [k2tog, yo] twice, k1, yo, k2tog, k1, k2tog, yo, *k11*, yo, k2tog, k1, k2tog, yo, k1, [yo, k2tog] twice, k2. **52** K1, yo, k2tog, k1, k2tog, yo, k1, yo, k2tog, k1, k2tog, yo, *k13*, yo, k2tog, k1, k2tog, yo, k1, yo, k2tog, k1, k2tog, yo, k1. Rep Rows 42–53, working 2 additional sts between the *'s in each pattern row.

Open Lace Edging Chart *Beg on 8 sts*
Row 1 Sl 1, k1, yo, k2tog, yo, k2tog, k1, [yo] 3 times, k1. **2** Sl 1, k1, p1, k7, k last chart st tog with first babushka st, turn leaving rem sts unworked. **3** Sl 1, k1, yo, k2tog, k1, yo, k2tog, k4. **4** Sl 1, k9, k last chart st tog with next babushka st. **5** Sl 1, k1, yo, k2tog, k2, yo, k2tog, k3. **6** Bind off 3 sts, k6, k last chart st tog with next babushka st. Rep rows 1-6 for Open Lace Edging.

Mitered Corner Chart *Beg on 8 sts*
Row 1 Sl 1, k1, yo, k2tog, yo, k2tog, k1, [yo] 3 times, k1. **2** Sl 1, k1, p1, k6, turn leaving rem sts unworked. **3** Yo, k2tog, k1, yo, k2tog, k4. **4** Sl 1, k6, turn. **5** K2, yo, k2tog, k3. **6** Bind off 3 sts, k1, turn. **7** K1, [yo] 3 times, k1. **8** Sl 1, k1, p1, k7, k last chart st tog with center point st, turn. **9** Sl 1, k1, yo, k2tog, k1, yo, k2tog, k4. **10** Sl 1, k2, turn. **11** K3. **12, 13** Rep rows 6-7. **14** Sl 1, k1, p1, k4, turn. **15** K1, yo, k2tog, k4. **16** Sl 1, k8, turn. **17** Yo, k2tog, k2, yo, k2tog, k3. **18** Bind off 3 sts, k6, k last chart st tog with next babushka st.

Scalloped Edging Chart *Beg on 6 sts*
Row 1, 3 Sl 1, k4, k last chart st tog with next babushka st. **2, 4** Sl 1, k5. **5** Sl 1, k3, pass first 3 sts over 4th, k1, k last chart st tog with next babushka st. **6** Sl 1, k2, cast on 3. Rep rows 1-6 until all edge sts are joined to scalloped edging.

Open Lace Edging Chart

Beg on 8 sts

Mitered Corner Chart

Beg on 8 sts

Scalloped Edging

Beg on 6 sts

Legend:
- ☐ K on RS, p on WS
- ▨ P on RS, k on WS
- ⊡ Yo on RS
- ⧄ K2tog on RS
- ◁ K3tog
- ⏝▽ Sl 1, k3, pass first 3 sts over 4th
- ⊻ K in front and back of st
- ⌒ K last st from chart tog with 1 st from shawl
- ⊖ Bind off
- ⊖ Cast on
- ⊻ Sl1 on RS

Note for working Magenta Babushka Chart: Chart shows RS rows only. Knit all WS rows.

Magenta babushka

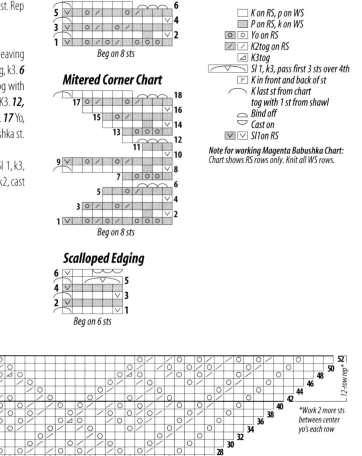

12-row rep

Work 2 more sts between center yo's each row

Cast-on

Hypotenuse

If scaling up for a shawl, remember that a triangle <u>twice</u> as deep will be <u>four</u> times as large over all.

2 3 4

1

99

Backward loop cast-on

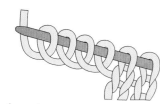

Chain cast-on

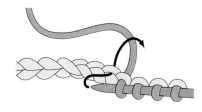

Invisible cast-on

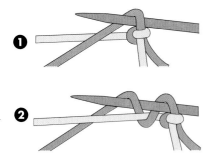

Long tail or one-needle cast-on

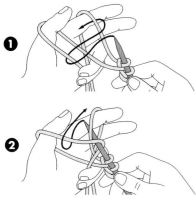

I-cord

Backward loop cast-on *Uses* To cast on a few sts for a buttonhole or the start of a sleeve. Form required number of backward loops.

Chain cast-on *Uses* As a temporary cast-on.
Chain desired number with scrap yarn. With main yarn, knit up 1 stitch in each chain, inserting needle into back loops of crochet.

Invisible cast-on *Uses* As a temporary cast-on, when access to the bottom loops is needed: to knit, graft, attach a border, or for an elastic hem.
1 Knot working yarn to contrasting scrap yarn. With needle in right hand, hold knot in right hand. Tension both strands in left hand; separate the strands with fingers of the left hand. Yarn over with working yarn in front of scrap strand.
2 Holding scrap strand taut, pivot yarns and yarn over with working yarn in back of scrap strand.
3 Each yarn over forms a stitch. Alternate yarn over in front and in back of scrap strand for required number of stitches. For an even number, twist working yarn around scrap strand before knitting the first row. Later, untie knot, remove scrap strand, and arrange bottom loops on needle.

Long tail or one-needle cast-on
Make a slip knot for the initial stitch, at a distance from the end of the yarn (about 1½" for each stitch to be cast on).
1 Arrange both ends of yarn in left hand as shown. Bring needle under front strand of thumb loop, up over front strand of index loop, catching it . . .
2 . . . and bringing it under the front of the thumb loop. Slip thumb out of loop, and use it to adjust tension on the new stitch. One stitch cast on.

Knitting-on
Uses A cast on that is useful when adding stitches within the work.
1 Make a slip knot on left needle.
2 Working into this knot's loop, knit a stitch and place it on left needle. Repeat step 2 for each additional stitch.

Emily's circular beginning
You need to use a crochet hook, but you do not need to know how to crochet, just follow the diagrams. Make a ring with the short end below (This ring can be roomy; it will be tightened later.) *Chain through the ring **A** Chain through the last chain **B** Chain B is the first stitch and waits on the crochet hook. Repeat from * until there are as many loops on the crochet hook as stitches to be cast on. Distribute the loops on 3 or 4 double-pointed needles. **C** After working around in pattern for several inches, you may pull on the short end to close the ring.

I-cord I-cord is a tiny tube of stockinette stitch, made with 2 double-pointed needles.
1 Cast on 3 sts (or desired number of sts).
2 *Knit across. Do not turn work. Slide stitches to right end of needle. Rep from *.

ssk *Uses* ssk is a left-slanting single decrease.
1 Slip 2 sts separately to right needle as if to knit.
2 Knit these 2 sts together by slipping left needle into them from left to right. 2 sts become one.

Knitting-on

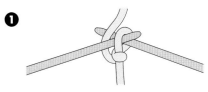

Emily's circular beginning

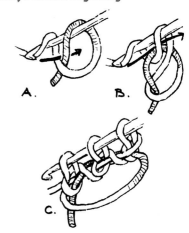

Illustration courtesy of Schoolhouse Press from Elizabeth Zimmermann's Knitting Workshop.

ssk

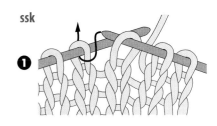

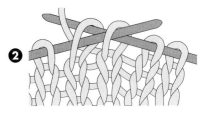

S2KP2, SSKP, sl2-k1-p2sso

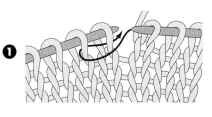

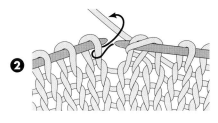

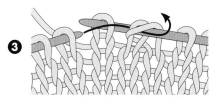

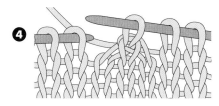

S2KP2, SSKP, sl2-k1-p2sso *Uses* A centered double decrease.

1. Slip 2 sts together to right needle as if to knit.

2. Knit next st.

3. Pass 2 slipped sts over knit st and off right needle.

4. Completed: 3 sts become 1; the center st is on top.

Sk2p, sl1-k2tog-p2sso *Uses* A left slanting double decrease.

1 Slip one stitch knitwise.

2 Knit next two stitches together.

3 Pass the slip stitch over the k2tog.

Make 1 (M1) *Uses* A Single increase.

1. With right needle from back of work, pick up strand between last st knitted and next st. Place on left needle and knit through back (or purl through back for M1 purlwise).

2. This increase can be used as the left increase in a paired increase (M1L).

3. For the right paired increase, with left needle from back of work, pick up strand between last stitch knitted and next stitch. Knit twisted.

4. This is a right M1 (M1R).

Short rows wrap *Uses* Each short row adds two rows of knitting across a section of the work. Since the work is turned before completing a row, stitches must be wrapped at the turn to prevent holes.

Work a wrap as follows:

1 With yarn in back, slip next stitch as if to purl. Bring yarn to front of work and slip stitch back to left needle as shown. Turn work.

2 When you come to the wrap on a right-side row, make it less visible by working the wrap together with the stitch it wraps.

Grafting

Uses An invisible method of joining knitting horizontally: row to row. Useful at tips of mittens, hats and for joining edgings together.

Stockinette graft

1 Arrange stitches on two needles.

2 Thread a blunt needle with matching yarn (approximately 1" per stitch).

3 Working from right to left, with right sides facing you, begin with steps 3a and 3b:

3a Front needle: yarn through 1st stitch as if to purl, leave stitch on needle.

3b Back needle: yarn through 1st stitch as if to knit, leave on.

4 Work 4a and 4b across:

4a Front needle: through 1st stitch as if to knit, slip off needle: through next st as if to purl, leave on needle.

4b Back needle: through 1st stitch as if to purl, slip off needle: through next st as if to knit, leave on needle.

5 Adjust tension to match rest of knitting.

Garter stitch graft

1 Arrange stitches on two needles so stitches on one needle come out of purl bumps (lower needle) and stitches on the other needle come out of smooth knits (upper needle).

2–4 Work as for stockinette graft except: on 3b, go through the stitch as if to *purl*. On 4b, go through 1st stitch as if to *knit*, and through next st as if to *purl*.

Make 1

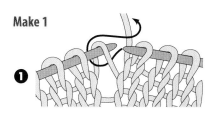

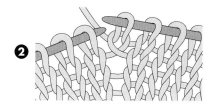

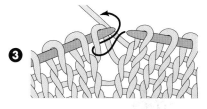

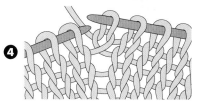

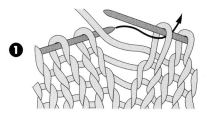

Grafting **Stockinette graft**

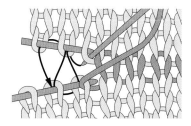

Grafting **Garter st graft**

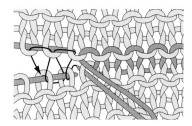

Short rows wrap

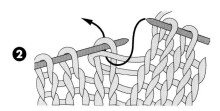

K, yo, k

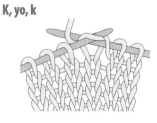

K, yo, p

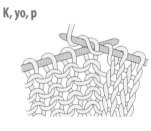

Yo twice

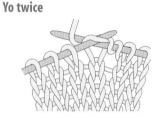

Start with a yo

Knit, yarn over, knit (k, yo, k) After knitting a stitch, the yarn is behind the RH needle. Bring the yarn under the needle to the front, take it over the needle to the back (where it is in position to knit), and knit the next stitch.

Knit, yarn over, purl (k, yo, p) Knit, bring yarn under the needle to the front, over the needle to the back, then back under the needle to the front before you purl the next stitch.

Yo twice Wrap the yarn around the needle twice before working the next stitch: two loops over the RH needle. The principle is the same for a triple yo (three wraps, three loops). The extra wrap makes a larger hole, more stitches can be worked into it on the next row.

Start with a yo At the beginning of a row, simply bring the yarn under the needle to the front and take it back over the needle before you work the first stitch. This creates a lacy edge.

Fringe
Cut a piece of cardboard the desired length of the fringe. Wrap yarn around it. **1** Cut yarn at one end. Hold 4 strands (or desired number) tog and fold in half. With RS facing, insert crochet hook from front to back at corner of short edge of shawl. Pull folded end of fringe through to form loop. **2** Pull cut ends through loop and tighten. **3** In same way, attach fringe across, spacing as desired. Trim ends.
Overhand knotted fringe Divide each fringe in half and, with an adjoining strand fringe group, tie an overhand knot, about 2½" from edge. Repeat across. Form diamond shapes by tying another set of overhand knots near edge of fringe.

Tassels
1 Wrap yarn around a piece of cardboard that is the desired length of the tassel. Thread a strand of yarn, insert it through the cardboard and tie it at the top, leaving a long end to wrap around the tassel.
2 Cut the lower edge to free the wrapped strands. Wrap the long end of the yarn around the upper edge and insert the yarn into the top, as shown. Trim the strands.

Blocking
There are numerous ways to block shawls and scarves. Many tips are included at the end of individual projects. In general, the piece is washed and then pinned in place to dry. Here's one suggested way:
  Wash the shawl gently, roll it in a towel to absorb excess moisture. Place the piece on a table or protected floor large with enough area to spread out the shawl or scarve. A carpeted floor covered with towels or a sheet with towel underneath is ideal for pinning into. If the piece is extremely large or long, you may want to fold it in half.
  Pin it out (using plenty of pins), stretching gently to make a perfect square or whatever shape it should be. This takes time, and a tape measure is essential to properly line up your measurements. Often pinning out the points of a lace edge is essential to the finished look.
  Allow to dry completely before lifting (12-24 hours).

Fringe

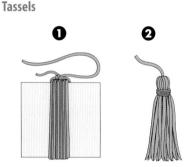

❶ ❷

❸ ❹

Overhand knot

Tassels

❶ ❷

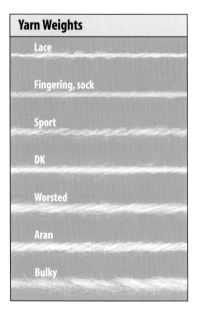

Yarn Weights
Lace
Fingering, sock
Sport
DK
Worsted
Aran
Bulky

Metrics
To convert inches to centimeters, multiply the inches by 2.5.
For example: 4" x 2.5 = 10cm

To convert feet to centimeters, multiply the feet by 30.48.
For example: 2' x 30.48 = 60.96cm

To convert yards to meters, multiply the yards by .9144.
For example: 4 yds x .9144 = 3.66m

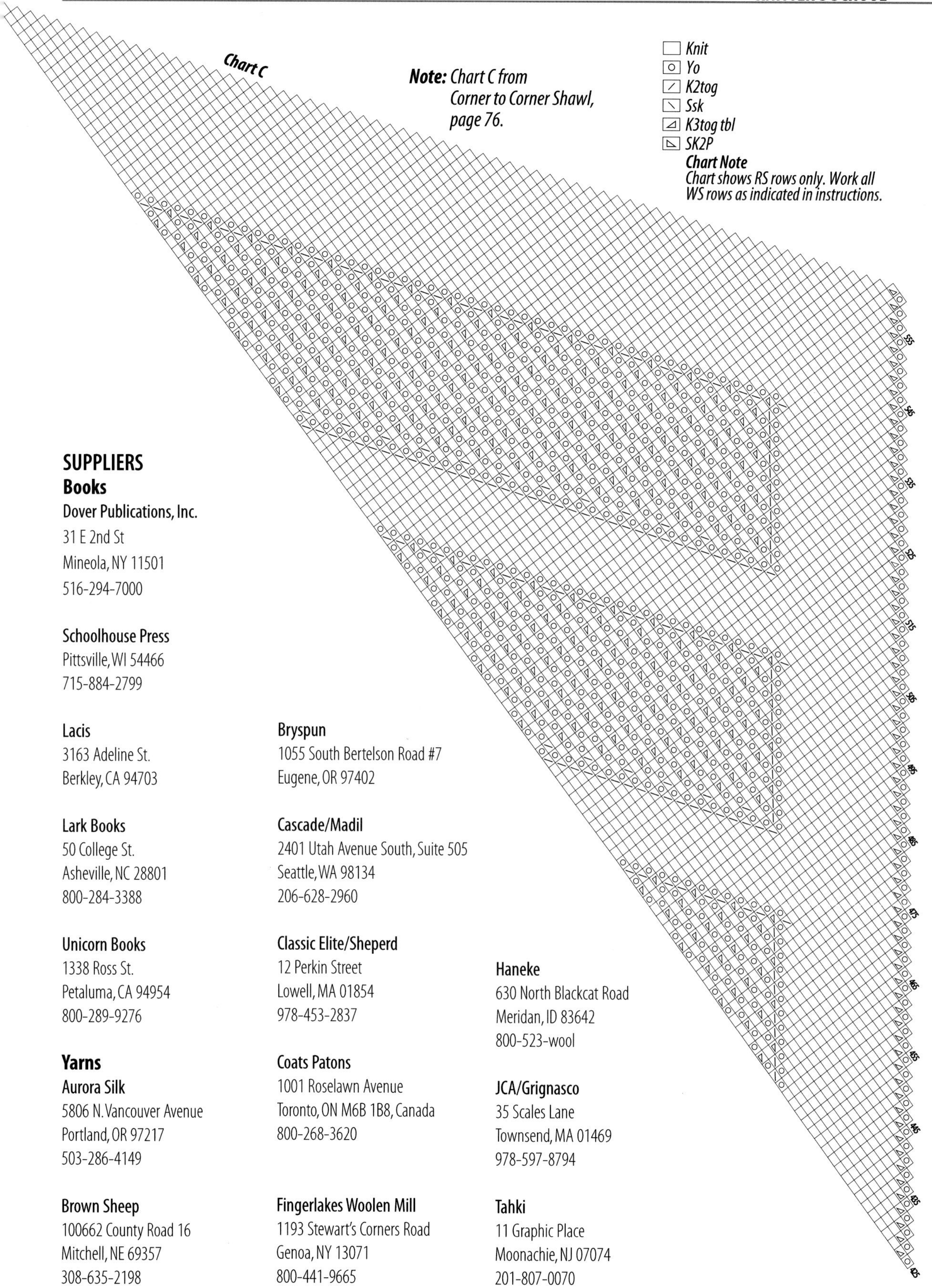

Chart C

Note: *Chart C from Corner to Corner Shawl, page 76.*

☐ Knit
☑ Yo
☑ K2tog
☑ Ssk
☑ K3tog tbl
☑ SK2P

Chart Note
Chart shows RS rows only. Work all WS rows as indicated in instructions.

Abbreviations

approx approximate(ly)
beg begin(ning)(s)
CC contrasting color
cn cable needle
cm centimeter(s)
cont continu(e)(ed)(es)(ing)
dec decreas(e)(ed)(es)(ing)
dpn double pointed needle(s)
foll follow(s)(ing)
g gram(s)
" inch(es)
' foot(feet)
inc increas(e)(ed)(es)(ing)
k knit(ting)(s)(ted)
lb pound(s)
LH lefthand
m meter(s)
mm millimeter(s)
MC main color
oz ounce(s)
p purl(ed)(ing)(s)
pat(s) pattern(s)
pm place marker
psso pass slipped stitch(es) over
rem remain(s)(ing)
rep repeat(s)
rev reverse(d)
RH righthand
RS right side(s)
rnd round(s)
sl slip(ped)(ping)
ssk slip, slip, knit 2tog
st(s) stitch(es)
St st stockinette stitch
tbl through back loop
tog together
WS wrong side(s)
wyib with yarn in back
wyif with yarn in front
yd(s) yard(s)
yo yarn over

SUPPLIERS

Books

Dover Publications, Inc.
31 E 2nd St
Mineola, NY 11501
516-294-7000

Schoolhouse Press
Pittsville, WI 54466
715-884-2799

Lacis
3163 Adeline St.
Berkley, CA 94703

Lark Books
50 College St.
Asheville, NC 28801
800-284-3388

Unicorn Books
1338 Ross St.
Petaluma, CA 94954
800-289-9276

Yarns

Aurora Silk
5806 N. Vancouver Avenue
Portland, OR 97217
503-286-4149

Brown Sheep
100662 County Road 16
Mitchell, NE 69357
308-635-2198

Bryspun
1055 South Bertelson Road #7
Eugene, OR 97402

Cascade/Madil
2401 Utah Avenue South, Suite 505
Seattle, WA 98134
206-628-2960

Classic Elite/Sheperd
12 Perkin Street
Lowell, MA 01854
978-453-2837

Coats Patons
1001 Roselawn Avenue
Toronto, ON M6B 1B8, Canada
800-268-3620

Fingerlakes Woolen Mill
1193 Stewart's Corners Road
Genoa, NY 13071
800-441-9665

Haneke
630 North Blackcat Road
Meridan, ID 83642
800-523-wool

JCA/Grignasco
35 Scales Lane
Townsend, MA 01469
978-597-8794

Tahki
11 Graphic Place
Moonachie, NJ 07074
201-807-0070

other publications from XRX, Inc.

Socks, Socks, Socks

Sally Melville Styles
Sally Melville

Magnificent Mittens
Anna Zilboorg

Ethnic Socks and Stockings
Priscilla A. Gibson-Roberts

The Great American Afghan

Knitter's Magazine

Weaver's Magazine

 BOOKS

XRX Books would like to hear from you!

We can't publish all the knitting books in the world—only the finest.

We are knitting enthusiasts and book lovers. Our mission is simple: to produce quality books that showcase the beauty of the knitting and give our readers inspiration, confidence, and skill-building instructions.

Publishing begins as a partnership between author and publisher. XRX Books attracts the best authors and designers in the knitting universe because we share their passion for excellence. But books also require a shared vision: photographer Alexis Xenakis and his team bring the garments and fabrics to glorious life. This is where our journey begins.

Cutting-edge computer technology allows us to focus on editing and designing our publications. XRX Books Editor Elaine Rowley can exchange files from South Dakota with our knitting editor in New York or our authors, wherever they happen to live, within a matter of minutes. Our digital consultant, David Xenakis, and his team insure accuracy of color and texture in our images. Graphic Artist Bob Natz, believing that design is not good unless it functions well, produces beautiful, easy-to-read pages.

Now those pages are in your hands and your journey begins.

Tell us what you think:

•by mail	•by phone	•by fax
XRX Books	605-338-2450	605-338-2994
PO Box 1525		
Sioux Falls, South Dakota		
57101-1525		

•by e-mail
erowley@xrx-inc.com

•on xrx-inc.com
You may visit our XRX Books site on the World Wide Web: www.knittinguniverse.com

•On our Knitter's OnLine forums:
Join the conversation and post your reactions and comments in our book discussion bulletin boards:
www.knittinguniverse.com/script/webx.dll?knitalk

We look forward to hearing from you. New journeys are under way.